Zarzuela

Music in American Life

A list of books in the series appears at the end of this book.

Zarzuela

Spanish Operetta, American Stage

Janet L. Sturman

University of Illinois Press
Urbana and Chicago

Publication of this book was supported by the Provost's Author Support Fund and a Fine Arts Research and Development Grant from the University of Arizona and by the Program for Cultural Cooperation between Spain's Ministry of Education and Culture and United States Universities.

♾ This book is printed on acid-free paper.

Library of Congress Cataloging-in-Publication Data
Sturman, Janet Lynn.
Zarzuela : Spanish operetta, American stage / Janet L. Sturman.
p. cm. — (Music in American life)
Includes bibliographical references and index.
ISBN 0-252-02596-2
1. Zarzuela. I. Title. II. Series.
ML1950.S78 2000
782.1'2—dc21 00–008032

Contents

Acknowledgments

Over the past fifteen years many people have helped me to uncover the continuing story of zarzuela in the United States, far too many to list them all here. The text's numerous citations, however, should alert readers to these individuals' invaluable contributions to this work. Nevertheless, I take full responsibility for any remaining errors or oversights.

A few persons, however, must be singled out for their exceptional roles. I owe my beginning interest in zarzuela to the late Josefina Trelles Solomon, a former neighbor and longtime friend. The solid guidance I received from Professor Dieter Christensen at Columbia University continued to serve me as I prepared this book. Other New York residents who were exceptionally generous with their time and resources included Silvia Brito, René Buch, and Pablo Zinger. I am thankful to all who granted me interviews and sent me programs, tapes, and literature. Miguel De Grandy, Gonzalo Madurga, and Blanche Artis Lewis went out of their way to call me and send me material.

Joseph McClain, Stuart Mattingly, Oscar Macchioni, and Carmen Doris helped me to prepare the manuscript for publication. My colleagues who constitute our writer's group at the University of Arizona, Jay Rosenblatt, Robert Clifford, Laura Atwood, and Donnalee Dox, offered countless useful suggestions and much appreciated moral support during a summer of revisions.

Judith McCulloh, assistant director and executive editor at the University of Illinois Press, has been wonderfully patient and always encouraging. I am also grateful to Theresa Sears, managing editor, and Bruce Bethell, manuscript editor, for the many improvements they made to the manuscript. The reviewers who read an earlier draft of this manuscript offered exceedingly valuable advice, and I especially want to thank Craig Russell for directing me toward resources and individuals that enriched my life as well as the text. John Koegel was exceptionally generous and shared a rich array of resources with me.

My family gave up countless hours to make certain that I finished this book. Thanks always to my parents, John and Dorothy Sturman, and to my parents-in-law, Ernest and the late Eva Weiss. Above all, my love and gratitude go to my delightful and patient children, Michael and Andrea Weiss, and to my wonderful husband, Arthur Weiss.

Editorial Conventions

Narratives involving more than one language always raise problems of format, and it can be difficult to decide which language's customs should prevail in various situations. I have chosen to render titles of zarzuelas and other dramas using contemporary U.S. conventions rather than Spanish ones. In other words, whereas Spanish style capitalizes only the first word and all proper nouns in a title (e.g., *El barberillo de Lavapiés*), the title appears frequently on programs and cover pages of scores as *El Barberillo de Lavapiés.* I chose this latter format, which is also the standard English-language format, for all titles of zarzuelas, dramas, and related productions. Translations of titles appear in parentheses following the original Spanish and retain the same capitalization (e.g., *The Little Barber of Lavapiés,* a neighborhood in Madrid). Sometimes a direct translation offered little guidance as to a work's subject, so I occasionally opted for a less literal and more practical translation. Untranslated terms are virtually always proper nouns (e.g., Luisa Fernanda is the name of the central female character in the zarzuela so titled).

For references in endnotes and the bibliography, however, I follow the conventions of the original language. Translations of foreign-language titles capitalize only the first word of the title and subtitle, as well as any proper nouns and adjectives.

In general I use the American spelling *theater* rather than the British *theatre,* except when the word is part of a proper name, such as the Thalia Spanish Theatre, or used in a title.

Lastly, a few important names appear in formats that may seem wrong to those unacquainted with them. Most Spanish speakers would expect the surname De Grandy to be presented as de Grandy, which is in fact how the name was shown in Cuba; after moving to America, however, the family preferred the former spelling. A similar rationale guides the spellings for the names Paco D'Rivera and Delia D'Campos. "The International Festival de la Zarzuela" is correct in neither English nor Spanish, but that is the official title. Some write "international Festival de la Zarzuela," which works better but is less common.

Zarzuela

Introduction

From Experience to Study

Entering the theater's lobby (see fig. 1), I immediately sense a special electricity in the air. To some degree this feeling characterizes all events at this theater, but there is more spark than usual tonight, for the performance is both a musical production and the opening of the company's latest zarzuela, *La Generala* (The Lady General). A distinctive brand of Spanish operetta, zarzuela attracts a diverse audience, including many patrons who might not normally come to see the non-musical Spanish plays presented here.

"¿Quiere una copa?" a smartly dressed young woman asks me as she proffers a tiny glass of sherry. The lobby of the Teatro Repertorio Español, located in the Gramercy Park area of lower Manhattan, is crowded. A few English words stand out in the conversational blur, but most of the people speak Spanish. An elderly nun waits at the doorway and is soon joined by her companions, a tall, dark man who strides in holding hands with his five-year-old son sporting a sparkling white suit. A few teenagers huddle in a corner, gazing with studied New York aloofness past the crowd and occasionally stopping to tease one another or glance at their notebooks. For these teens, attending this evening's performance is a school assignment.

The renowned flamenco dancer Pilar Rioja arrives. Soon thereafter Silvia Brito, director of a "competing" Spanish theater, the Thalia (located in the New York borough of Queens), steps into the lobby accompanied by a few cast members from *Los Claveles* (The Carnations), the zarzuela running at her theater this same week and into the summer. The presence of these two women contributes something of a celebrity aura to the crowd.

Everyone seems to stop at the box office, more to chat with Gilberto Zaldívar, the executive director of Repertorio Español, than to pick up their tickets. Many patrons appear to know one another well. Phrases such as *reunion, party,* and *social*

Figure 1. Exterior of the Teatro Repertorio Español, 138 E. 27th St., New York, New York. Photo by Janet Sturman, 1989.

gathering seem to be fitting descriptions of this event. Patrons are treated as guests rather than anonymous individuals in the audience.

Once the audience members find their places in the darkened theater (which seats 141), animated conversations continue to intertwine as people greet one another, often leaving their seats and moving up and down the aisles to visit with friends and family. Any newcomer to this group senses that the core audience is more than a group of acquaintances; these people's lives and views intersect in many places.

"Encantado de verlo," greets director René Buch as he moves down one aisle, shaking hands and welcoming patrons: "Bueno, ¿qué tal? Nos hablamos después." He really seems delighted to see each person and will indeed find time to speak afterward with most of them.

Even before the curtain rises, the sounds of the overture alert the audience to the special nature of this performance. The musical director, a virtuoso pianist, commands attention as he dives into the overture's opening chords. The piano is augmented by synthesized sounds, and two additional musicians play assorted percussion. The lushly harmonized melodies, built on unmistakable Spanish syncopations, immediately engage the "newcomers" in the audience, Spanish speaking or not (see figs. 2 and 3).

The curtain rises on a chorus of four women sporting blond wigs (à la Marilyn Monroe) and wearing white silk pajamas emblazoned with black polka dots. They "smoke" cigarettes held at a distance by glistening black cigarette holders. This evening's production of the comic zarzuela *La Generala* has begun. Patrons are treated to a characteristic blend of spoken Spanish dialogue and sparkling Spanish songs, in this case including Iberian, English, French, and even Viennese rhythms (the plot is set in England and concerns exiled royalty, passions for tea and tennis, and Scottish Highlanders).

Like all productions at the Repertorio Español, *La Generala* features sophisticated stage design; geometric and abstract, the set relies more on shadows and shapes than color and concrete furniture. In this production the stage is set with five large mirrors, and black and white are the only colors used in the costumes. The resulting look evokes deliciously decadent manners and yawning elitism engagingly appropriate for this romping musical comedy premiered in 1912.

Like much zarzuela, Amadeo Vives's music displays an affinity with opera. I am reminded of Rossini as I listen and note the work's vocal demands coupled with the playful staging. At times the spoken narrative resembles the frenetic dialogue of modern *telenovelas,* the popular soap operas shown by virtually every Spanish-language television station in the United States and abroad.

The crowd is clearly pleased by this unique production. The party atmosphere that preceded the show resurfaces in post-show celebration as patrons stay to greet performers and groups disperse for home or other gathering sites.

That production of 1988 was not the first zarzuela that I attended, nor was it my last. Over the years, as I continued to attend zarzuela productions in various locales, I have always felt a similar combination of musical, theatrical, and social electricity.

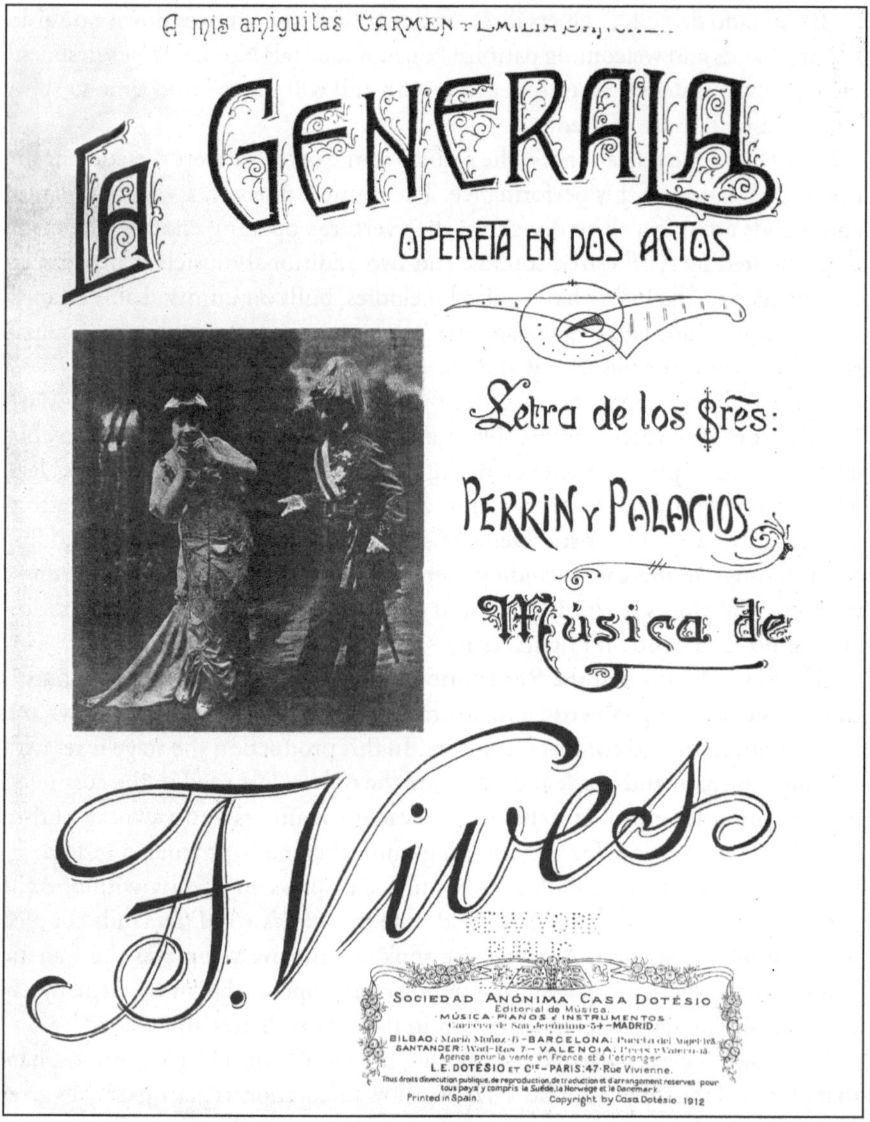

Figure 2. Cover of the piano-vocal score of *La Generala,* by Amadeo Vives. *La Generala,* operetta in two acts, music by Maestro Amadeo Vives. Book by Mr. Perrín and Mr. Palacios. Madrid: Sociedad Anónimo. Casa Dotésio, Editores Madrid [1912].

Figure 3. Opening bars of the "Marcha Militar" from *La Generala. La Generala*, operetta in two acts, music by Maestro Amadeo Vives. Book by Mr. Perrín and Mr. Palacios. Madrid: Sociedad Anónimo. Casa Dotésio, Editores Madrid [1912].

As I write this introduction in 1999, I look back fondly on my introduction to zarzuela. In 1983 my neighbor Josefina, an energetic Cuban American woman then in her midfifties, insisted I accompany her to the Spanish theater to see a full-scale zarzuela. She knew of my interest in Hispanic arts in New York, and she had accompanied me to many musical events. With patience and a certain amusement, she had watched me learn to dance to the Latin rhythms of salsa and, through the walls of our old apartment building on Manhattan's upper West Side, had listened to me practice *montunos* on my piano. She also knew that I had been trained as a classical musician and ethnomusicologist, and she was eager for me to experience what she called "another side of Hispanic culture."

We went to see Repertorio Español's compelling production of *Doña Francisquita,* a bubbly drama with enchanting, frothy music also by Amadeo Vives. The story is based on a drama written by the great Spanish playwright Lope de Vega. Soon thereafter we traveled to Sunnyside, New York, to see Tomás Bretón's joyful masterpiece of Castillian spirit *La Verbena de la Paloma* (The Festival of Our Lady of the Dove).[1] This slice-of-life drama revolves around courtship, confusion, and reconciliation as working-class residents of Madrid prepare to attend the festival honoring that city's patron saint, Mary, the Virgin of the Dove. It was offered by the Thalia Spanish Theatre, the company that would become New York's most devoted champion of the genre.[2] In both cases I was charmed by the music, but I was equally captivated by the production decisions, the friendly atmosphere, and the social dynamic that supported the whole event. These features seemed worthy of serious study.

By 1985 several New York companies were regularly offering zarzuela, and I was regularly attending those presentations. Occasionally someone would inquire, "Why are you so interested in zarzuela? You are not Hispanic, are you?" I would answer that I was not but that I enjoyed the music and the atmosphere. And of course, ethnic background neither precludes nor ensures an interest in any one kind of music. Nevertheless, zarzuela's growing popularity in New York certainly did seem to be linked to the genre's Spanishness, and this also interested me. As an ethnomusicologist, I have always observed the relationship between the projection of ethnic identity and musical creation, performance, and reception.

Full-scale productions in New York were limited to companies with directors, performers, and clientele of Hispanic heritage. Few of those involved were of direct Spanish ancestry, however, and the majority would identify themselves as Cuban, Dominican, Colombian, or Puerto Rican. I found myself asking how Spanish zarzuela was relevant to an American experience, be it Caribbean, Latin American, or North American.

To many readers the claim that zarzuela could have anything to do with American music might seem preposterous. Topically, linguistically, and musically, zarzuela always highlights distinctly Spanish perspectives (even when the plots address foreign themes), although colonial variants and productions sometimes expressly oppose the dominating politics and language of Spain.[3] Given this tradition, it is natural to question how zarzuela could represent anything American. Over time, however, I became increasingly aware of relationships between musical performance and complexities of ethnic identity that are at once American and global in nature.

Another issue intrigued me. I quickly learned that zarzuela had a mixed reputation.[4] Indeed, Réne Buch, the artistic director of Repertorio Español, once wryly noted, "If people want to show they have bad taste, they tell you they like zarzuela."[5] Why then, I wondered, would a theatrical company with ambitions to national fame mount zarzuela in any format? Certainly the genre straddles conventional categories: it embodies elements of classical and popular art, it is neither opera nor serious drama, and yet it requires both trained singers and good actors. The content is neither purely folkloric nor high art; it is too popular for some and too classical for others. The nature of the genre has changed over time, and its days of mass popularity are over, but without question the music and characters of this stage tradition have touched the lives of many listeners and deserve contemporary consideration, both scholarly and artistic.[6]

In a more serious tone, Buch reminded me that for all the hastily written zarzuelas offered by many underrehearsed companies, there exist genuine gems worthy of contemporary attention and professional production.[7] Something about zarzuela appeals to contemporary singers and actors who are willing to look beyond hasty dismissals of the genre as mediocre. Buch's daring productions of zarzuela, for example, could never be labeled conventional. I found myself wondering whether the frequently maligned popularity of zarzuela, its status as lyric theater belonging to the people, and the genre's connections to classical forms were the very features that made it particularly susceptible to fresh interpretation and thus attractive to new groups that might claim ownership.

These questions became the starting place for my dissertation, which focused on the history of zarzuela and its performance traditions in the New York metropolitan area.[8] Over the ensuing decade I continued to follow the activities of the New York artists who promoted zarzuela, but I began to expand my survey to look at zarzuela across the United States. New study of the impact of productions in other major cities, such as Miami, Chicago, Los Angeles, and Washington, D.C., and additional attention to production in the American Southwest, especially in El Paso, added other facets to my story and thus inspired this book.

Although some of the questions behind my dissertation have guided my subsequent research, I widened the scope of my investigation to better address recent developments. First, the general public has grown more aware of zarzuela. More zarzuelas were produced across the United States during the late 1990s than at any time since the 1930s, when the genre peaked in popularity. Hence, while New York remains the principal focus of my investigation, this book also notes connections among productions across the United States. The network of relationships among those working with the genre transcends geographic boundaries in ways I have only recently come to appreciate fully. Not surprisingly, the Internet has become an important tool for strengthening that network.

Finally, the production standards for American presentations are increasingly influenced by the standards of professional opera and theater. The transformation of grassroots efforts into full-scale professional enterprises gets more attention in this book than in my earlier writing, as it must if readers are to understand why I have come to regard zarzuela and its production as a critical force in the shaping of a Hispanic American identity.

Zarzuela occupies a complex position in America's music, one that builds on the genre's history both in Spain and in the New World. Understanding this position is essential for understanding why artists and audiences respond as they do to the genre and its possibilities.[9] Chapter 1 outlines this peninsular history, but it begins by emphasizing critical contrasts between modern productions and those that defined the genre in past centuries. Contemporary producers and patrons consider the history of the genre to be important, but they read it selectively.

Chapter 2 is devoted to the arrival of zarzuela in the New World and looks at the influence of Spanish touring companies on lyric drama in the former colonies. Chapter 3 focuses on creole responses to this foreign import and examines how Cuban artists and audiences used zarzuela and related genres to create expressions of national identity. The prominence of Cuban producers, artists, and supporters for zarzuela, especially in New York, calls for special attention to the history of Cuban lyric theater. If anything, the Cuban influence is even stronger in the 1990s, as presenters have found new ways to bring creole variants of zarzuela to North American stages without compromising their larger goal of using Spanish zarzuela to unite Hispanic patrons of diverse nationalities.

Historically theatrical troupes, not individual performing artists, brought zarzuela to the Americas. The production of zarzuelas in the United States is intimately connected to the development of Spanish theater in this country. Over the years the genre has continued to enjoy more regular production in theaters than in concert halls or even on recordings. Paradoxically, the theatrical aspect of the genre both enhances and limits its popularity in North America. The non-Spanish-speaking majority more readily supports zarzuela as music detached from the drama, but professional Hispanic theaters are the most consistent and thorough sources of production. Moreover, although some patrons of Hispanic theater require an introduction to the genre, a sizable portion of that clientele is already familiar with the tradition, if not each specific work.

Hispanic or Latino theaters[10] have goals as diverse as the many national backgrounds and various ancestries that constitute the Hispanic American population. Nonetheless, Hispanic Americans have found theater to be a powerful resource for defining identity and for controlling their experience in the United States. Music has consistently been an integral part of that theatrical effort. Luis Valdez, founder of California's El Teatro Campesino, a theatrical company that has gained widespread mainstream attention for its efforts to serve as a mouthpiece for the Mexican American, or Chicano, experience, has always argued that theater should do more than reflect experience; it should shape it. Theater, he says, should "inspire audiences to social action by illuminating specific points about social problems . . . and by showing or hinting at a solution."[11] The lyric theater I examine in this book realizes this potential. My primary focus, however, remains on activities centered in or connected to New York City. The companies that embrace zarzuela as part of their repertoire contrast in many ways with the aggressive activism of troupes such as the justly celebrated Teatro Campesino. New York's Repertorio Español and Thalia Spanish Theatre have not been as quick to reject the white European proscenium traditions Valdez criticizes.[12] Whereas El Teatro Campesino is a mouthpiece for Chicano concerns, companies featuring zarzuela typically speak for, and to, a more broadly defined Hispanic population.

As I imply in the scenario that opens this introduction, the audience is an important part of my study. I am more interested in the reception of zarzuela than I am in the genre's intrinsic characteristics per se. Consequently, chapter 6 is devoted to a examination of the people who attend zarzuela productions. Here I again concentrate on groups in the New York metropolitan area. The profile of these patrons is preceded by a consideration of the complexities of ethnic identity and the ways those complexities pertain to experience of audiences for zarzuela and related Spanish-language lyric theater.

With a clear sense of the audience for zarzuela, we are in a position to evaluate the relationship between production practices and the projection of ethnic identity. The goals of contemporary producers balance artistic vision with larger social goals. Thus, chapter 7 analyzes the choices presenters make regarding repertoire, approach, and general practice.

Chapter 8 examines the financial backing and publicity required to support zarzuela. The way a presentation is promoted and financed is frequently linked to the values that guide production and presumably influence reception. In recent years I have become increasingly aware of the connections between the systems supporting zarzuela in New York and those supporting classical Spanish music and theater across the United States. This network of support has developed with surprisingly little assistance from broadcast media and recording, arguably the two most potent forces, worldwide, in performance today.[13] Chapter 8 concludes by reflecting on the advantages and disadvantages of this remarkable support system.

Chapter 9 presents my conclusions regarding the contributions of zarzuela and related Spanish lyric theater to Hispanic American identity, past and present. Productions of zarzuela in the contemporary United States reflect both artistic capital and visions of an inclusive, yet esteemed, social status. As I will show, zarzuela proves to be remarkably flexible, allowing it to serve, and even define, a specific constituency of Americans with Hispanic ancestry.

1

From the Spanish Court to Madison Square Garden

Royal Origins and Public Reception

Madison Square Garden bears little resemblance to the first Teatro de la Zarzuela, the palace theater located on the wooded grounds on the outskirts of Madrid where, legend claims, the Spanish monarchs Prince Philip IV and Mariana of Austria attended the premiere of *El Laurel de Apolo* (The Wreath of Apollo) in 1657.[1] Unlike La Zarzuela's elegant, intimate stage, the Garden's cavernous arena swallows its audience amid cold, gray cement and molded plastic seats. Here New Yorkers are more likely to root for their favorite sports heroes or rock stars than to delight in music set to the measured verse of the Spanish baroque poet Calderón de la Barca.

Zarzuela—especially the genre's early court varieties—seems out of place in Madison Square Garden, as do classically trained actors and singers of Plácido Domingo's caliber. Although Domingo has sung in larger arenas, we more typically associate his performances with the crystal chandeliers and the black-tie regulars of venues such as New York's Metropolitan Opera House. Nonetheless, it was in the Garden during July 1985 that New York audiences experienced both Calderón's verse and Domingo's performance as part of José Tamayo's *Antología de la Zarzuela* (Zarzuela Anthology), a theatrical extravaganza produced with the avowed intention of reviving interest in the zarzuela both in Spain and abroad.

Tamayo's *Antología* offers a useful lens through which to consider important aspects of the genre's history. The apparent anachronism of staging a zarzuela in a sports arena shows rather strikingly how attitudes toward the genre have changed. Nevertheless, the history of the zarzuela is no more interesting than are the ways in which contemporary presenters understand and use that history. Tamayo's *Antología* provides a good starting point.

Staging a Glimpse at History

Tamayo's show opens with the *loa,* or introduction, to the zarzuela *El Laurel de Apolo* (see fig. 4). The choice reflects an awareness of history, for not only does the prologue unfold as a defense of a theatrical genre new to seventeenth-century patrons,[2] but *El Laurel de Apolo* is generally acknowledged to have been the first zarzuela written, even though Calderón did not so label it.[3] Among the musical numbers in this work is a *seguidilla* (a verse form featuring four- or seven-line strophes, frequently set to music in 6/8 or triple meter) sung by a shepherdess. Calderón's assumed collaborator, the composer Juan de Hidalgo, set an important precedent by including such a rustic dance song in a work acknowledging courtly taste and aristocratic manners. Regional dance numbers would later come to characterize the zarzuela, and though Tamayo does not include the *seguidilla* from *El Laurel de Apolo,* the next item on his program is the beloved *seguidilla* from Barbieri's 1874 zarzuela *El Barberillo de Lavapiés* (The Little Barber of Lavapiés, a Madrid neighborhood).

Tamayo offers only one scene from *El Laurel de Apolo* as a way of introducing audiences to the history of the genre. After this opening, his *Antología* quickly moves to more popular, and better known, nineteenth- and twentieth-century repertoire. The notes to Tamayo's 1986 New York program position *El Laurel de Apolo* at the beginning of "the 278-year history of the Zarzuela (1657–1936) . . . synthesized in this program." Nevertheless, these two dates mark traditions as different from each other as are Madison Square Garden and the palace theater in La Zarzuela on the royal site of the Pardo.

Tamayo's show indicates that contemporary producers selectively read the history of the zarzuela. With rare exceptions, notably the Chicago Opera Factory's 1999 fully staged production of *La Púrpura de la Rosa* (The Color of the Rose, a story of Venus and Adonis), the Baroque court tradition is certainly not what most patrons experience today.[4] Patrons and presenters alike value the zarzuela, however, in part because of its distinguished history. This reality calls for an overview of the genre's history.

The following overview defines zarzuela and its relatives at different points in time. The historical frame permits a better understanding of terms such as *sainete, zarzuela grande,* and *género chico.* Contemporary audiences regularly encounter these designations in connection with zarzuela presentations but do not always differentiate them, although historically important distinctions existed. Answers to questions regarding which aspects of the zarzuela's lineage mattered to people in the past and why promise to help illuminate the concerns that matter to those

By Arrangement with Mel Howard
Under the Patronage
of the Spanish Government

presents

ANTOLOGIA DE LA

ZARZUELA

The Music and Dances
of Spain's "Teatro Lírico"

Created and Directed by
José Tamayo

JOSEFINA ARREGUI
JESUS CASTEJÓN
CARMEN GONZÁLEZ
EMELINA LÓPEZ
FRANCISCO MUDARRA
ANTONIO RAMALLO
MARI CARMEN RAMÍREZ

with
PEDRO LAVIRGEN

BALLET ESPAÑOL "ANTOLOGIA"
Directed by and Featuring
MARIA DEL SOL
and MARIO LAVEGA

Choreography by ALBERTO LORCA

Scenery designed by
RAFAEL RICHART

THE RONDALLA LÍRICA OF MADRID
Manuel Gil, Director

CHORUS OF MADRID
José de Felipe, Director

THE ORQUESTA DE
CAMERA LIRICA OF MADRID
Manual Moreno-Buendía,
Musical Director

Exclusive Management:
MEL HOWARD ENTERPRISES, INC.

Presented under the patronage of the Spanish Government, Ministerio de Asuntos Exteriores, Instituto de Cooperación Iberoamericano, Dirección General de Relaciones Culturales, Ministerio de Cultura

"Loa" of the Zarzuela
"El Laurel de Apolo"

Original by Pedro Calderón de la Barca
Music by Manuel Parada from the original themes of Hidalgo
First performed in 1657 before His Majesty Phillip IV

In 1657 in a building called La Zarzuela (located in the Real Sitio de El Prado), the Spanish monarchs Phillip IV and Mariana of Austria attended the first performance of a comedy by Pedro Calderón de la Barca, which had been set to music by Maestro Juan de Hidalgo. This comedy was titled *El Laurel de Apolo*. Though no one was aware of it, a musical genre – not exactly opera as cultivated in Italy – had blossomed. One of the characters of the *Lao* (prologue) says "It is not a comedy, but simply / a short fable / which, in an Italian mode / is sung and performed." Zarzuela is the name of the character.

Through music, dance, and song, the 278-year history of the Zarzuela (1657-1936), when *La Tabernera del Puerto* by Sorozábal was first performed, is synthesized in this program "*Antologia de la Zarzuela*."

Iris CARMEN VILLA
Eco ANTONIO RAMALLO
Zarzuela MARIBEL ALCALÁ

Four musical groups represent the four continents: Asia, Africa, America, and Europe.

El Barberillo de Lavapiés

Words by Luis Mariano de Larra
Music by Francisco Asenjo Barbieri
First performed at the Zarzuela of Madrid in 1874

Goya's Madrid. The people conspire against Grimaldi, the Minister of Charles III. Lamparilla, the flatterer of Lavapiés (a character based on Figaro de Beaumarchais) protects the young Marchioness Estrella and her lover, accomplices in the revolt. "Since I was born on Paloma Street that name was jokingly given to me when I was a little girl," sings one of the principal characters, amid the romantic, Goyaesque Madrid populace celebrating at a fiesta.

Seguidillas, Song of Paloma, Duet of Paloma and Lamparilla, Caleseras
BALLET and the RONDALLA
Soloists CARMEN GONZÁLEZ and JESÚS CASTEJÓN

Así Nació la Zarzuela (Poem)

Written by José Herrera Petere

CARMEN VILLA
ANTONIO RAMALLO

El Niño Judío

Words by Enrique García Alvarez, Antonio Paso, and Antonio Fanosa
Music by Pablo Luna (1879-1942)
First performed at the Apolo of Madrid in 1918

Samuel, a young bookseller in Madrid, and his sweetheart, Concha, travel to India in search of the rich Jew who must be Samuel's father. Concha sings of her pride in being Spanish: "From Spain I

continued

Figure 4. Program for José Tamayo's *Antología de la Zarzuela* (1986). Mel Howard Enterprises, with support from the Spanish Government. Used with permission.

involved with contemporary productions. In short, my overriding question is this: can the history of zarzuela offer perspectives regarding the relationship between identity, language, and musical expression that may relate to contemporary activity in the United States?[5]

Early Spanish Musical Drama: Using the Language of the People

To answer this question, I began by looking at theatrical forms that pre-dated the zarzuelas of Calderón. The practice of combining spoken drama with music and dance is an old and proud Spanish tradition, dating from the twelfth-century religious dramas known as *autos.* Indeed, the combination is characteristic of a range of dramatic genres, with zarzuela emerging in the seventeenth century and maintaining its status today as the genre most strongly identified with Spanish national music theater.[6]

The concept of zarzuela has varied since its birth and is further complicated by the tendency of laypersons and scholars alike to lump together all nonoperatic, Spanish musical theater under the term *zarzuela.* The overlapping nomenclature begins to make sense only when zarzuela is examined historically and alongside other Spanish dramatic practices. For example, as Tamayo's extravaganza suggests, the genre's status, its prestige and identity, stems from its appropriation of literary practices that distinguished sixteenth-century Spanish literature worldwide. Poetic, musical, and theatrical genres all appropriated the epic content and the meter of the *romance.*[7] Invoking situations, times, and places associated with these epics allowed authors to exalt community values in new artistic formats. As definitions and views of zarzuela changed throughout the ages, so also did the genre's status and popularity. Patronage, public support, and foreign influence all played important roles in these changes.

A goldsmith from Seville, Lope de Rueda (fl. ca. 1540–67), and his group of traveling actors produced *comedias,* a clever combination of poetic and prose dialogue in four to six acts, in public squares or in the courtyards of city buildings known as *corrales.*[8] Many of Rueda's comedias featured musical numbers, frequently titled as romances. Romances were based on dances and popular songs of the era.[9]

Singers frequently performed these numbers from behind an old blanket that served as the backdrop for the crude stages that actors set up in city squares.[10] Musicians also supplied music onstage in the form of songs added to support the plot, divide the drama into scenes, or provide diversion between acts.

Golden Age Pedigrees

The parts for singers in the *comedias* of Lope de Rueda are hardly showcase vehicles, and music is not at the center of these works. Perhaps this explains why such works rarely appear on modern stages. Audiences in the past thrilled to the elegance of the verse and the energy of live performance. More important than a balance of music and verse was the fact that skilled playwrights were creating works for the general public.

Contemporary audiences are more likely to encounter the next generation of Iberian musical dramatists. Nonetheless, although present-day actors find the *comedias* of Cervantes and Lope de Vega rewarding to perform, singers aspiring to high status within their profession are less likely to jump at the chance to do so. The annual Siglo de Oro festival of Spanish-language drama in El Paso, Texas, shares many features with the Shakespeare festivals that exist on both sides of the Atlantic. The literary merit of works by the playwrights of Spain's Golden Age is a source of tremendous pride and overshadows any musical component in these dramas.

Works by Lope Félix de Vega Carpio (1562–1635) and Miguel de Cervantes Saavedra (1547–1616) are important in the history of zarzuela because they represent a standardized ratio of music to spoken verse. De Vega used music to add realistic support for dramatic content (wedding songs at weddings, reaping songs for harvests, etc.), to delineate the structure of the drama by dividing it into smaller units, or to cover the noise of stage machinery, especially with instrumental sounds. Indeed, de Vega is responsible for defining the new *comedia* of the seventeenth century into three main acts built around polymetric verse, mixing tragedy with comedy in the projection of plots on almost any topic as long as they were credible and served to mirror society in a decorous manner.[11]

Lope de Vega is most frequently cited by modern promoters of Spanish theater in the United States when they publicize the historical ties between the modern zarzuela and Spain's Golden Century dramatists.[12] Nonetheless, the first work to bear the designation *zarzuela* was written by another of Spain's great dramatists, Pedro Calderón de la Barca y Henao (1600–1681). Cotarelo points out the close relationship between Calderón's invention and the *comedia:* "This great poet, almost without wanting it or knowing it, invented for Spain a new dramatic genre as a result of only two creative factors: he reduced the three acts previously common in comedies to two, and he gave the music, and above all song, an importance almost equal to the spoken poetry. He then gave the new development in literature and art the name it carries today: zarzuela."[13]

Calderón's serendipitous formulation is one of the beloved legends that zarzuela aficionados share with one another. Elaborations of this origin story appear in many American programs, including the one offered by José Tamayo and those distributed at the Thalia Spanish Theatre in New York. Readers of program notes and artist interviews will learn that the name *zarzuela* was taken from the name of one of the royal residences of King Felipe IV. The palace located in the neighborhood of the Pardo, the royal estate not far from Madrid, served as the king's hunting lodge and was known as la Zarzuela because of the many *zarzas* (bramble or blackberry bushes) surrounding it.[14] The following description by Cotarelo finds its way into many an American program: "To entertain [the king] on days when bad weather did not permit hunting, actors [*cómicos*] from Madrid were imported to present short plays, without elaborate settings and in which instrumental music and song were paramount. Such functions, because of the setting in which they were produced, came to be called '*fiestas de la Zarzuela.*'"[15]

It soon became customary to refer to a *fiesta de la Zarzuela* simply as a zarzuela. The first work entitled "*fiesta de la Zarzuela*" was Calderón's *El Golfo de las Sirenas* (The Gulf of the Sirens). It was subtitled a "piscatory eclogue," a designation stressing both its fishing theme and its compact form. This one-act drama, framed by musical minidramas, was performed at La Zarzuela on January 17, 1657.[16] Nine years earlier, however, Calderón had presented a lyric drama entitled *El Jardín de Falerina* (Falerina's Garden) in the two-act format that would later become the standard pattern for the seventeenth-century zarzuela.[17]

Calderón's later work *El Laurel de Apolo* is generally acknowledged to be the prototypical zarzuela because it is in two acts and the sung episodes form an integral part of the drama. In addition to incorporating popular song and dance (the *seguidilla* mentioned earlier), Calderón combined features of the masque, the spectacle play, and native musical and theatrical traditions, as well as practices from Italian opera.

Despite the new zarzuela's debt to opera, however, zarzuela decidedly did *not* mirror Italian practice. This issue, often ignored by contemporary American performers, mattered greatly to Spaniards at the time, for then, as now, musical choices were governed as much by identity concerns as by aesthetic preference. Louise Stein points out that the Calderonian zarzuela was "not merely an alternative to opera, it was anti-operatic—easier to produce, enthusiastically cultivated, and ultimately more visible."[18] Although it was a cultivated form, it had a populist appeal.

As it did in the *comedia,* music served structural goals in zarzuelas. It was based on popular tunes and texts, sometimes rearranged in polyphonic settings. It was especially important in contributing a sense of realism in rustic scenes and provided the medium for mystical, supernatural, and anonymous voices and dialogue. In general, the use of recitative, characteristic of opera, held limited appeal to Spanish playwrights and composers. Louise Stein notes that Spanish composers preferred to reserve the speechlike recitative, which was popular in early Italian opera, for divine or otherworldly characters. Humans sang in a natural voice and in forms the Spaniards had enjoyed for decades, such as *coplas, estribillos, romances, tonos,* and *tonadas,* most typically set as solo songs and homophonic choruses (see the glossary for these and other terms).[19]

In and Out of the Shadow of Opera

Many contemporary performers evaluate zarzuela in terms of opera, perhaps because the Spaniards themselves did so. During the eighteenth century the aristocracy welcomed several Italian queens who exerted considerable influence in musical affairs. The first Italian-born consort of Philip V (Felipe V) was María Luisa Gabriela de Saboya. She was followed by Isabel de Farnesio. Philip's heir, Ferdinand VI (Fernando VI) married Bárbara de Braganza, a talented instrumentalist and composer who welcomed the renowned composer Domenico Scarlatti to her court and continued to support the great singer Farinelli.[20] Meanwhile, the public in the *corrales* grew increasingly infatuated with the work of operatic troupes.[21] Thus a predilection for Italian music took root in the first half of the century and continued to exert influence thereafter.

By 1740 the balance between Spanish and Italian features in zarzuela had shifted in favor of the Italian style. Bussey cites as an example of this shift a zarzuela premiered in 1743, *Viento Es la Dicha de Amor* (The Wind Is the Messenger of Love). The text, by Antonio de Zamora, is set by José de Nebra, whom Chase calls the "Lope de Vega of Spanish music" because of his musical fecundity.[22] The majority of vocal numbers in Nebra's score are set in the *da capo* aria format characteristic of Italian opera. Chase claims that the repetitive ABA form never before held much appeal to the Spaniards, who saw it as halting the dramatic pace. More important, Nebra follows Italian convention and employs cadenzas and highly ornamented (melismatic) vocal lines, particularly in the returning *da capo* section. Such passagework requires far more virtuosic singing than that found in early zarzuelas. In *Viento Es la Dicha de Amor,* as in opera, the musical drama supersedes the importance of textual clarity.[23]

This change in focus significantly affected the development of zarzuela during the eighteenth century. Cadenzas and highly ornamented musical lines obscure the meaning of the text and attract attention to the music rather than the spoken dialogue and beautifully crafted verse that were the genre's original focus. This emphasis on music continued into the nineteenth and twentieth centuries, and today most contemporary devotees would argue that the music is by far the most memorable component of the zarzuelas they know.

Most Spanish lyric drama from the eighteenth century has been relegated to the dustbin of history, even though the short and immensely popular forms that emerged during this period, including the *tonadilla* and *sainete,* left a lasting impact on musical production, consumption, and evaluation both on the Iberian Peninsula and in the colonies. Eighteenth-century audiences wanted entertainment, not edification, and elite musical language, along with the heroic and mythological plots characteristic of zarzuela before 1760, did not satisfy this desire.

It was the highly original Spanish playwright Ramón de la Cruz (1731–94) who rescued the zarzuela with *Las Labradoras de Murcia* (The Working Women of Murcia).[24] This drama, which premiered in 1769, focuses on the lives, loves, and customs of a group of peasant women who travel from farm to farm reaping the fields at harvest time. Cruz collaborated with Antonio Rodríguez de Hita (1724–94), a celebrated Spanish theorist and composer of sacred music. Rodríguez de Hita's score exhibits his absorption of Italian opera buffa style but also incorporates overt references to folk song and dance from the region of Murcia. A popularly cited example of such a reference occurs in the scene set in a silkworm nursery. A storm breaks, and it is the local belief that the silkworms will die from fright at the sound of thunder. To prevent this the workers rush onstage—carrying guitars, castanets, mandolins, and tambourines—to perform a *jota murciana,* a lively, regional dance accompanied by cheerful singing and boisterous music, which they hope will drown out the storm. This brilliant attempt to convert the raw material of local custom into nationalistic art is what prompts Chase to refer to *Las Labradoras* as "the masterpiece of the Spanish popular lyric drama in the eighteenth century."[25]

Cruz had found the dramatic mode that would later make zarzuela "the most popular form of entertainment [in Spain] short of the bullfight."[26] Despite his success, Cruz grew to feel that zarzuela had absorbed too many of the formulaic practices associated with opera, and he soon turned to the shorter, more flexible genre of the *sainete.*

Contemporary audiences are likely to encounter works designated as *sainetes.* For example, the still-popular *La Verbena de la Paloma,*[27] completed in 1894, is billed as a *sainete.* This nineteenth-century drama exemplifies the persistence of the genre. *Sainete* plots tend to be humorous and satirical, frequently exploring the customs of common folk. The music typically mirrors this emphasis on local color and features dances and songs identified with regional practices.

Another form, the *tonadilla,* also emerged in the eighteenth century to compete with the zarzuela.[28] Like the *sainete,* this one-act musical drama ultimately influenced later developments in zarzuela. Although *tonadillas* were frequently performed in the salons of aristocratic homes, their tremendous popularity resulted from an infatuated bourgeois public. Chase writes: "The rate of consumption was terrific. The maximum life of a *tonadilla* was seven days. Fecundity and facility were prerequisites for the composer of *tonadillas,* who was obliged to drive his talent to the utmost in order to earn a living and satisfy an eager, but insatiable public."[29]

Although the *tonadilla* unfolded in a single dramatic act, the material frequently fell into three parts. The first part, the introduction, typically featured verses offering an initial presentation or conversation concerning the principal subject matter. The second part was the main body of the work, during which a succession of verses, or *coplas,* appeared. The third part highlighted a final number, typically a *seguidilla,* a *tirana,* a *polaca,* or a free development in keeping with the time and place.[30]

These one-act forms, which championed current events over classic tales and nationalism over internationalism, enjoyed a short-lived but general appeal. Their structure and emphasis placed them at odds with the goals of the increasingly isolated Spanish aristocracy. The incorporation of popular elements established an aesthetic standard on which all subsequent composers were to build, even those who scorned the return of zarzuela because they wanted to develop Spanish national opera instead.

The immediate appeal of the *sainete* and *tonadilla* contributed to their demise. They were ultimately disposable forms, and by 1830 both had "run their course."[31]

Values and Reception in the Nineteenth Century

The history of zarzuela in the nineteenth century is also a history of its relationship with formal institutions of higher learning. Academic attitudes toward lyric theater may have had minimal effect on the general taste and consumption, but they did influence the attitudes of composers. The validation of the academy remains an issue today.

Some composer-librettist teams longed to write an opera in Spanish, while other Spaniards considered Italian to be the only language appropriate to the "divine art" of opera. The faculty at the Royal Conservatory (Real Conservatorio de Música), established in 1830, was strongly influenced by the champions of Italian opera, and Chase reports that students of voice and declamation were instructed in Italian but never in Spanish.[32] The twentieth-century musicologist Federico Sopeña Ibañez argues that not only was zarzuela inferior to Italian opera, but attentions to zarzuela prevented Spanish composers from developing a national operatic tradition to compete with Italy's.[33] Given this debate, it seems ironic that early nineteenth-century efforts to create a Spanish national opera led not to the start of a new operatic tradition but to the resurgence of the zarzuela. It is even more ironic that this revival of zarzuela was due in part to the efforts of a shrewd Italian composer named Basilio Basili.

In 1839 the writer Manuel Bretón de los Herreros collaborated with Basili to write a one-act work entitled *El Novio y el Concierto* (The Lover and the Concert). It was billed as a *comedia-zarzuela,* and the score contained typically Spanish dances and rhythms. This marked the first use of the designation *zarzuela* since the turn of the century. The announcement for *El Novio* states: "This comic piece, as the name indicates, makes use of music and verse, similar to the French *vaudeville,* but with the difference that the sung portions are motivated by the spoken dialogue."[34]

Bretón de los Herreros's plot offers a platform for airing the early nineteenth-century debate over Spanish versus Italian music. The story involves an affianced young tenor who, being Spanish, is dismayed at the prospect of a career singing only in Italian. He finds himself attracted to the Cinderella-like cousin of his fiancée, who has a talent for singing Spanish songs—especially songs from Andalusia. Her finesse with regional ornamentation, especially those trills known as *gorgoritos,* is irresistible. With the help of his uncle, the young fellow initiates a competition between the cousin and his fiancée, matching Italian music against Spanish music, obviously the principal objective of the drama.[35]

Basili continued to collaborate with Bretón and others during the first half of the nineteenth century to write short, often farcical zarzuelas that portrayed the music and customs of the Spanish people, particularly the Andalusians. As revived by Basili and others, zarzuela now featured contemporary themes and carried on in the popular spirit of Ramón de la Cruz and the *tonadilla,* bearing little resemblance to the heroic zarzuela of the early eighteenth century. The new form was such a success that in 1848 the Spanish government established a zarzuela company to operate in the Cruz theater so that drama could alternate with French ballet.[36]

A Plethora of Formats

By the middle of the nineteenth century, the public had grown tired of pretty farces and sought more substantial theatrical fare. An expanded version of the zarzuela, the *zarzuela grande,* arose in response to this search. Works of this sort characteristically featured three acts rather than the one or two acts favored in the second quarter of the century, and most examples were written in verse.

In 1851 the newly formed Zarzuela Society presented *Jugar con Fuego* (To Play with Fire) in the Circo theater. This three-act *zarzuela grande* featured poetry by Ventura de la Vega and music by the most important of all nineteenth-century composers, Francisco A. Barbieri. Cotarelo cannot resist comparing it with Italian opera and notes that *Jugar con Fuego* is a dignified work. The additional length, previously thought impractical, facilitated the development of more serious subject matter. He notes that Barbieri "did not try to obtain laughs from ridiculous old ladies, nor bandits, nor Gypsies, nor proud Andalusian characters."[37]

The *género grande,* as this form is known, became quite popular and remained in vogue until the 1880s. The dramatic themes varied, but historical subjects were by far the favorite, especially those involving Spanish history as seen in the courts. Political intrigue under Carlos III, for example, provides the subject matter for Barbieri's *El Barberillo de Lavapiés.* Salter calls this "the most celebrated classic in the repertory."[38] His judgment is supported by the attention the work has received lately in Madrid and from recent New York artists and audiences, who patronized at least four productions of the work in the 1980s.[39]

Despite its longer, more serious format, the nineteenth-century *zarzuela grande* was promoted as popular, public entertainment. Another format, the *género chico,* also emerged during this period and further solidified zarzuela's public appeal. The growing popularity of zarzuela shaped the nation's performance venues. From 1851 to 1880 the Circo Theater presented primarily zarzuelas and as a result was renamed Teatro Lírico Español. Earlier, in 1857, the Sociedad de Artistas, a group devoted to the cultivation of zarzuela, sponsored the construction of a new theater called El Teatro de la Zarzuela, which still stands in Madrid today.[40]

By 1867 the Spanish economy had weakened as a result of political upheavals.[41] In that same year the *teatro por horas* (hour-long theater) originated as an attempt to combat now declining theater attendance. Bentivegna describes it thus: "The idea was to present in the Recreo theater a series of *funciones por horas* [hour-long events] instead of the four or five hour *funciones completas* presented in the rest of the theaters in Madrid. This project would make possible a much lower ticket price and would attract people for its cheapness, as well as for the convenience of being able to choose any hour for attending the theater."[42] The idea was a huge success.

Such a format demanded a different type of entertainment from the *zarzuela grande,* and the *género chico,* a shorter, simpler type of zarzuela that could be produced within an hour, emerged as a new twist on the old taste for short comic sketches and collective self-examination. The *género chico* did not always incorporate music, but the lyric versions enjoyed unparalleled popularity in major theaters throughout Madrid. Lionel Salter compares the extraordinary popularity of the *género chico* to that of the *tonadilla* of the previous century. So great was the public's demand for this new form that in the 1890s eleven theaters in Madrid were devoted entirely to the performance of the *género chico.*[43]

Bentivegna notes that Madrid itself—"her people, her buildings and streets, and her traditions"—is "the single greatest theme of the zarzuela of the *género chico.*"[44] For instance, the lower classes of Madrid are characterized in arguably the most famous of all *género chico* dramas, *La Verbena de la Paloma,* a work that continues to attract audiences today both in the United States and in Spain.[45] Given how beautifully the music of Tomás Bretón y Hernández captures the spirit of Madrid, it is difficult to accept that he saw the minor genre as secondary to his serious interest in writing Spanish opera and *zarzuela grande.*[46]

Today, when zarzuela and its variants no longer dominate theatrical offerings, the *género chico* is considered a kind of zarzuela. The term *zarzuela* has always been a fairly elastic designation, but after 1880 it became even more so. Depending on the circumstances of performance and plot, designations such as *jugete, revista, sainete, parodia, humorada, apropósito, écloga, pasatiempo,* and others were applied to various types of theatrical presentation featuring music. All these forms were considered to be close relatives to zarzuela, and examples of them were frequently billed as such, despite the composers' labels.[47] This practice continues today, especially in New York, where the larger non-Spanish-speaking public has only recently become acquainted with the term. Tomás Bretón may have labeled his *La Verbena de la Paloma* a *sainete,* but in the United States it is promoted as a *género chico* zarzuela.

International versus National Recognition: The Opera Debate Rekindled

The success of the *género chico* did not eradicate Spanish composers' desires to create a national opera tradition that would position Spain as a serious player on the international music circuit. There were three basic perspectives on the best way to accomplish this task, and all of them have influenced contemporary attitudes toward zarzuela.

The first view held that serious zarzuela, *zarzuela grande,* could serve as a foundation for Spanish opera. All that was needed was to replace the spoken dialogue with sung recitative. This is exactly what Emilio Arrieta did in 1871 when he presented the revised version of his 1855 zarzuela *Marina.* Arrieta was one of many composers who wrote both zarzuelas and operas, relying, as Chase notes, "on the latter for prestige and the former for cash."[48] Critics of the revision approach claim that the recitatives were too Italianate.[49] Armando de María y Campos, however, describes *Marina* as "one of the greatest triumphs of the Spanish lyric theater" and notes how Mexican audiences from 1869 to 1946 thrilled to it both as an opera and reset as a zarzuela.[50] Contemporary aficionados of zarzuela know *Marina* only as an opera, but many feel that it does not play well.[51] Today it is usually performed in concert format, and few recall staged versions of it.

In opposition to those who felt that zarzuela should be elevated to the artistic heights of opera, another contingent felt that serious zarzuela was already a sufficiently distinctive national form; altering it to make it more like opera would damage it. Cotarelo y Mori is the most eloquent spokesperson for this perspective. He states: "There is no valid foundation whatsoever for the idea of inferiority that some persons attribute to this class of genuinely Spanish lyric drama. . . . The zarzuela was and is dramatic, and even tragic, because it is a complete lyrical dramatic form just as much as the opera, and without limitations of any sort. It differs from the opera only in that a considerable portion of the text is not sung but is spoken."[52]

The third compositional perspective was to ignore zarzuela altogether and devote all energy to composing opera. The composer and musicologist Felipe Pedrell (1841–1922) is the most important figure to espouse this means to develop a truly Spanish opera. In the prologue to his tripartite lyric drama *Los Pireneos* (The Pyrenees), he states that Spanish opera must be based on a fusion of artistic and popular traditions, including large doses of "living folklore." The composer Amadeo Vives (1871–1932) began his career writing operas based on Pedrell's principles. Vives achieved moderate success with *Maruxa* (1913), a zarzuela that is labeled an *écloga lírica* but sung throughout, as with opera. Ironically, however, his fame rests with his zarzuelas *Los Bohemios* (The Bohemians) and *Doña Francisquita.* The latter is considered a classic in modern Spain and was performed hundreds of times in Latin America and the Caribbean. It is also one of the zarzuelas presented most frequently in New York today.

The Twentieth Century: From Craze to Revival

Early twentieth-century zarzuelas tended to involve more suggestive material, more spectacular and elaborate productions, and in general a more sentimental tone than did previous works. The *género chico* remained popular, although it was soon overshadowed by the more risqué *género ínfimo,* a genre based on the French variety shows and described by Salter as a "crude revue sketch."[53]

A related development was the rise in popularity of the *revista.* Formerly presented as an elaborately staged commentary on current events, the *revista* became a huge spectacle with chorus girls and fancy stage effects. It enjoyed great success throughout the first half of the twentieth century both in Spain and in Latin America. A survey of current theater listings in *El Fígaro,* a Madrid newspaper, reveals that Spanish audiences continue to enjoy *revistas,* although there are far fewer of them than there were fifty years ago.

Spanish composers used the term *opereta* for works exhibiting the gay, graceful qualities admired in the operas of Gounod and Delibes as well as in the waltzes of Strauss. One work popular with contemporary American audiences, *La Corte de Faraón* (Pharaoh's Court), written in 1910 by Perrín y Palacios with music by Vicente Lleó, is designated as an *opereta* and exhibits just such tendencies. The story makes use of risqué jokes and phrases with double meanings as it parodies Verdi's *Aïda* as well as the biblical story of Joseph and the wife of Potifar ("Putifar" in Spanish). Its exotic setting also allows for elaborate staging.

Many scholars cite Federico Moreno Torroba (whose serious zarzuela *Luisa Fernanda,* written in 1932, is a current favorite in the United States) as one of the last composers to work in a climate supporting zarzuela creation.[54] The renowned Spanish operatic tenor Plácido Domingo, whose parents performed and produced zarzuela, challenges that view somewhat. In his biography he writes about activity in the 1940s: "A great many zarzuelas were being written. . . . In those days zarzuela singers performed once or twice every weekday and twice or three times on Sundays. Many works were given a hundred or even two hundred performances and as soon as a company stopped performing one zarzuela, another was immediately mounted."[55]

Despite the activity Domingo recalls, and despite continued production outside Madrid, especially in Barcelona, the fact remains that after 1934 productions of new zarzuelas in Spain gradually tapered off. The disastrous effects of the Spanish Civil War (1936–39) initiated a decline later reinforced by the emergence of television as the primary mode of popular entertainment.[56] In the past twenty years theatrical companies have focused primarily on presenting classics of modern zarzuela, all of which were written between 1870 and 1940.

By 1951 reporters no longer noted new works and a flurry of zarzuela production but referred instead to "a revival of zarzuela."[57] The birth of the long-playing record in the 1950s made it possible for Montilla, Soria, Angel, London, and Columbia to distribute excerpts from "the most enduringly popular pieces."[58] The Spanish government under the regime of General Francisco Franco tried to encourage the production of zarzuela and lent support to a series of zarzuela recordings devoted to documenting the genre. These efforts helped to turn a handful of works into classics. At the same time, however, official censors banned some of the more spicy works, including Lleó's *La Corte de Faraón,*[59] a work that remains appealing to contemporary New York audiences.

By 1960 zarzuela had become a dated genre. In 1966 Spanish impresario José Tamayo organized a show of excerpts of music and dance designed to provide a whirlwind tour of zarzuela's 300-year history. With partial support from the Spanish Ministry of Culture, Tamayo's *Antología de la Zarzuela* has toured the world over the last thirty years as a means of stimulating interest in the genre. A series of televised films of zarzuela productions, produced in 1968, spurred additional interest.[60] In 1979, however, when Tamayo presented his *Antología* in a huge gala performance at Madrid's Monumental Bullring, the entertainment weekly *Variety* reported that "many observers had serious doubts that the old musical form had enough adherents to justify such a mammoth endeavor."[61]

Richard Traubner noted in the early 1980s that staged zarzuelas had not regained the enormous popularity they once enjoyed. Today he seems more optimistic about the new productions that have come largely, but not exclusively, from Madrid, during the past decade or so. Although he laments that "Madrid's Teatro de la Zarzuela, in spite of its name, now only does short seasons of three or four zarzuelas a year, interspersed with grand opera presentations,"[62] there are other nodes of activity to indicate that Spaniards may be ready once more to support their unique lyric drama.

Among the new efforts is the series of authoritative versions of full zarzuela scores being prepared by the Instituto Complutense de Ciencias Musicales, an educational affiliate of the Spanish Society of Authors and Publishers (SGAE) working with the patronage of the Ministry of Culture. These publications have led to new performances and an equally well crafted set of new recordings on compact disc (released on the Auvidis Valois label with both French and Spanish support).[63] In addition to the government, private foundations, such as the Fundación Guerrero, have taken the lead in promoting new interest in zarzuela. In 1995 the Fundación Guerrero cosponsored the International Zarzuela Congress in Madrid, which attracted scholars from around the world.

The new productions that have been appearing at Madrid's major theaters are perhaps the best sign of a serious revival; many of these are truly exciting. Richard Traubner is equally enthusiastic about the productions he has seen in more intimate venues, mounted by smaller companies such as the Opera Cómica de Madrid.[64] Most of these productions continue to feature old favorites of the repertoire, such as Vives's *Doña Francisquita,* Moreno Torroba's *Luisa Fernanda,* or Guerrero's *Los Gavilanes.* (It seems that audiences need to travel to Latin America or the United States for the rare opportunity to hear a freshly composed zarzuela, such as the Argentine production of *Viva la Verbena,* by Luis Aguile, or the New York production of *Los Jíbaros Progresistas,* by Puerto Rican born composer Manuel Fernández.)

Despite the new activity, support for zarzuela is limited. Traubner writes, "Paradoxically, the very Spanishness of zarzuela has, on the one hand, prevented its exportability in other languages and, on the other, made it too tritely and narrowly nationalistic for sophisticated young Spaniards. They disdain its mass appeal, its too catchy song hits (drummed over the radio to the delight of Madrid taxi drivers), its old-fashioned association with their grandparents' tastes."[65] Zarzuela faces stiff competition from rock and other forms of popular music that now entertain youth at their late-night parties.

Basic Values and Historical Legacies

The memory of Tamayo and Domingo at Madison Square Garden provides a guide to the features that most concern contemporary performers and supporters of zarzuela. Just as in the past zarzuela afforded an opportunity for Spaniards to assert their individuality in the face of domination by Italian and Central European standards, today the genre continues to stand for a distinctive Hispanic legacy.

Repertoire that highlights a legacy of literary excellence, or music that offers a vehicle for vocal display and regional color, remains attractive to contemporary performers. Although the term *zarzuela* has been used to refer to significantly different kinds of lyric theater, it has always indicated a distinctly Spanish format connected to national identity. The Spanish pedigree remains of value to proponents in the United States, and this has facilitated the genre's importation.

Structurally the zarzuela format has relied heavily on combining spoken dialogue with song and dance, allying the genre with theatrical interests as much as with musical ones. Even when composers incorporated foreign musical traditions, their insistence on the primacy of the Spanish language continued to distinguish zarzuela from other traditions of lyric drama.

Another consistent trait of zarzuela is the continual blend of popular and elite concerns, a trait that manifests itself both in the design of individual works and in the kind of attention the genre came to attract. This blend is essential to the success of zarzuela in the United States. Calderón's zarzuela incorporated pastoral scenes and a few songs in popular style, despite the writer's attempt to cater to the prevailing court taste. Even in the nineteenth century, when zarzuela was viewed primarily as popular entertainment, it attracted the attention of Spain's most celebrated classical musicians, including Albéniz, Granados, and de Falla.

Finally, it seems impossible to talk of zarzuela and not also mention opera. Zarzuela has always been compared to opera and perhaps always will be. Certainly the decision by the editors of *Opera News* to devote their July 1997 issue to zarzuela is evidence of this continuing, though virtually unidirectional, association. At times opera offered inspiration to Spanish composers, and at other times it provided opponents, but few opera composers or performers have turned to zarzuela for inspiration. This uneasy relationship with opera may have accounted for much of zarzuela's popularity through its various stages, and it certainly accounts for the kind of attention the genre has received from musicologists and critics. This battle for status and recognition, as well as for creative options, followed the genre to the colonies, increasing its attraction to performers, audiences, and promoters in the New World. As I will show, Plácido Domingo and José Tamayo are neither the first nor the only artists to capitalize on zarzuela's curious blend of elite models and populist appeal.

2

Zarzuela in the New World

Peninsular Imports and Creole Responses

If Americans know only a single example of touring zarzuela performers who promoted both new and beloved zarzuelas across the Atlantic, that example is the celebrated team of Plácido Domingo Sr. and his wife, Pepita Embil. Their famous son, Plácido Jr., has kept their memory before the public with his fond recollections of their work. Domingo shared his memories of his parents' tours to the Americas with composer and producer Federico Moreno Torroba. "To me," he said, "the melodies of zarzuela were the lullabies of my childhood."[1] He recalled the family's subsequent move to Mexico, the site from which they operated their own touring theatrical company, with which he performed as a youth. The Domingos constitute comparatively recent examples of a long history of Iberian artists who carried peninsular fashions in lyric drama to Spain's colonies. The popularity of zarzuela in Latin America and the Caribbean is due in no small measure to such traveling artists and to those, like the Domingos, who settled in the Americas and influenced local production.

Although it is not surprising that immigrants from Spain, such as the Domingos, would be interested in presenting lyric drama recalling the customs and practices of Iberia, it is harder to conceive that Latin American and Caribbean audiences in the nineteenth century, especially during the years of struggle for independence, would welcome these imports so readily. It is even more of a wonder that people of Caribbean and Latin American ancestry residing in the United States—people often several generations removed from a direct connection to Spain—would find much with which to identify in peninsular zarzuela.

The same may be said today, for time has not changed the general perception that zarzuela represents a distinctly Spanish perspective. When the Cuban-born theater director René Buch asked me, "What interests you in zarzuela?" I found myself wondering the same for him. Cuban American patrons seem especially supportive of zarzuela. Why is that so? Does the history of the genre in Latin America and the Caribbean help to explain which groups of people support it today?

The annals of zarzuela in Latin America offer some answers to such questions. The primary concern of this text, the response of North American audiences (still largely Hispanic) to zarzuela, is certainly related to the genre's popularity in countries south of the border, but zarzuela's reception in Latin America and the Caribbean has its own history and ultimately turns on a completely different set of social, political, and cultural concerns. Among such concerns is the nature and status of national identity and the promotion of creole (native-born) views versus peninsular (Iberian or European) perspectives. Thus the arrival of zarzuela to the Americas is just part of the story; another part concerns how Latin Americans responded to these traditions and to what degree they made them their own.

Criollismo: A Prefatory Discussion of New World Appropriation and Self-representation

Criollismo is a perspective that takes pride in recognizing the non-European contributions to blended ancestry that were devalued during colonial rule.[2] Applied to musical drama, the term denotes works that reflect the values and concerns of local people. Regional tastes, goals, and colonial experience influenced the development of locally born (creole, or in Spanish, *criollo*) lyric traditions that competed with, even as they were based on, European models. The historical overview that follows this introductory discussion shows that the interaction of Spanish-born performers with local artists led not only to new forms but also to new perspectives regarding imported ones.

Latin American perspectives guiding new composition and performance strategies often reflected regional politics between several different social groups: *peninsulares* (Iberian-born immigrants), *creoles* (native-born residents claiming European ancestry), *indígenas* (indigenous people, i.e., American Indians and their ancestors), and *esclavos* (slaves, mostly those of African ancestry, although others, such as Chinese laborers, fell into this class). Complicating matters were those whose heritage included more than one of these different ancestries. Social politics often pitted Creoles (who benefited from their ancestral links to the colonial power even though their status was customarily lower than that of the Spanish-born *peninsulares*) against residents with indigenous or African ancestry. In general, across the Americas hierarchies of social status turned on issues of ethnicity and placed *peninsulares* at the top, Creoles on the rung below, and those of so-called mixed blood still lower. The dilemma of self-representation became more acute as each of Spain's colonies gained independence, and music, like literature and art, became a powerful if sometimes controversial tool in establishing new national identities.

The term *creole,* whether applied to people or forms of lyric drama, is not simply defined. Although it designates someone, or something, of European ancestry born in the New World, the exact composition of ancestry varies depending on circumstance, status, and locale. Entire volumes have been devoted to defining the term, and some of the New World's most celebrated writers, including the Caribbean-born authors Aimé Césaire and Frantz Fanon, have explored the nature and dilemmas of Creole identity—especially the problem of having to create a non-European self-identity using European forms (language and, among other things, musical genres).[3]

In many Caribbean countries (as in the state of Louisiana, where the term is part of general vernacular) the designation *Creole* (*criollo* in Spanish) indicates an emphasis on European ancestry as a distinctive component of heritage, whatever the remaining contributions. In contrast, "Creoles of color," although not always so labeled, reflect a blend of European and African ancestries, and perhaps other heritages as well. Terms used to emphasize the non-European component of Creole ancestry—in some cases used to quantify it—include *mulato* (descendent of a black and white parent), *pardo* (light brown, a synonym for *mulato* in Cuba), *moreno* (dark in color, sometimes used as a title), *trigueño* (the color of dark wheat, darker than *pardo,* a synonym for *moreno*), and *mestizo* (a descendant of an Indian and white parent).[4] Most of these terms are ascribed labels with a pejorative taint, not positive self-definitions. In certain situations, especially in circumstances calling for an unequivocal distinction from the colonial presence, the inclusion of African or Indian ancestry served, and continues to serve, as a badge of distinction separating New World identities from European colonial ones.

Latin American nations may share many patterns of development, but they have significantly different histories. The developments covered in my historical examination highlight the interactions among Cuba, Mexico, and Spain while touching on comparable musical activity in other Latin American nations. Although most of Spain's colonies gained independence in the early 1800s, Cuba remained a colony almost until the end of the century. Slavery was not abolished on the island until 1868, and well into the 1870s Cubans continued secretly to import slaves to work the sugar plantations on which much of the economy depended. Thus slavery continued long after the United States abolished the practice and Cuban officials had formally prohibited it.[5] This had obvious repercussions for racial and ethnic politics. It also had important musical implications.

Just as Cuba was an important trade site for the importation of slaves to the

New World, artistic traffic to and from the island helped to transmit African-influenced genres and styles throughout Latin America. Spanish fashions in music, as in other domains, enjoyed privileged status in Cuban culture throughout the nineteenth century. The ten-year war for independence (1868–78) was inconclusive, and it was 1895 before the Cuban leader José Martí led the country in a war that developed into the Spanish-American War, culminating in the establishment of the Cuban Republic in 1898 (with a U.S. governor until 1902).

Commenting on some of the musical repercussions of differing political and economic development across Latin America, Robert Stevenson writes: "Since most of the Spanish colonies in the New World revolted during the same decade, 1810–1820, it has often been assumed that culturally as well as politically the colonies had all reached approximately the same stage in their development around 1810. This is an untenable assumption, however. When other colonies were at the crest of their wave, musically speaking, Mexico was in a trough."[6] Among the reasons he cites for this low level of musical development is Mexico's relatively stable economic position, which attracted foreign talent, thus creating a cultural environment that did not encourage the development of native-born talent.[7] As long as foreign work provided the standard by which all local creation was judged, creole forms were regularly dismissed as populist or light fare (and therefore not to be taken seriously).

As the following historical overview will show, zarzuela and its related light forms offered particularly amenable templates for absorbing local influence. Works in these new forms were often performed alongside ones imported from Spain. The local dramas were rarely accorded high status in circles of power, however, since they were local creations based on popular models. Imported forms of music and drama developed strong roots from an early date and have continued to dominate the musical stage well into the twentieth century.

Transported Traditions: The Dominance of Peninsular Models

When the Spaniards first arrived in the New World at the end of the fifteenth century, they found indigenous theater traditions. Little is known of these traditions because the conquistadors, with the aid of the Catholic church, quickly suppressed and eventually eradicated such rituals of Amerindian culture. Consequently, indigenous practice had little influence on the development of lyric theater in Latin America. It was not until the late nineteenth century, as a result of efforts to create art from an identifiably nationalistic perspective, that Latin Americans again began to take interest in their native traditions.

Although the first European settlers landed in the Caribbean, the most influential early settlements were established in Mexico and Peru in the 1530s. Mexico City in the north and Lima in the south served as the two great centers for the dissemination of Spanish culture to the New World. Cuba, too, quickly became one of the most important centers of New World musical activity, in part because of the cultivation of local talent and activity and also because practically all ships traveling from Spain to Latin America stopped in Cuba.

In the sixteenth and seventeenth centuries, colonists in Latin America used drama primarily to further the instructional intentions of the Catholic church. *Autos sacramentales, coloquios,* and *entremeses* were imported to the Spanish colonies, and it was not until the seventeenth century that a purely secular theater took hold.[8] Even then, Spanish music and theater, including the early zarzuela, were enjoyed primarily by those in the viceregal courts of Mexico City and Lima. Gilbert Chase writes: "In these two cities, as to a lesser extent elsewhere, the musical art of Spain was duplicated in all its manifestations. The Spanish drama, which as we know, was almost invariably associated with music, flourished with notable vigor at Lima during the sixteenth and seventeenth centuries. The plays of Calderón, especially, were held in high esteem there, his popularity enduring even longer than it did in Spain."[9]

Far from simply paralleling the fashions of Europe, colonial expressions represented a lingering fascination with genres past their prime in their lands of origin. When opera and zarzuela were the current new rage in seventeenth-century Lima and Mexico City, the *loas, autos, mojigangas, bailes,* and *entremeses* of the previous century survived in other South America capitals, in minor cities, and even in remote religious missions where, according to Vega, they surfaced in honor of specific occasions, such as grand ecclesiastical festivals, coronations, royal weddings, and personal receptions.[10]

Regional Preferences: Performance and Repertoire

While drama was imported from Spain, new works were created by Latin American composers and playwrights who took their cues from peninsular fashions. As early as 1701 Calderón's *La Púrpura de la Rosa* was performed in Lima with new music by the Spanish-born Peruvian Tomás Torrejón y Velasco.[11] Eleven years later the second New World opera, *La Parténope,* based on a book by Silvio Stampiglia and with music by the Mexican-born chapel master Manuel de Sumaya (also spelled "Zumaya"), premiered at the viceregal palace in Mexico City. Sumaya's music in this work presumably featured a blend of influences from seventeenth-century liturgical choral practice (such as the imitative polyphony and voice pairing alternating with homophonic passages found in his extant *villancicos*) as well as approaches drawn from late baroque Italian opera, including recitatives and *da capo* arias with demanding virtuoso passages for the soloist.[12] In the New World as in Spain, lyric theater responded to the larger European fascination with Italian opera. Sumaya's work also illustrates the close relationship between church and theater in the Spanish colonies. In these eras before conservatories of music existed, church musicians were among the few with formal education in music and literature, and their influence extended far beyond chapel walls.

Despite this early start with opera, Koegel points out that few Mexican composers followed Sumaya's lead. Operas were not regularly performed in Mexican theaters until the nineteenth century, although individual arias by Italian and Mexican composers were performed in cathedrals and probably other settings.[13]

In the second half of the eighteenth century the *tonadilla escénica* (intermission scene designed for a small number of singers, similar to the intermezzo in Italy at this time) enjoyed popularity throughout Hispanic America. Both the *tonadilla* and the *sainete* appeared in Buenos Aires around 1770, in Chile in 1777, and probably earlier in Lima. Vega reports that until 1850 the *tonadilla* and *sainete* "enthused audiences and irritated critics of the New Republic [of Argentina]."[14]

The adoption of the *tonadilla* and *sainete* signaled the development of new venues and audiences for lyric drama. The center of dramatic influence moved from the cathedrals and palaces to the bourgeois salons and the public theaters that were springing up throughout the eighteenth century. The association between theaters and salons was greater than we might think today. The salon represented a principal concert locale; indeed, Mayer-Serra notes that until the 1890s, Mexican concerts resembled salon gatherings more than they did the staged public concerts cultivated in nineteenth-century Europe.[15] In these more intimate and flexible American concert settings, excerpts from musical dramas were favorite material.

Intimacy and flexibility did not prevent Latin American theaters from carrying status. The Cuban attitude toward public theater reveals the symbolic weight of both the venue and any performances associated with it, and by 1900 every Cuban city of any importance had a theater of its own. In his brief history of Cuban theater, Rine Leal explains that for Cubans, a theater symbolized not just culture but also aristocratic influence and political strength.[16] In the theater one could see all types of spectacles, from dramatic tragedies to ballets, opera to circus acrobats. Leal emphasizes the glamour of the Cuban theaters, noting their continued programming of Spanish drama, especially zarzuela. He writes: "The island was abloom with theaters, mimicry imposed the norms of elegance, the Italians gave the aesthetic touch, and in the *palcos* and *grilles* ladies and gentlemen gallantly circulated, while the *zarzuela* or *drama español* was repeated night after night."[17]

Leal also suggests that music, rather than spoken drama, made these productions worth attending. "I don't think, in truth, that the quality of these early seasons was very brilliant, but what was most agreeable was the scenic music: *tonadillas, tiranas, zarabandas, seguidillas, boleros, jácaras, dengues, jarabes, minuets de corte, gavotas, pan de xarabe, polkas, cacuchas,* and much more."[18]

Although opera was considered the highest form of theater in Cuba and elsewhere in Latin America (Stevenson refers to the 1800s in Mexico as "the operatic century"), the general public continued to prefer drama that combined spoken dialogue with song.[19] To please this public, operas were often translated to Spanish or converted into zarzuelas. Béhague offers an early example of this trend with his description of an 1806 performance of Cimarosa's *El Filósofo Burlando* (The Scoffing Philosopher) in Mexico's Teatro Coliseo, which transformed the Italian opera buffa into a zarzuela by substituting spoken dialogue for the recitatives.[20]

The *Sainete* and Its Influence on New World Drama

Although New World composers continued to write in styles reflecting Spanish tradition, public taste favored more local subject matter, especially outside the centers of the viceroyalties, where aristocratic manners held less sway. Audiences throughout Latin America responded so favorably to the *sainetes* of Ramón de la Cruz that other New World dramatists eagerly adapted his format to create native forms. According to Pasquariello, Cruz's dramas enjoyed more popularity in the Americas than in Spain. They were performed in Mexico as early as 1778, appeared in Lima and Bogotá before 1800, and remained in favor in the New World, especially in Argentina and Chile, much longer than in Spain.[21] Given the simmering revolutionary climate during this period, it is not surprising to find audiences responding eagerly to forms that provided opportunity to express popular views and celebrate regional identities.

In Argentina the Spanish *sainete* gave birth to the *sainete gauchesco,* in which the Argentine "cowboy," or *gaucho,* replaced local Spanish characters.[22] By 1800 Argentine customs and dances began to supplant Spanish tradition in a new dramatic form known as the *melólogo,* which combined elements of both the *tonadilla* and the *sainete.*[23] Such adaptations were common throughout Latin American but were even more assiduously developed later in Cuba.

Despite this emerging interest in creole forms of music and drama that reflected local custom, the continued reliance on foreign work throughout Latin America is all but overwhelming.[24] Such an emphasis is made clear in the fascinating history of Manuel Areu (1845–1942), a touring performer, composer, author, and director of musical theater, that was compiled by Mary Montaño and expanded and analyzed by Sally Bissell. Areu's story provides rarely documented details regarding the activities of touring zarzuela troupes. The analyses of Areu's extended residencies in Cuba, Mexico, and the United States offer unparalleled insight into zarzuela's journey to Hispanic America and in particular highlight the regular artistic exchange between Cuban and Mexican stages.[25] The vicissitudes of life as a traveling musician, from serendipitous contacts to the draining competition and power struggles among performers, are well illustrated by Areu's experience. Equally important is the insight the accounts offer regarding performance practices and the politics surrounding public reception of zarzuela and other types of music and drama. Examined in the context of other daring nineteenth-century artists who traveled from Spain to Latin American with their dramatic companies, Areu's example makes the details of history come alive.

Nineteenth-Century Zarzuela Comes to the Americas

Not long after interest in zarzuela revived in Spain during the 1850s, theatrical companies were formed to tour the provinces. Shortly thereafter some of these groups traveled to Latin America to present the latest repertoire in theaters there. Vega reports that audiences in Buenos Aires saw their first season featuring the romantic zarzuela in 1855, and a decade later a regular season of zarzuela performances was established there. Touring companies dedicated to the production of zarzuela appeared in Mexico in 1855 and Chile in 1857. Vega speculates that zarzuela appeared in Lima prior to 1855, but the country first to receive romantic Spanish zarzuela was Cuba, in 1853.[26]

Zarzuela was also carried to Puerto Rico, where audiences in San Juan enjoyed presentations by foreign companies as early as 1858. From that year until 1914, theaters in San Juan featured at least one visiting troupe of zarzuela performers. Between 1874 and 1929 there were at least ten companies actively producing zarzuela in Puerto Rico.[27]

A second wave of performers departed Spain for the New World in the 1860s, Manuel Areu among them. Born in Madrid, Areu began his career in the 1850s as a violinist for various theatrical companies in that city and in the Spanish provinces. In 1864 Areu's parents, both actors, collaborated with José Rogel, a musician colleague, and formed a zarzuela troupe known as the Areu-Rogel Zarzuela Company. They toured the provinces for three years playing in Burgos, Valladolid, Pamplona, Santander, Vitrios, and Valencia, with their son as an integral member.[28]

In 1868, partly in response to the struggles that Madrid theaters faced after the war and partly in response to the invitation of Cuban impresario Don José Albisu, the Areu family traveled to Havana and began a new zarzuela company bearing the name of its promoter. Here the newly formed Albisu Zarzuela Company faced a fresh set of challenges, including competition from another Spanish troupe led by the famous composer Joaquín Gaztambide. Arriving in Cuba, the company was greeted by political unrest as Cubans entered their own war, the ten-year struggle for independence. The competition between the Gaztambide and Areu companies points to the great influx of European troupes, performers, and works that flooded the stages of Latin America, particularly those of Cuba and Mexico, during the watershed year of 1868. Throughout the rest of the century, foreign entertainment dominated the stages, and at least one foreign zarzuela company operated in each capital city.[29]

In Cuba, Manuel Areu encountered firsthand the identity and power struggles of those under colonial rule. His sympathies for creole arts did not surface on this trip, but in subsequent years Areu worked closely with artists who championed creole expression, and he began to incorporate regionalisms into his own compositions. In 1868 he was made aware of the economic impact of identity politics, for frequent clashes between *peninsulares* and *criollos* dampened theatrical attendance. A move from Havana to Matanzas did not improve matters, so the company relocated in Mexico to finish their contract with Albisu.[30]

Travel itineraries indicate that, like other traveling troupes, the Albisu company offered zarzuelas and other dramatic productions in provincial towns as well as in major cities. After their ship arrived in Veracruz early in 1869, the Albisu company traveled by stagecoach to Jalapa, Puebla, and Apizaco, performing in each town, and then continued on to Mexico City, where they opened at the Iturbide Theater on March 4, 1869, to a warm welcome.[31] Their first season included several works that might be familiar to fans of zarzuela today, such as *Campanone* (Loud Mouth), *Luz y Sombra* (Shadow and Light), *El Relámpago* (Lightning), *Marina*, *El Caballero Particular* (The Peculiar Gentleman), *El Juramento* (The Oath), *El Postillón de la Rioja* (The Postilion of Rioja), *Un Pleito* (A Lawsuit), *El Diablo en el Poder* (The Devil in Power), *El Valle de Andorra* (Andorra's Valley), *Los Diamantes de la Corona* (The Diamonds of the Crown), and *El Sargento Federico* (Sergeant Federico).[32]

The move to Mexico did not stem the rivalry between the Albisu company and that of Gaztambide, for the composer also took his troupe to Mexico City. This competition was augmented by the capital city's growing fondness for French opéra bouffe, a form with which neither company was then prepared to compete, and by the end of 1869 both troupes had disbanded.

The popularity of the new French form of entertainment, opéra bouffe, resulted from a series of political and social upheavals that marked the second half of the nineteenth century. Bissell notes that the peak popularity of this genre corresponds exactly with the reign of Napoléon III (1852–70). The corruption, hypocrisy, and grand delusions of the period were material for these operatic parodies and burlesques, which assumed two contradictory roles. First, opéra bouffe served as an outlet for social criticism, a role that was generally tolerated by official censors since the genre was considered to be carefree entertainment. Second, the genre captured visions of everyday life. The pretensions of the court of Napoléon III were fair game, and critiques were often disguised as components of "crazy, incredible tales" or updated myths.[33] The most celebrated proponent of this genre was Offenbach. Lightly orchestrated but memorable melodies and dance rhythms, based on such fashionable dances as the waltz, polka, quadrille, or cancan, characterized the musical numbers in this genre. Spoken dialogue tended to dominate the musical components.

For a short time (from approximately 1866 to 1871), Spanish composers imitated opéra bouffe and created their own lyric *bufo* dramas, some by well-known zarzuela composers such as Arrieta, Barbieri, and Oudrid.[34] Translated works of Offenbach and other French composers were also presented in Madrid. These works traveled to Latin America with various touring companies. Areu's memoires indicate that while in Mexico and Cuba, his parents' troupe performed representative *bufo* works such as Rogel's *Los Infiernos de Madrid* (The Infernos of Madrid), Arrieta's *Un Sarao y una Soirée* (A Spanish Gathering and a French Party) and *El Potosí Submarino* (The City Underwater), and Barbieri's *Robinson,* as well as translations of Offenbach favorites. Reception was not the same in each locale, but the works enjoyed lasting popularity throughout the century in Mexico. Bissell notes the Mexican audiences' remarkable enthusiasm for the cancan but suggests that Mexicans welcomed opéra bouffe because of the similarities between the dictatorships of Porfirio Díaz and Napoléon III. Although each man built his country's economic and industrial structures, both did so with little regard for long-term social form. Like Napoléon, Porfirio considered *bufa* drama to be rather harmless and promoted it as entertaining theater and as a sign of his goodwill.[35] Opéra bouffe was less successful in Cuba, where Spanish rule and stricter censorship were still in place. Also, Cubans were developing their own *bufo* theater, which owed a measure of debt to the French form as well as to the *sainete* and *género chico.*

Again, the story of Manuel Areu illuminates larger patterns of activity, for his activities confirm that even in Mexico the influence of Cuban *bufo* drama began to compete with Spanish zarzuela. To sustain himself and his family, Manuel Areu performed with the Cuban *bufo* company in residence at the Teatro Principal in Mexico City (Cuban *bufo* is discussed in the following chapter). This position, as well as Areu's later friendships with Cuban artists seeking to create distinctively national art, underscores the intersection of regional and imported theater. The job led to the formation of a new zarzuela company at that theater, directed by Areu and incorporating most of the former members of the Albisu company. Following disputes regarding leadership, José Joaquín Moreno emerged as the impresario of the group, which toured the Mexican provinces in 1873 and 1874 as the Moreno Company.[36]

The fate of Areu and his fellow performers from this point offers insight into performance customs and venues that are likely to be unfamiliar to audiences today but were important options for Latin American audiences in the nineteenth century. When disputes within the Moreno Company led to a split, Areu and those who sided with him aligned with the company of José Poyo, an artist who specialized in performances organized for the popular theatrical format known as *tandas,* which were rather like the *funciones por horas* discussed in the previous chapter.

Género chico works were natural choices for *tandas,* and in the case of longer works, such as a two- or three-act opera, each act would be considered a *tanda.* Both the *tanda* format and the *género chico* were tremendously popular in Mexico, and the Teatro Principal became known for both. Magaña Esquivel quotes a journalist from this era who wrote: "The Teatro Principal has become an article of absolute necessity. I can conceive of life without eating, but I cannot imagine living without *tandas.*" The same writer also enthused: "The only perfect type of entertainment that we have in Mexico is the hour-long zarzuela [*zarzuela por horas*]."[37]

Tandas were frequently performed in temporary, tent-covered outdoor stages known as *jacalones.* In Mexico City the Poyo-Areu Company operated a *jacalone* known as "La Zarzuela," which burned to the ground in 1874. Although no one died, the fire destroyed the company's costumes and scenery, forcing Areu and other performers in the company once again to seek new alliances.

More stable touring companies sometimes achieved legendary status, even during their lifetimes, as they built audiences throughout the New World. So popular was the Aragonese couple José Jarques and Isidora Segura, for example, that the Chilean musicologist Eugenio Pereira Salas refers to the decade 1872–82 as the "Decenio Jarques."[38] The Jarques Company brought zarzuela to Chile, Argentina, Peru, Bolivia, Uruguay, and France. They also helped to organize local companies. A list of some of the works they performed during this period, primarily featuring *zarzuela grande,* offers some indication of the repertoire that crossed the ocean to the New World and also indicates that many works arrived long after they premiered in Spain (the dates in parentheses). Between 1872 and 1882 the Jarques toupe offered *Jugar con Fuego* (1851), *Galanteos en Valencia* (Flirtations in Valencia, 1853), *Los Diamantes de la Corona* (1854), *Catalina de Rusia* (Catherine the Great, 1854), *El Sargento Federico* (1855), *Marina* (1855), *La Hija de la Providencia* (Daughter of Providence, 1856), *Dos Coronas* (Two Crowns, 1861), *Llamada y Tropa* (Reveille, 1861), *Pan y Toros* (Bread and Bulls, 1864), *El Molinero de Subiza* (The Miller of Subiza, 1870), *La Marsella* (1876), *El Salto del Pasiego* (The Leap from Pasiego, 1878), and *El Anillo de Hierro* (The Iron Ring, 1878).

While the Jarqueses were touring Latin America, Manuel Areu's career took a turn that highlights the nature of the exchange that took place between Cuba and Mexico in the last quarter of the century. In 1879, after traveling along the Gulf Coast of Mexico and into New Orleans during the 1870s, Areu and his family of performers returned to Cuba. With the war ended, theater once more flourished in Cuba, which became an important site for fresh creativity. Theater records and Areu's personal memoirs indicate not only regular performances in Havana theaters such as the Tacón, the Albisu, and the Cervantes in 1879 but also his engagement to perform *tandas* at the Teatro Principal in Mexico City on October 31, 1880.[39]

While traveling between Mexico and Cuba, Areu also formed his own company for Mexico City's Teatro Principal. The Areu Company performed *tandas,* and their repertoire included a zarzuela by Cuban composer José Maurí, whose work will be noted in the following chapter.

From 1880 to 1895 Areu traveled back and forth between Cuba and Mexico. In Cuba his work revolved around theaters in Havana, Guanabacoa, and Cárdenas (including venues famous for *bufo* dramas). In Mexico he worked in the capital city as well as in Orizaba. The years from 1894 to 1902 were spent almost exclusively in Cuba, where he and his family took permanent residence. In addition to producing presentations of his own, he was often employed by other companies, such as the Cuban zarzuela company directed by Havana composer Modesto Julián, and he made occasional trips to Spain and other cities in Mexico and elsewhere in Latin America.

During the period when he lived and worked in Cuba, Areu had time to compose music for theater and salon pieces. As I have shown, it was not uncommon for theatrical composers to serve as the director of a zarzuela troupe. Areu's activity as a composer is noteworthy because he made special efforts to accommodate local culture and concerns, reminding us that composers did not have to be native-born to advance the concerns of local residents. Among his theater pieces are five one-act zarzuelas. Among the four musical numbers in *Una Suare de*

Confianza (A Group in Confidence, 1885) is a *guaracha* (an African-influenced Cuban dance song), and *Un Çonato de Coburgo ó Dos Loterías* (The Kept Man of Coburgo, or Two Lotteries, 1890) concerns a poor man's marriage to a wealthy high-society woman, a union the Cubans call a "*conato.*" The cast of characters in the drama, including the standard Creole character of a *mulata,* interact in a Havana hotel. The music features a *guaracha* and an *habanera.* Areu did not limit his attention to Cuban culture. He addresses the concerns of Mexican miners and their political struggles in his 1912 zarzuela *El Minero, ó Lucha de Amor* (The Miner, or Struggle for Love).[40]

Many other Spanish companies either toured Latin America or established extended residency in a major city between 1870 and 1890. Pereira's observations regarding Chile's place on the circuit make clear that these companies contributed to theatrical culture in a profound way: "Except for the romantic impulse of the literary movement of 1842, nothing else has had as strong an influence on the development of Chilean theatre. . . . [The Spanish zarzuela promoted the] rediscovery of our popular customs, of our idiosyncrasies, and fueled a passion for the vernacular that infused new breath into the theatre."[41] Such remarks apply to other Latin American countries as well.

Pereira laments that the *zarzuela grande* seemed to inspire only Chilean writers. Chilean composers did not initially try to mimic the music of the romantic zarzuela, nor did they try to combat foreign influence by creating lyric drama with a nationalistic flavor in the manner of their Argentine and Cuban colleagues. Only after the arrival of the *género chico* near the end of the century did Chilean composers turn to writing lyric theater with a *costumbrista* flavor (enriched by the inclusion of local rhythms, customs, and character types).[42]

Fascination with the *género chico* was not limited to Chile. No single work roused Hispanic audiences more than Bretón's *La Verbena de la Paloma,* the most famous example of the genre. The reception given the initial presentation of this *zarzuelito* (little zarzuela) indicates how quickly and how deeply the *género chico* charmed New World audiences. The work became an instant success in 1894 throughout South America, where it was heard simultaneously with its first Madrid run. An Argentine edition was published the same year that the original edition appeared in Spain, and a Mexican edition was published a year later, in 1895. Chase claims: "No other Spanish piece ever knew such popularity; every available theater staged it. In Buenos Aires, for instance, it was sung in five theaters at the same time and four times an evening in some of them."[43] Quite possibly the most beloved of all zarzuelas, *La Verbena de la Paloma* is regularly programmed today in the United States, as well as in Latin America, as a period classic of the *castizo* (authentic *Madrileño*) taste.

By 1889 productions of the *género chico,* also known as *revistas líricas* (lyric revues) or *espectaculos de hora* (hour-long shows), had invaded Buenos Aires. Vega explains that in Argentina both the zarzuela and the *género chico* served as parents to local traditions of lyric theater that embodied the songs and folkloric dances of that nation: "Principally vehicles of European music, and instruments of hybridization, these theatrical forms were soon converted into agents for the propagation of popular Argentine music."[44] Vega acknowledges that the folkloric music woven into these dramas was not authentic; rather, it was arranged to match cultivated European tradition, similar to the way in which composers in Spain orchestrated regional music such as the *fandango* and *jota* and incorporated these arrangements into a zarzuela.

Native Composition and Regional Perspective

By the 1890s the array of foreign works that dominated Latin American stages included French and Italian operas refashioned as zarzuelas. Vega's lament that Argentine perspectives never really generated a large body of native zarzuela (though there was more success with the regional *sainete*) reminds us that native responses to the zarzuela were not uniform across Latin America. In part this variation was due to widely different political circumstances.

In Mexico many companies operated by Spaniards offered zarzuela and related genres, but relatively few native composers composed zarzuelas before 1890. Bissell reports that between 1890 and 1892 only twenty-three Mexican zarzuelas appeared on stage, with only nine receiving a measure of success.[45] She writes: "Most of these works appear to be patterned after foreign models. . . . Nevertheless, creole elements also appeared through the incorporation of patriotic themes and local customs in the texts, and the inclusion of popular melodies in the music."[46] In the last decades of the nineteenth century, however, Mexican-born composers became more active in creating new zarzuelas.[47] Miranda lists over 350 zarzuelas by Mexican composers composed between 1877 and 1920.[48] Indeed, the years between 1890 and 1910 were ones of uncommon activity, and Miranda illustrates these works' extraordinary popularity by pointing to the enormous success of *Chin-chun-chán* (1904), with music by Mexican composer Luis G. Jorda and text by Rafael Medina, and its more than two hundred continuous performances, culminating in a performance in Barcelona in 1907. He cites the exotic zarzuela *Zulema* (An Arab Slave Girl), with music by Ernesto Elorduy, as exemplifying the high quality of musical composition that many of these works exhibited and their largely unacknowledged influence on the development of both an original, nationalistic perspective and a Mexican opera tradition.

Despite the late surge of activity in Mexico, the creation of a native lyric theater was pursued more energetically in Cuba. Working earlier and more vigorously than their counterparts in Mexico, Cubans used zarzuela to explore the very nature of Creole identity, placing in high relief the politics of ethnicity. Because of the substantial impact that Cuban forms had on the development of lyric theater elsewhere in the Americas, especially in Mexico and the United States, the following chapter will explore Cuban zarzuela and its relatives.

Twentieth-Century Trends and Imports Linking the Americas

Both the zarzuela and the *género chico* remained tremendously popular throughout the New World well into the 1930s. In addition to regional groups, Spanish traveling troupes continued to entertain audiences across Latin America and the Caribbean, venturing into the United States as well. The next chapter's discussion of Quinito Valverde's traveling zarzuela troupe shows the impact of such groups in the United States.

During the 1940s Latin Americans struggled with economic problems and began to rely once again on imported productions to complete their theatrical seasons. In 1946 one of the troupes welcomed by New World audiences was that of the Spanish composer Federico Moreno Torroba. Torroba, whose zarzuela *Luisa Fernanda* has brought audiences to tears throughout the Spanish-speaking world, took his company to Puerto Rico, Mexico, and finally Cuba over two years. Two of the performers with Torroba's troupe were Pepita Embil and Plácido Domingo Sr. When the tour ended, Embil and Domingo returned to Spain, collected their children, and moved to Mexico City, where they established their own zarzuela company in 1948. According to Plácido Jr., the Domingos and Company regularly toured the Mexican provinces and the Caribbean basin; they once spent as long as eight months in Puerto Rico.[49]

Puerto Rican experience with zarzuela is important to this study since Puerto Ricans constitute the largest segment of New York's Hispanic population and thus form a large potential audience (as I will show, an array of conditions, including prior exposure and economic status, limit Puerto Rican support for zarzuela in the United States). Chronicles of Puerto Rican theater indicate substantial cultural exchange with other Latin American countries, particularly those bordering the Caribbean basin. In addition to Puerto Rican companies, contributors to the seasons of zarzuela presented at the Tapia Theatre in San Juan and in other major Puerto Rican cities (in the Caribbean, even more so than in Spain, zarzuela is a distinctly urban taste) include troupes from Cuba (second in number only to local productions), Spain, Mexico, and occasionally Argentina. Production continued well into the 1960s and beyond, although it slowed in the 1930s with the growing popularity of film and revue-style comedies. This kind of exchange continues to the present, but most recent zarzuela productions have been mounted by local companies that travel within a confined region.[50]

Not all exposure comes from professional performance. Popular melodies and the preponderance of spoken verse over serious singing give zarzuela a special appeal for amateur groups. Dower mentions that Puerto Rican children staged zarzuelas or performed excerpts on their school programs, just as North American children might perform shortened versions of Gilbert and Sullivan operettas or American musicals. Leopoldo Escalante, a Venezuelan-born pianist and musical director of zarzuela in New York, remembers that his first encounter with zarzuela came as a child attending puppet-show productions presented by Cuban performers (Teatro Guiñol).[51] Immigrants from Argentina, Chile, Venezuela, and Cuba describe similar experiences with zarzuela when they were children.[52]

Zarzuela's modern reputation as light theater, accessible to amateur performers, helps to explain the mixed response it receives from serious musicians. Many acknowledge the genuine beauty of much zarzuela music but lament the unprofessional performance traditions that have come to be associated with the genre. Plácido Domingo tells how his voice instructors at the Conservatory of Music in Mexico City initially did not take him seriously because he sang too much zarzuela. Domingo's own comments indicate the nature of zarzuela performance practice and the uneven standards still associated with the genre. His conflicting sentiments are shared by many.

> I owe my love of music to the zarzuelas I so often heard from the time I was a small boy. They fascinated me then and they still do now—to a point. When one grows up, one unfortunately tends to see more clearly the defects in the things one loves. But just as in other art forms there are great, good, so-so, bad, and terrible works, the same is true of zarzuela. . . . The composers of some of the shorter works were lazy; they would write precious little music and leave most of the piece as spoken dialogue. Still the musical quality of some zarzuelas is very high indeed. . . . What used to disturb me most is that the comic, secondary roles were usually given to people with terrible voices and I would often leave performances during these numbers and come back for the serious singing.[53]

The performance practices Domingo recalls still occur, although many producers attempt to address some of his concerns. Modern responses to these traditions are discussed in chapter 7.

Concluding Concerns and Shared Processes

Several issues that pertain to modern American productions surface in the previous historical survey. First, transported to the New World, the Spanish zarzuela competed with several local variants that exploited the genre's potential to serve as music of the people. Songs from all these dramas, sometimes despite the substantial demands they placed on performers, entered the popular repertoire. In other cases, long after the vogue of the theatrical traditions diminished, the music lived on in the hands of independent singers and instrumentalists who appropriated individual songs and dances and kept them alive in renditions suited for popular local ensembles, such as the mariachi in Mexico and marimba ensembles in Central America. As a result of such popular circulation, and as the origins of these songs and dances from lyric theater became increasingly obscure, the material acquired a folkloric status.[54]

Despite the popularity of working-class characters and rural types in the music and plots of *drama lírico,* the urban middle-class continued to be the principal supporters of zarzuela and its *costumbrista* cousins. The growth of lyric drama in Latin America was closely tied to the development of public theater in general, as well as the salonlike concert, and audiences delighted in its ability to embrace both classical and popular traditions.

The development of local forms based on Spanish models helped to secure zarzuela's position as an artistic medium in Latin America, although for some composers the ultimate and more prestigious goal was to establish a national style of opera.

As with the Spanish form, Latin American zarzuela is one development in a long tradition of lyric theater. In both cases the genre developed from its aristocratic roots to serve as entertainment for a cosmopolitan, urban public. Zarzuela suffered continual comparison with opera, and according to operatic criteria it frequently lost. Opera offered both composers and performers promise of international recognition and cultured status. Zarzuela was more accessible, more popular, and frequently more relevant but not as distinguished.

The most important distinction between the peninsular history and the New World experience is that in Latin America zarzuela was a foreign genre. Colonial domination facilitated its acceptance, but across Latin America composers and audiences sought ways to adapt European forms to project local identities. The process of forging national varieties of zarzuela is shared across Latin America, but local goals and specific creole forms varied. The Argentine *sainete,* Mexican zarzuela, and Cuban *bufo* dramas enjoyed limited periods of popularity and differing degrees of status, but all exerted some influence on attitudes concerning the ways lyric drama should serve the needs of local patrons.

Although the procedures associated with modern productions of zarzuela in the United States differ in many ways from those discussed in this chapter, the development of creole approaches to lyric theater across Latin America, and especially in Cuba, highlights a process of appropriation and representation that characterizes later developments in the United States.

This brief historical overview reveals that in Latin America the most popular Spanish zarzuelas were regularly performed and remained in regular circulation well into the twentieth century, despite local competition. This situation is due in large measure to the influence of immigrants from Spain, the popularity of international touring companies, and the persistence of conservative views that continued to deem peninsular imports more worthy of respect than works by local creators.

These points provide a starting framework for considering how Hispanics in the United States have responded to zarzuela. As will be discussed in chapters 4 and 5, familiarity with the performance tradition and repertoire, as well as general perceptions regarding the zarzuela, vary in fairly predictable ways depending on the ethnicities, educational status, and social backgrounds of potential patrons. Notably, the rich history of the zarzuela and related creole forms in Cuba has influenced support for zarzuela in the United States far beyond what one might expect given the numbers of Cubans compared to other Hispanics. However, the North American population that supports zarzuela has substantially different needs from its counterparts in Latin America, particularly regarding the conception of identity. A more detailed look at approaches in Cuba will illustrate some of those needs and differences.

3

A Side Trip to Cuba

Costumbrista Attitudes toward Lyric Theater

Cuba played a pivotal role in zarzuela's development and transmission in Latin America and the Caribbean. Equally distinctive is the extent to which Cubans manipulated and reformulated Spanish zarzuela. After the romantic zarzuela arrived in Cuba in 1853, its great success inspired a range of vernacular variations, such as *pequeñas zarzuelas cubanas, pequeñas revistas, juguetes, cómicos,* and *líricos cubanos,* as well as parodies of French, Italian, and Spanish works. *La Vía Grande* (The Big Street), by the famed violinist Brindis de Salas, offers a later example of a Cuban parody of the extremely popular Spanish zarzuela *La Gran Vía* (The Grand Avenue).[1]

As discussed earlier, the Cuban predilection for zarzuela and other representations of Spanish culture reflects the island's political history. Cuba was one of the last of Spain's colonies to gain its independence. The country retained close ties to Europe (turning to France as well as Spain for cultural models) far later than did most Latin American colonies. The most distinctive Cuban treatments of zarzuela and its relatives developed as part of a rich array of approaches labeled *costumbrista* (employing local customs and characters).

Although Cubans never let Spanish standards completely dominate their stages or social interactions, European ancestry remained a badge of high status. The search for a successful balance between local needs and European standards guided those working with lyric theater in Cuba, and it remains a concern to Cubans working in the United States. The following examination of Cuban *costumbrista* theater provides a useful background for understanding the perspectives and influence brought by Cubans who support zarzuela productions in the United States.

Importing and Exporting: Havana as a Hub of Musical Exchange

Cuba's geographical location facilitated continual access to zarzuela traditions. Havana was a major Caribbean harbor for European trade and an important refueling port for ships bound for the Americas. As a consequence, virtually all zarzuela troupes on their way to South and Central America scheduled a stop in Cuba.[2] Havana became both a destination and a launching site for zarzuela throughout the Americas.

Richer by far than many of its Latin American and Caribbean neighbors, Cuba enjoyed a prosperity that allowed it to exert considerable influence throughout the Hispanic world. Latin American musicians came to study in Cuba during the nineteenth and early twentieth centuries. For example, Dower notes that many Puerto Rican musicians and composers received their training in Cuba.[3]

Cuban companies specializing in zarzuela and *teatro costumbrista* frequently left the country on tour. Pasarell mentions numerous performances in Puerto Rico by various Cuban zarzuela companies, and Mayer-Serra describes how Afro-Cuban dance forms brought by a company of *bufos habaneros* affected Mexican lyric drama. The company of Leopoldo Fernández traveled throughout Latin America, particularly in Mexico, Venezuela, Colombia, and Peru. The company also traveled to cities in the United States, such as Miami, New York, Chicago, Los Angeles, and San Francisco—places where the performers could count on support from a large Hispanic population. Until Castro's revolution, actors and composers, including the celebrated *zarzuelero* and popular bandleader Ernesto Lecuona (1896–1963), formed their own touring theatrical companies to promote their works.

Francisco Covarrubias and Early Cuban Approaches to Lyric Theater

Cuban approaches to zarzuela were rooted in a rich history of creole theater. Throughout Latin America the eighteenth-century Spanish *sainete* inspired local writers to create regional drama, but appropriation of the *sainete* was exceptionally vigorous in Cuba. The form served as a model for the short farces of Francisco Covarrubias (1755–1850), Cuba's first noted dramatist. Covarrubias was both a performer and a writer, and for many years he was also the most celebrated comic in Cuba. His work led to the development of a new Cuban theatrical tradition, *bufo* drama, discussed later in this chapter.

Cuban theater benefited indirectly from the Napoleonic wars, for they prompted many artists to leave Spain and relocate on the island. As a dramatist and actor, Covarrubias worked to great advantage with a group of Spanish actors, musicians, and dancers who came to Cuba in 1810, just after the Napoleonic invasion.[4] For twenty-one years Covarrubias and this group worked to regenerate public interest in the *tonadilla,* but they presented it as an enriched form that emphasized dance as an integral component and featured musical structures more reminiscent of comic opera.

Covarrubias rejected purely Spanish models. As a connoisseur of light theater, he recognized at an early date that the characters who animated the peninsular forms could be replaced with Creole types. Beginning in 1812 Covarrubias replaced the *majos, chisperos, catalanes, gallegos, payos, gitanos, moros,* and *mendígos* of the Madrilenian dramas with *guajiros, monteros, carreteros, peones,* and other popular island characters and rural types.[5] In his hands, *Las Tertulias de Madrid* (*Tertulias* of Madrid) became *Las Tertulias de la Habana* (*Tertulias* of Havana). (A *tertulia* is a salon-style gathering of intellectuals, artists, and musicians.) He also turned to Afro-Cuban rituals for inspiration and in so doing "Cubanized" the *sainete* by incorporating the character and traditions of the *negrito* into his dramas. This nod toward the distinctive African components of Cuban culture was not without prejudice. *Negrito* roles were generally stereotypical and played by white actors wearing blackface.[6]

Even more important than Covarrubias's character substitutions was his incorporation of Cuban melodies and hit songs into his *criollo* dramas. Using local music made the drama more believable, but it also paved the way for other composers to develop an entirely Cuban theatrical genre, the *bufo cubano* (Cuban comic drama).

Teatro Bufo Cubano

Creators of *teatro bufo* took *costumbrista* theater to new extremes and positioned it as an alternative to European theater rather than an adaptation of it. *Teatro bufo* developed alongside the very genres it opposed. While the socially elite were admiring foreign forms of musical drama, such as Italian opera and Spanish zarzuela, artists sensitive to popular taste were creating forms, such as *teatro bufo,* that highlighted African slaves' non-European contributions to Cuban life.

Bartolomé José Crespo y Borbón and Enrique Guerro were two composers who helped to establish the Afro-Cuban element in *teatro bufo* after 1847. In their works they replaced the *seguidilla, villancico,* and *aria tonadillesca* with the *guajira, guara-*

cha, canción cubana, and other distinctively Afro-Cuban musical forms. The titles of dramas written after 1850, such as *Los Ñáñigos* (an Afro-Cuban confraternity), *Tu Madre Es Conga* (Your Mother is Congolese), and *La Negrita* (The Little Black Girl), clearly reveal the Afro-Cuban emphasis.

Carpentier points out that *bufo* dramas consistently featured dances and songs such as the *contradanza, danzón, rumba,* and *son*—music that captured the rhythmic vitality associated with Afro-Cuban music but also appealed to the elite white sense of nationality by building on the European *contradanza.*[7] The popularity of the later development of the *contradanza,* the *danzón,* best illustrates the ambiguities of sociocultural identification. By 1920 the *danzón* had become so popular that it was considered the national dance of Cuba. It found its way into all kinds of events, including theatrical ones, and new *danzones* were composed on themes of beloved operas and zarzuelas.

The principal supporters for public theater in Cuba came from the white middle-class or Creole population—individuals who, though not European-born, owed their privileged social position to their European ancestry.[8] The racial and class conditions for theatrical support, so obvious in the Cuban context, are equally important to the story of Hispanic lyric theater in the United States.

Teatro bufo became a nineteenth-century sensation. In 1868 a company called Los Bufos Habaneros devoted its efforts to popularizing the *bufo cubano.* In that same year the Teatro Cervantes was dedicated solely to the production of the *género bufo cubano. Teatro bufo* achieved success almost overnight, and in eight months there were eight companies in Havana devoted to its production. The genre found its most perfect expression in the repertoire of the Teatro Alhambra, which for twenty or thirty years acted as a stronghold for daring *costumbrista* theater, operating, in Carpentier's words, as "a true conservatory of nationalistic rhythms."[9] Composers associated with the Alhambra would go on to experiment with other forms of lyric drama, including zarzuela.

The rebellious nature of *teatro bufo* made it politically potent during 1868–78, when Cubans were fighting the unsuccessful "Ten Years War" for their independence. Carpentier reports that while composers with aristocratic leanings continued to write *contradanzas* to flatter the colonial government, the authors of the *bufos* were becoming increasingly audacious and satirical in their jabs at the "imperialist" regime.[10]

Teatro bufo helped to develop a broad audience for nationalistic lyric theater, and historians of Cuban theater agree that the *bufo* genre transformed the country's dramatic tradition. Leal writes: "With these elements [vernacular figures, music, and dance], *Los Bufos Habaneros* went out to fight against Italian opera,

Spanish zarzuela, and the post-romantic drama. They triumphed precisely because they recognized our national features."[11]

Tolón identifies a Cuban collective perception—namely, that theater had the power to define both national identity and political position. He writes: "Fixed in the Cuban mind was the idea that the rise of *los bufos cubanos* broke with the typical Spanish theater and was a symbol of *cubanidad* [Cubaness]. In the *bufos cubanos,* one always finds a rejection of authority."[12]

Teatro bufo also transformed the musical landscape. Carpentier explains: "The role of the *bufos* in the evolution of popular Cuban music was considerable. Thanks to them all types of songs and dances, both rural and urban, were brought to light, diffused, and mixed. Scenic requirements gave birth to diversified genres, all branches of the same tree. The Negro acquired a definitive force."[13]

Despite the resounding popularity of the *bufo cubano,* its vision of national identity was ultimately too jocular and too oriented toward parody. Parallels in the United States would be the ambivalent portrayals of black culture transmitted first by traveling minstrel theaters and developed later on the vaudeville stage. Although these traditions were distinctly American in style and drew freely on African American music and dance, they did little to elevate the status of black Americans or to integrate them into the national identity. Similarly, the *bufos* made the public aware of black cultural contributions but refused to take them seriously.

Some of the *bufos* made their way to New York and other American stages, where they competed with American vaudeville (see chapter 4 as well as appendixes A and B). After 1884, however, Cuban interest in the *bufo* declined. The dramatic texts were generally "without literary value, and the language used was increasingly coarse."[14] Twentieth-century patrons sought a more refined vision of national lyric theater. Once again composers looked to the possibilities in zarzuela, but the national experiment with *bufo* drama would leave a lasting mark.

Cuban Zarzuela (and Opera)

By the end of the nineteenth century, just as the island was finally to win its independence from Spain, Cuban composers and librettists developed a *teatro costumbrista* with more status and finesse than the earlier *teatro bufo.* The newer works featured dramas revolving around political themes, used vernacular expressions—particularly creole phrases—and were written with a characteristically spicy wit. The music was always very Cuban, rich in creole rhythms. This new *costumbrista* theater, best described as an approach rather than a genre, achieved great popularity. The composer Federico Villoch wrote 400 *costumbrista* works, and Panchito y Gustavo Robreño wrote 259.

Teatro costumbrista is difficult to separate from Cuban zarzuela or even Cuban opera. *Costumbrista* composers include Jorge Anckermann, Manuel Maurí, Raimundo Valenzuela, Rafael Palau, Modesto Fraga, Jaime Prats, Luis Casa Romero, Francisco Rojas, Justo Soret, and Eliseo Grenet, many of whom are also known for their operas and zarzuelas. Eliseo Grenet (1893–1950), whose name appears regularly in New York theatrical annals from the 1930s, illustrates the flexible attitudes of these composers. Grenet was a composer, an actor, and a bandleader and traveled widely. He appeared as often in New York City nightclubs as he did in comparatively more elite Hispanic theaters (see chapter 4). Of Afro-Cuban ancestry himself, he formed a company entirely of Afro-Cuban artists called Cubanacán to perform his works throughout Latin America, the United States, and Spain. In 1935 his zarzuela *La Camagüeyana* (The Girl from Camagüey, a city in the southeastern half of the island) was staged with great success in Barcelona's Teatro Nuevo. According to Livermore, Grenet's *La Virgen Morena* (The Black Madonna), a one-act *sainete* conceived with the more serious tone and ambition of a zarzuela, had the longest run in Spain of any Cuban work.[15]

A distinctly Cuban tradition of *zarzuela grande* did not really bloom until after 1920. Ernesto Lecuona (1896–1963) is another Cuban composer known for his popular and semiclassical works, including *zarzuela grande.* His *María la O* appeared in 1930, featuring the Catalan soprano Conchita Bañuls and the Cuban tenor Miguel de Grandy, whose influence on zarzuela productions in Miami and New York is discussed in subsequent chapters.[16] To this day *María la O* is one of the most popular of the Cuban zarzuelas. Even this mature work, obviously influenced by romantic opera, can also be described as *costumbrista.* Lecuona wrote for classically trained voices and instrumentalists, a characteristic that Cuban *zarzuela grande* shares with its Spanish counterpart.

Cuban zarzuelas typically feature plots addressing racial issues, often mixing Galician (a term that in Cuba refers to Spaniards generally, not just those from the province of Galicia) and Negro characters and incorporating representative music from both groups. The hybrid of regional music and characters in works such as Lecuona's *Rosa la China* (Rosa, the Chinese Girl) reflects the blend of races and backgrounds that makes up the Cuban population. In 1932 the celebrated *Cecilia Valdés,* by Gonzálo Roig (1890–1970), premiered in Havana's Teatro Martí and allowed audiences another vision of their character. The story, based on Cirilo Villaverde's celebrated 1882 novel bearing the same title, explores race relations and colonialism in a plot that links interactions between a typical nineteenth-century Cuban planter family and a slave family to the despotic manipulations of big-city politics. An ill-fated romance between an aristocratic young man and a *mulata* (a woman of mixed African and European ancestry) leads to death and dishonor. The score features typical Cuban forms, including the *canción, habanera, danza, contradanza,* and *guaracha.* Tolón describes the work as "the most valuable jewel in our popular lyric theater."[17] *Cecilia Valdés* remains a beloved zarzuela outside Cuba as well.

Reception and Promotion of Zarzuela in Cuba

The most famous period of *zarzuela grande* in Havana took place from 1927 to 1937 and occupied stages in several theaters, including the Teatro Martí, the Teatro Principal de La Comedia, and the old Teatro Nacional. Fewer local zarzuelas were produced during the depression and throughout the 1940s, and touring productions from Spain dominated Cuban theater in the major cities. As before, these visiting companies focused on the most famous zarzuelas, thus reinforcing local appreciation for the "period classics," as Livermore calls the gems of Spanish zarzuela created before 1940. Even as they developed their own zarzuelas, Cubans continued to support Spanish forms.

The Cuban zarzuela tradition stands out among Latin American approaches to the genre because of its enormous popularity and the extent to which it developed. Zarzuela was more than entertainment in Cuba; it had genuine cultural and political influence. Cuba's most famous composers wrote zarzuela; Havana's best theaters hosted both local and foreign productions. Performers were obliged to acquaint themselves with the tradition, and many devoted their careers to zarzuela or, as a result of it, to lyric theater. This last point may be most important, since many of those directly responsible for producing zarzuela in New York and elsewhere in the United States are Cuban immigrants.

Many artists left Cuba for the United States in the 1950s and 1960s. In 1969 a group of Cuban performers led by Marta Pérez, Pily (Píli) de la Rosa, Miguel De Grandy II, and Demetrio Mendéz formed the Sociedad Pro-Arte Grateli to produce Spanish and Cuban zarzuelas and *operetas.* This Miami-based society enjoyed support from the growing population of Cuban immigrants, many of whom paid monthly dues to sustain productions. This first wave of immigrants for the most part comprised highly educated urbanites of middle-class or elite standing who had enjoyed plenty of exposure to lyric theater and zarzuela. Many of them had participated in the production of musical theater as part of the salon concert movement that characterized well-mannered life during the 1930s and 1940s.

Even today older Cubans residing in New York recall *asociaciones culturales,* community organizations that included amateur and professional performers who would present zarzuela in many of Cuba's major cities. These immigrants remember zarzuela as Cuban activity, not merely as imported Spanish practice.

Cuban sentiments regarding zarzuela are especially strong, in large part because of the intrinsic relationship between the genre and virtually all other musical activities of the elite and aspiring classes. Cubans brought those views with them to the United States and found others of Latin American ancestry who shared those sentiments in varying degrees. Nonetheless, these views led to new directions in U.S. contexts.

4

Creating *The Land of Joy*

Zarzuela and Hispanic Theater in the United States

Sitting on my blanket for an open-air concert of zarzuela arias offered in New York's Prospect Park (Brooklyn, New York) in July 1986, I wondered why this repertoire was so little known in musical circles. This was the first time I had heard American singers perform zarzuela arias with full orchestral accompaniment. Later I would learn of a few theatrical organizations and festivals where zarzuelas were mounted with full orchestra, but concert audiences remained unlikely to hear the genre treated so seriously in New York and elsewhere in the United States. Although most patrons love zarzuela for its music, North American audiences have historically had to turn to theaters (or theatrical organizations) rather than musical institutions to encounter regular and respectful treatments of zarzuela (although even in these theaters "respect" may not entail a full orchestra). This situation prompts several questions regarding the history of zarzuela in the United States and its position in New York's musical scene. When and how did the zarzuela arrive in the United States? Where and by whom was it promoted and accepted? How has that history affected current attitudes toward the genre? How does New York's reception of zarzuela compare with that elsewhere in the United States? The answers to these questions require a look at the history of Spanish theater in the United States, a story that makes clear the powerful linkage between Spanish-language theater and zarzuela production in New York City and in the United States in general.

Preliminary Observations Regarding Spanish Theater in New York

New York may not have the longest history of Spanish theater, but it is one of the United States' most important cities for Hispanic theater, a role it has played since the nineteenth century. As the nation's center for professional theatrical activity, New York operates as a hub connecting a constant influx of international and national influences. Although the New York theatrical scene has a character all its own, the circuit of influences shaping that character has always been linked to other American cities. Hence, the history of Spanish theater outside New York forms part of my story.

These connections are especially important when we look at the role zarzuela has played, and continues to play, in anchoring theatrical activity in Spanish theaters and in promoting positive self-identification among Hispanic residents. New York has always embraced Hispanics of widely diverse backgrounds, distinguishing it from other American cities where the Spanish-speaking population has been more homogeneous. From an early date theatrical presentations addressed this diversity. Nicolás Kanellos, a renowned scholar of Hispanic theater in the United States, notes that the New York stage has always reflected a kind of pan-Hispanic culture and states that it was "a model for solidifying diverse Hispanic nationalities on stage."[1] Much of the following discussion, although indebted to his work, moves beyond his views as it sets the stage for later discussions of how New York–based presenters have actually helped to forge new conceptions of Hispanic identity as they worked to establish professional companies and build cohesive audiences. Zarzuela has served as a particularly potent vehicle for this kind of identity construction.

Southwestern Roots

The earliest roots of Hispanic theater in the United States can be found in the American Southwest. Professional and semiprofessional companies found a home there well before the Spanish-American War in 1898, but activity prior to 1848 tended to be spontaneous, impermanent, and largely amateur. Theatrical and musical activity in the early missions and military stations was an important but temporary diversion from the hardships of frontier life. The American Southwest was subject to many of the same hardships faced by those in the Mexican Sonora: war taxes, revolts by Yaqui Indians, raids from the Apache, and general political chaos. Such hardships argued against a settled arts community. Permanent theaters and resident companies were uncommon until after 1850, but the region did support local amateur activity and receive visiting performers.

The earliest recorded performance date of a Spanish-language play in the United States is 1598. The drama, written by Marco Farfan de los Godos, preceded the earliest English-language production in the United States by six years and was staged near what we now call El Paso. It most probably included music and bore a similarity to the *autos sacramentales* mentioned in chapters 1 and 2.[2] This event established El Paso as a nodal site in the history of Spanish-language theater in North America.[3]

In the 1800s successful California trade centers that had developed from earlier Spanish and Mexican settlements, notably Los Angeles and San Francisco, attracted the attentions of traveling troupes from Mexico, Spain, and Cuba, and they soon became entertainment centers that supported local theatrical productions in the Spanish language. These cities were additionally attractive destinations because they could be easily reached by ship.

In both cities and countryside, the influx of population and income that began around 1848 with the Gold Rush made possible stronger public support of music and theater. John Koegel notes that before the Gold Rush, Spanish-speaking Californians living in rural areas and towns on Mexico's northern frontier had no direct access to large-scale formal musical and theatrical establishments, such as those available in central Mexican cities. "Cathedral choirs, professional drama, opera and musical theater, orchestra (apart from Indian musical groups in the California missions), artistic salons, formal concert life, and professional music teachers and performers only came to California during the American period [after 1846]."[4] Much the same can be said for other regions in the American Southwest. Inland or border cities that could be reached by stagecoach, such as Tucson, El Paso, and San Antonio, were also treated to visits from traveling troupes, but with less frequency.

Things began to change after 1850 with the establishment of dedicated theater buildings. The Eagle Theater in Sacramento, California, opened in October 1849 and was one of the earliest theaters west of the Mississippi. As might be expected, permanent theatrical venues surfaced somewhat later inland. In southern Arizona the first theaters were built in the 1870s.[5]

Once in place these venues encouraged development of both imported and local talent. As the number of formal sites for music and theater increased in San Francisco, the city began to compete favorably with arts centers to the east, including New York, Philadelphia, Boston, New Orleans, and Cincinnati. Although San Francisco offered many more events than did Los Angeles, the latter enjoyed more public events presented expressly for Hispanic audiences.[6] One of the earliest commercial theaters dedicated to Hispanic arts in Los Angeles remains standing today, the Teatro Merced, or Merced Theater. First opened in 1870, it was for eight years the principal home for touring Mexican troupes and a place for local Mexican American musicians to perform.[7]

The tour circuit for troupes that appeared at the Merced, such as the Mollá company from Mexico, used stagecoach routes and railroad lines. It looped through several California cities; continued into Arizona (Tucson), New Mexico (Santa Fe, Albuquerque, and Las Vegas); and moved on to Texas (the transportation and hence arts hub of San Antonio, as well as border towns). At various points the route dipped south into Mexico, and any of the northern Mexican states of Sonora, Sinaloa, Baja California, Chihuahua, Coahuila, Tamaulipas, Durango, and Nuevo León were possible stops on this circuit.[8]

A city's location along standard transportation routes was one of the most important factors determining how theater developed and who performed. Gipson claims that the stagecoach journey between Fort Worth and San Diego was an arduous one, and the only theatrical and musical companies to brave the trip were Spanish-language troupes. In contrast, North American companies from the East rarely ventured into the western interior; in the 1850s, when performing artists arrived to inland sites such as Tucson from elsewhere in North America, they came as solo acts.[9] Harbor cities that had become major trade centers enjoyed an obvious advantage, sparing travelers grueling (and at times dangerous) land routes, and hence artistic offerings were more diversified there. Spanish companies that once toured Latin America and the Caribbean (e.g., Areu's company, noted in chapter 2), began to settle in cities such as Tucson and Santa Fe and operated as local repertory companies. By the 1870s performers from the United States outnumbered those from Mexico and Spain.[10] This shift corresponded to changing population demographics. For example, in 1864 people of Mexican and other Latin American ancestry formed 64 percent of the population of Tucson, Arizona. By 1881 this same group was only 30 percent of Tucson's population. Given such changes, it is not surprising that Hispanic influence on the general character of theater in southwestern cities began to wane.[11]

Despite the growing U.S. influence after 1870, Hispanic audiences and other receptive patrons could enjoy a fairly steady diet of Spanish melodramas, Mexican and Cuban plays, and zarzuelas in formats and venues geared to family audiences and a broad segment of the Hispanic community, not merely the elite.[12] Entertainment superseded reverence for individual works in these late nineteenth-century performances. A company from Mexico might offer a single act from Giuseppe Verdi's opera *Attila* in conjunction with a series of shorter musical or dramatic interludes. The social tone of the event was determined, to a large degree, by price, venue, and the reputation of the performers and sponsors. These factors were more likely to determine the class and ethnic composition of the audience than was the specific work performed or the language of the presentation. Shows featuring Italian opera, French grand opera and operetta, and Spanish and Mexican zarzuela attracted wealthy and middle class-patrons, including merchants and socially prominent landowners among the Mexican American elite. Italian opera also drew working-class Mexicans, especially when coupled with musical comedy, vaudeville, circus, and variety acts and when presented in low-cost formats such as tent shows and *tandas.*[13] Program formats were adjusted to appeal to a wide audience and to keep each element happy.

Promotional strategies in California and the Southwest reveal the mix of attitudes that surrounded these presentations. Local Hispanic musicians and theatrical performers in California were sometimes billed as "Spanish," in part to help deflect the prejudice of the general Anglo-American majority against the Mexican or Hispanic minority in these cities.[14] Koegel notes that this was not the case for all non-English productions: the German community proudly presented theater and music in German without fear of criticism or sanction.[15] Clearly for a majority of U.S. citizens, a Latin American origin was not as prestigious as a Spanish one, but even peninsular efforts did not always succeed in the eyes of Americans who aspired to match Central European standards. This Eurocentric focus was bolstered by commonly expressed fears that immigrants from Mexico and elsewhere in Latin American competed with Anglo-Americans for jobs.

Overall, theater in the Southwest was characterized by flexibility and an emphasis on Mexican perspectives. Certain areas came into their own during the twentieth century. Successive waves of immigration to Los Angeles helped to sustain a regular audience for Hispanic theater, and Koegel points out that such activity peaked between 1910 and 1940. Well into the twentieth century, performers trained in classic theater and zarzuela found themselves creating works that addressed regional concerns and performing vaudeville and variety acts, especially popular during the depression.

The theatrical traditions emerging in the West and Southwest were not isolated from New York. Touring companies from Mexico, Spain, Cuba, and occasionally Argentina or another Latin American country traveled along circuits that connected the East and West Coasts of the United States. In addition to the Southwest tour circuit described previously, a northern circuit also existed, and some of the larger companies that toured the Southwest linked the two. Troupes taking northern routes typically began in New York, frequently after a run in Cuba, and then moved through Philadelphia, Cleveland, Detroit, Chicago, and on to points west, ending in Los Angeles.

A third touring circuit existed between New York and the Florida cities of Tampa and Miami, where Cuban immigrants fleeing the wars for independence quickly established an active theatrical scene. The theater buildings they built soon housed visiting companies from Havana and Spain in addition to serving the needs of resident amateur and semiprofessional groups. These companies offered zarzuela and other dramatic entertainment for workers in the tobacco factories and their families. Many of the performers hired to entertain this discriminating audience continued north to perform in New York.[16] New York newspapers from the turn of the century indicate that a New York–to–New Orleans circuit flourished as well. This route facilitated the exchange of Spanish theatrical trends between southeastern and the northeastern American cities.

New York Prior to 1960

The Hispanic culture found in New York differed from that of the Southwest. It is important to remember that Spanish speakers resided in the Southwest and California long before English-speaking Americans took over. After the Spanish-American War, theater in border cities received impetus from the large-scale migration from Mexico to the United States. These areas provided a ready-made clientele for Spanish theater, as well as for local Hispanic drama. On the East Coast the situation was different. In New York the Spanish-speaking population was an immigrant one not built on a resident base. The first wave of Spanish-speaking immigrants to New York consisted of expatriate Sephardic Jews who arrived in 1654. Even later, in the 1820s, when Spanish culture began making a mark in New York's publishing industry, it reflected a mixture of national backgrounds; it was not dominated by those of Mexican ancestry, as was the norm in the West.

The relative size of the Hispanic population constituted another difference between New York and the West. In contrast to those in the western regions of the United States, Spanish-speakers in nineteenth-century New York made up a marginal portion of society. This population, like New Yorkers in general, primarily looked to Europe for cultural ties, resources, and models.[17] The glance toward Spain was modified somewhat in the 1890s when, according to Kanellos, "New York became an organizing and staging center for Cuban, Puerto Rican, and Dominican expatriates seeking the independence of their homelands from Spain."[18] During this period numerous performances supporting revolutionary efforts (including some of the *bufos cubanos* described in the previous chapter) supplemented the traditional repertoire of melodrama and zarzuela.

At the turn of the century New York's Hispanic residents could not claim any theaters as their own, as could Hispanic communities in Los Angeles, San Antonio, and Tampa, and impresarios offering Spanish-language fare had to rent available theaters around town.[19] The New York performances of the Spanish-born actor Manuel Noriega and his company (see appendix A and B) show how frequently a company might adjust venue, repertoire, and even identifying name to court audiences.

Noriega embodies the international nature of Spanish theater: he was born in

Spain; made a name for himself as an actor in Mexico; worked for years in Havana; and moved to New York in 1916, where he founded the Compañía Dramática Española and proceeded to offer Spanish comedies, *sainetes,* and zarzuelas in the Teatro Leslie, the Amsterdam Theater and Opera House, and Carnegie Hall (see appendix A). Once settled, he hired more actors, mostly Cuban, Mexican, and Spanish, and his repertoire expanded to feature Galician or Catalonian works as well as Cuban blackface comedy. As audience support fluctuated between sell-out crowds and small showings, Noriega formed new partnerships (one with a Greek businessman), changed the name of his company to El Gran Compañía de Opera y Zarzuela, and moved to the Park Theater, renaming it El Teatro Español.[20]

The support base for Spanish-language theater was less predictable in New York than in the Southwest. Especially until impresarios began to control their own theaters, success in New York meant having the musical and business savvy to gain recognition and support from diverse populations, not just within the Spanish-speaking community but also outside it. The curiously mixed reviews and resulting influence of one early zarzuela performance highlights the complexities of such conditions.

In 1917 a Spanish troupe took New York by storm with its performance of *La Tierra de la Alegría,* a zarzuela billed as *The Land of Joy* in English and also identified as a *revista.*[21] The story, written by José Elizondo and Estanislao Velasco and set to music by Quinito Valverde,[22] concerns two Americans who visit Spain and played with resounding success for twenty-two weeks to a mixed audience of Spanish and English speakers at the Park Theater. The audience attending *The Land of Joy* was apparently more Hispanic than Anglo, yet every major English-language newspaper in the city published a rave review of the production.[23] Critics lavished praise on the dancers, especially "La Argentina," around whom the show revolved, and on Valverde's music. Interestingly enough, the reviewers unanimously disapproved of the addition of American actors, whose purpose, it seemed, was to supply enough English dialogue to clarify the plot. All reviewers felt the production should have been staged solely in Spanish. Perhaps it is for this reason that Kanellos describes the production as "an unsuccessful run," a surprising conclusion given the enthusiasm of the contemporary press.

Carl Van Vechten, writing in 1918, described Valverde's opening as "unheralded, unsung and indeed, almost unwelcomed by reviewers who had to trudge to the out-of-the-way Park Theater." He speculated that those who chose not to attend that night might have (wrongly) reasoned: "It is all very well to read about the goings on in Spain, but it would never do here in America."[24] Perhaps non-attendee's felt that way, but most contemporary reviewers considered the show to have been a success, largely because of the music. In 1917 Burns Mantle wrote in the November 2 issue of the *New York Mail:* "But here, for once, the play was not the thing. The thing was the music of Valverde and the Spanish songs and dances, and their language is as universal as it is eloquent."

Valverde himself conducted the orchestra, and with the exception of the added American actors, the cast consisted of a troupe of fifty performers from Madrid. Mantle reports that an American impresario had spotted the troupe performing in Havana and asked it to prepare a New York performance. Among his concerns were the sets; though lavish, they were in poor repair and therefore not up to American standards.[25]

The condition of sets and costumes remains an issue for troupes today, perhaps reflecting different cultural perspectives. I regularly hear older Hispanic patrons remark that the costumes seen in contemporary New York zarzuela presentations "look too new, as if they've never been worn." Such remarks are offered when a patron is trying to explain how a recent production has been "Americanized." As if confirming the American expectation of bright new material, reviewers in the English-language press lamented the worn conditions of the sets and costumes when the José Tamayo's *Antología de la Zarzuela* arrived from Spain and appeared at Madison Square Garden in 1985 and 1986.

For the Hispanic community in New York in 1917, *The Land of Joy* was new only in format, for as already indicated, zarzuelas were fairly common fare for Spanish dramatic troupes performing in that city. For non-Hispanics, though, the show was, as one *New York Globe* reporter stated, "intoxicatingly exotic."[26] The *New York Times* review echoed this appreciation of foreign fare: "In the wilderness of musical comedies of native commerce, it is a pleasure to welcome a piece of the kind in which local color and character are as novel as they are genuine."[27]

The incredible success of *The Land of Joy* revealed the potentially broad appeal of Spanish lyric theater in New York. There is evidence that the run promoted genuine reflection regarding the general appeal of zarzuela within the Hispanic community as well. When Manuel Noriega's attempt to convert the Park Theater into El Teatro Español failed in 1919, critics at the Spanish-language newspaper *La Prensa* speculated that his choices for productions were insufficiently cosmopolitan and that *La Tierra de la Alegría* would have been a better choice than the operatic Galician idyll *Maruxa,* by Amadeo Vives, which Noriega chose for his final production in that venue.[28] The ensuing years revealed that continuing success would require good management as well as carefully chosen repertoire and that the exotic and musical appeal of the zarzuela, while a start, was not enough to sustain the attentions of non-Hispanic audiences. It would be many years before Spanish-language drama would again so captivate the non-Hispanic public.

The observation of the critic at *La Prensa* regarding the cosmopolitan expectations of New York audiences are worth further reflection. In the 1920s most Spanish speakers in New York had immigrated from Spain (see table 1). Figueroa reports that the largest Spanish-speaking communities were to be found in East Harlem and the Lower East Side, distinctions that remain true in Manhattan today. Moreover, just as today one might travel to Queens to find the largest concentration of Colombian immigrants, Spanish Americans in the first half of the century tended to live together based on the region of Spain from which they came. Many Galicians and Basques lived on Cherry Street, with others living further north in Greenwich Village, while Brooklyn was home for immigrants from Andalusia.

The names of clubs and cultural organizations often reflected the ethnic or geographical origins of the founders. Some notable examples are El Centro Andaluz (the Andalusian Center), El Centro Asturiano (for those from Asturias), and El Calpe Americano (Calpe is an old name for a rocky promontory, such as Gibraltar or the Peñon Ifach on the southeastern coast of the province of Alicante). These clubs frequently sponsored theatrical events and became especially crucial to the continuation of Spanish theater in New York during the 1930s,

Table 1. Origins of the New York Hispanic Population, by Decade, 1920 to 1970

Decade	Central and South America	Cuba	Mexico	Puerto Rico	Spain	West Indies
1920s	5,742	[a]	1,217	7,364[b]	10,980	8,732
1930s	14,268	[a]	2,152	44,908[b]	13,992	61,295
1940s	12,499	[a]	2,973	61,431[c]	13,583	13,344
1950s	45,865[d]	[e]	4,093	245,922	14,075	[e]
1960s	102,009 (101,033)	42,694	8,260	612,486[c]	24,438	121,915 (13,293)
1970s	415,906	98,479	7,893	874,471	23,225	162,755 (51,231)

Note: Most of the data were obtained from U.S. Census Reports. Allowances were made to accommodate changes in categories from year to year. Figures in parentheses indicate number from Spanish-speaking countries—that is, excluding individuals from, e.g., Brazil or Trinidad.

a. Included in total for West Indies.

b. Indicates figures obtained from Lawrence R. Chenault, *The Puerto Rican Migrant in New York City* (New York: Columbia University Press, 1938; repr., New York: Russell and Russell, 1970), 53.

c. Indicates figures obtained from Manuel Maldonado-Dennis, *The Emigration Dialectic* (New York: International, 1980).

d. Defined that decade as "Other America."

e. Included in total for "Other America."

when the depression, changing demographics, and the accompanying changes in public expectations placed new pressures on companies working in public theater (see appendixes A and B).[29] For example, from 1929 to 1931 El Centro Andaluz was periodically leased for productions by two professional companies that regularly performed at the Park Theater. Under various directors, theaters bore names suggesting ethnic meetings halls as much as performance stages. For instance, La Nacional (the National Theater) later became El Centro Español (the Spanish Center), and Webster Hall became Casa Galicia (the Galician House).[30]

In general Spanish theatrical seasons were prepared with an eye toward popular entertainment. Figueroa summarizes: "Theater was not presented for art's sake, but rather to captivate and entertain the audience. For this reason productions in the 1920s and 30s consisted predominately of zarzuelas, comedies, and melodrama, with a few classics and serious contemporary works added alongside."[31] Zarzuela, it seems, could count as both popular and more serious fare, depending on the production and venue. The low status that Figueroa assigns to zarzuela compared to serious drama prevails today and contributes to the ambivalence toward the genre that one still encounters among fans of zarzuela.

Many impresarios organized their productions less around repertoire than around a celebrity with box-office attraction. One regularly appearing headliner, Marita Reid, served as both stage star, director, and playwright for over three decades. Born in Spanish Gibraltar to a Spanish mother and an English father, Reid grew up bilingual and began performing at age seven. After touring southern Spain with various theatrical companies, she made her New York stage debut in 1921 with La Compañía de Teatro Español and toured with Fortunio Bonanova's Lyric Theater Company. Her work included performances in the zarzuelas *Las Corsarias* (The Pirate Women), *Los Cadetes de la Reina* (The Cadets of the Queen), *La Canción del Olvido* (The Song of Forgetfulness), *Maruxa*, and *Marina*. Her success in musical theater was equaled by her success in serious drama, and after touring with New York resident companies such as the Compañía de Zarzuela Española Antonio Trujillo, she formed her own companies at the Calpe Americano, Casa Galicia, and Ateneo. During the late 1930s and 1940s her work with these companies in the halls of various mutual aid societies and social clubs helped to keep Spanish theater alive. Her activities in political theater at some of these societies serve as a reminder of the behind-the-scene linkages that existed between commercial and political activities of Hispanic theater. Reid's influence was not limited to the Hispanic community, however. Her fame attracted attention from the mainstream press, and her fluency in English enabled her to act on Broadway, in American cinema, and on mainstream television during the 1950s.[32]

The 1920s and the early 1930s in New York were a kind of "Golden Period of Hispanic Theater."[33] The period was characterized by an abundance of highly skilled actresses and actors, eager audiences, the availability of large theaters suitable for regular productions, and an emphasis on comedies and light lyric productions, particularly zarzuela. During the later 1930s and 1940s, however, audiences for Spanish productions waned. This turn of events can be explained in part by the dramatic transformation of New York's Hispanic population. Areas of the city once dominated by Spanish immigrants now passed to Puerto Rican hands. The 1920 census reports 7,364 Puerto Ricans living in New York (see table 1). Figueroa estimates that by 1935 the Puerto Rican population had climbed to 50,000. Even allowing a generous margin for error, it is clear that the number of Puerto Ricans living in New York increased dramatically and rapidly in those fifteen years.

The backgrounds of the new Puerto Rican residents differed greatly from those of their Spanish-speaking predecessors. Most of the Puerto Rican arrivals had rural backgrounds and more limited educations than did the average immigrant Spaniard or Cuban who arrived before them. As chapter 2 indicated, zarzuela in Puerto Rico was an urban tradition; the majority of Puerto Rican migrants to New York had little exposure to, or taste for, formally staged drama of any kind. Few supported the European-influenced practices that had dominated New York's stage until then. Even the lighter genre of zarzuela relied too much on peninsular traditions to retain popularity with the majority of this new population.[34]

Despite shifts in population and audiences, musical theater did not vanish from the scene. The variety show, usually billed as a *revista,* began to dominate the Spanish stage. The overwhelming majority of these *revistas* offered a combination of comedy skits, circus acts, singing, and dancing. The format was closely related to the vaudeville sketch, still quite popular across the United States. The *revista* seemed a perfect solution for theaters struggling to compete with cabarets, nightclubs, and supper clubs, all of which offered extravagant musical revues in addition to providing an orchestra for dancing until the wee hours of the morning. The Puerto Rican composer and performer Rafaél Hernández (1896–1965), for example, managed to blend the popular and classical so skillfully that he regularly drew crowds from all backgrounds during his stays in New York between 1930 and 1934.[35]

The lines separating productions in a cabaret from those in a theater were often thin to nonexistent. The same performers would appear with virtually identical shows in each location. For example, the Afro-Cuban composer, actor, and bandleader Eliseo Grenet would appear one night at the Teatro Hispano and the next at the Cuban nightclub Yumurí. The popularity of Grenet, whose name dots newspapers between 1930 and 1940, signals the shifting tastes of New York's Hispanic population away from serious drama and toward popular culture.

Tastes were not the only thing that changed. Regional theaters changed owners and names regularly. As a rule, the new names increasingly indicated the owner's intention to attract Hispanics in general. Teatro Borinquen, for example, relinquished its name indicating Puerto Rican affiliation and became Teatro Latino.

Musical theater also had to compete with film in the 1930s. The designation *theater* became synonymous with movie house, yet some owners combined formats and offered live musical entertainment, including dramas or variety shows including music, alongside film. Presentation formats were fairly predictable: one movie and one stage show each night for a run of one or two weeks (see appendix B). During the 1930s the stage show was billed as the main attraction; the emphasis shifted the other way in the late 1940s.

These productions were dominated by Caribbean or Latin American performers rather than those from Spain. In October 1939, for example, La Gran Compañía de Bufos Cubanos y Zarzuela was especially popular at the Teatro Hispano (see appendix B). Its productions included works such as *España y Puerto Rico* (Spain and Puerto Rico), a *revista* clearly acknowledging the ethnic allegiances of the local audience.

The *revista* format was extraordinarily successful. During its 1937–38 season Teatro Hispano boasted of selling a half-million tickets—at a time when there were only 136,615 Hispanics living in New York.[36] The commercial viability of the *revista* lay in its ability to offer something for everyone without assuming any exposure to classical Spanish traditions.

By the late 1930s and throughout the following decade, traditional drama of any sort, including zarzuela, failed to attract a substantial or regular audience. Productions were still mounted, but production records support Figueroa's claim that works such as *Los Gavilanes* (The Sparrow Hawks) were not popular with a non-Spanish audience and were seen as "totally irrelevant" by most Hispanics in New York.[37] As previously noted, traditional Hispanic theater "went underground" for the next twenty years and continued largely because of the commitment and vision of a few dedicated individuals. Again, Marita Reid offers an example. In October 1936 the Spanish actress founded El Cuadro Artístico (the Artistic Scene), located at El Calpe Americano, 366 Third Avenue. As the name of her company suggests, she strove to recapture an audience for traditional forms of staged drama, including zarzuela, and offered one to three performances each weekend for the next seven years (see appendix A).

The productions at El Calpe typified the dominant attitude toward traditional Spanish drama at the time. To justify the small audiences, companies appealed primarily to the elite; theater was promoted as a leisure-time pleasure to be enjoyed by the educated or the well-to-do. According to Figueroa—who clearly wishes that Hispanic theater might attract more working-class patrons—Marita Reid and El Calpe promoted attitudes and "theater-going habits that still plague the Hispanic theater today."[38]

In the 1940s films won the battle and became the dominant form of popular theatrical entertainment, superseding even the musical reviews. It was certainly more profitable to run a film several times a day than to present a live stage show for which performers must be paid. This trend continued into the 1950s, when live theater was further devastated by the emergence of television.

Modern Hispanic Theater in New York (1950 to the Present)

While Spanish-language musical theater temporarily vanished during the 1950s, other dimensions of Hispanic theater began to develop a stronger New York identity. John C. Miller characterizes 1950–65 as the "nutritive stage."[39]

From 1950 to 1958 a group of actors headed by Edwin Janer operated as La Farándula Panamérica (Pan-American Showbusiness). Their productions integrated peninsular works with contemporary Spanish American plays. They offered three or four works per season at either the Master Theater, West 103d Street and Riverside Drive, or at the Belmont Theater, located on Forty-eighth Street. Their productions attracted a small group of patrons who were generally well-educated, middle-class Hispanic theater lovers.

La Farándula's first production to have a broad popular appeal was the overwhelmingly successful production of René Marqués's *La Carreta* (The Oxcart) in 1954. In addition to Marita Reid, artists involved with this production included Miriam Colón and Roberto Rodríguez, two artists who went on to form their own theatrical company in 1956 called El Nuevo Círculo Dramático (the New Dramatic Circle).

The opening of El Nuevo Círculo Dramático on Sixth Avenue between Forty-third and Forty-fourth Streets marked the establishment of a professional Hispanic theater with its own performance venue. The theater could seat only sixty people, and the actors worked largely for love rather than wages, but the effort marked a critical turning point for Hispanic theater in New York. With the emergence of El Nuevo Círculo Dramático came the first glimmers of renewed public support for traditional dramatic presentations, proving the healthy existence of an audience for staged drama in Spanish.

Three factors characterized the growth of Hispanic theaters in the 1960s and ultimately contributed to a resurgence of interest in the zarzuela in New York: renewed interest in traditional dramatic formats, innovative productions, and a concern for popular taste. Two developments signaled the increasing influence of Spanish theater in New York. First, the non-Hispanic population began to notice Spanish contributions. In 1964 the New York Shakespeare Festival began to offer productions in Spanish, and in 1965 *La Carreta* was produced off Broadway. Second, a group of influential Spanish theaters opened, most of which have remained open to this date. Many of the individuals associated with the 1960s theatrical surge have continued to play important roles in the New York theater scene and across the United States into the 1990s.

The genealogy of today's most active Spanish theatrical companies, including those directly responsible for the 1980s revival of zarzuela, begins in the 1960s. Figueroa reports that in 1966 a group of distinguished Hispanic actors, including Max Ferra, Oscar García, Antonio González-Jaén, Elsa Ortiz, Gladys Ortiz, Benjamín López, and Frank Robles, formed the ADAL Company (Asociación de Arte Latino, or Latin Arts Group), which later became INTAR (International Arts Relations, Inc.). In 1967 Miriam Colón established the Puerto Rican Traveling Theater, still in operation, and in 1969 Frances Drucker and Luz Castaños, of Barnard College, formed the Greenwich Mews Spanish Theatre, which would later become the Repertorio Español under the direction of René Buch.[40] Later that same year Luz Castaños left Greenwich Mews to form Nuestro Teatro (Our Theater), while Mágaly Alabu and Manolo Martín formed the experimental theater company DUO, and Herberto Dumé opened the Dumé Spanish Theatre. Silvia Brito would later refashion the Dumé Theatre into the Thalia Spanish Theatre, which along with Repertorio Español regularly offers zarzuela today.

The years between 1960 and 1980 were a period of exciting growth for Hispanic theater. They were also the years when zarzuela returned to New York stages and to the eyes and ears of the general public. In the 1940s individuals interested in presenting Spanish drama had turned their back on public taste and operated independently. This holds for zarzuela as well. Although at first few zarzuelas were presented as a regular part of any theatrical company's season, the genre began to reappear through special production efforts in venues and formats that highlighted the musical component over the dramatic script. Beginning in 1960 zarzuelas were offered in Carnegie Hall, Town Hall, and New York's City Centers (see appendix A and fig. 5).

In 1960–80 audiences could attend not only staged productions but also recitals featuring zarzuela excerpts, formats that remain popular today. During this

CITY CENTER OF MUSIC & DRAMA, INC.
Norman Singer, General Administrator
IS PLEASED TO PRESENT THE AMERICAN PREMIERE OF
"FIESTA IN MADRID"
A Musical Show based on the most popular zarzuela in the world,
"La Verbena de la Paloma" by T. Bretón

FIESTA IN MADRID
Adapted by Tito Capobianco From The Zarzuela,
"La Verbena de La Paloma" by Tomas Breton
starring
ISABEL PENAGOS
NICO CASTEL KAY CREED MURIEL GREENSPON
FRANCO IGLESIAS TERESA
CHAVO XIMENEZ ANTONIA REY
ROBERTO LORCA LUIS OLIVARES MANOLO RIVERA
and
CLARAMAE TURNER
Entire Production Conceived and Directed by
TITO CAPOBIANCO
conductor
ODON ALONSO
Associate Director ELENA DENDA
Production Associate CLIFFORD STEVENS
Choreography TERESA
Settings & Costumes JOSE VARONA
Associate Set Designer DAVID MITCHELL
Choral Director MARTINEZ PALOMO
Lyric Arrangement G. ROEPKE & J. VARONA
Lighting Designer HANS SONDHEIMER

Figure 5. Program for Tito Capobianco's 1969 *Fiesta in Madrid:* an early bilingual version of *La Verbena de la Paloma* (the songs were sung in Spanish and the dialogue delivered in English). City Center of Music and Drama, Inc. Stagebill used with permission.

time runs of staged productions were short-lived; producers generally offered only a single performance, a practice more common in the world of concert music than in the theater. Zarzuela productions that ran for longer periods stood out because they both accommodated theatrical convention and stressed the musical virtues of the works. The most notable examples were productions directed by Miguel De Grandy in the 1970s and Tito Capobianco's 1969 production of *La Verbena de la Paloma,* which ran for one week (see fig. 5). These efforts at reviving zarzuela ran parallel to the activities of the newly emerging theatrical companies. Not until the 1980s would these companies consider undertaking serious productions of zarzuela and adding representative works to their regular seasonal repertoire.

5

Profiles of Contemporary Producers of Zarzuela in the New York Metropolitan Area

The historical linkage between theatrical activity and zarzuela is clear, and the genre has always received its most consistent support from theatrical groups. Any consideration of zarzuela productions in New York—or in the United States generally, for that matter—must examine in some detail the background and activities of two New York theaters, Repertorio Español and the Thalia Spanish Theatre, companies that have regularly devoted energy to the genre since 1981. The questions I sought to answer include the following: What led these companies to produce zarzuela? What resulted from their efforts, and how do these remarkably stable organizations compare to others that present zarzuela?

A Profile of Repertorio Español

Of the two companies, Repertorio Español is the larger and more financially stable. It is one of a handful of genuine repertory companies in the United States and is acknowledged as the only U.S. repertory company operating totally in Spanish.[1] In 1968 René Buch, the company's artistic director, began working with Gilberto Zaldívar, who acted as producer for their first Spanish play together. The seed of the company was planted with that production. The following year the two joined Luz Castaños and Frances Drucker at the Greenwich Mews Theatre, calling themselves Las Artes and working to promote Spanish theater in New York. Castaños left the group later that year to form Nuestro Teatro.

Significantly, Las Artes was modeled after a theatrical organization in Cuba called Pro Arte. Like Pro Arte, Las Artes sponsored concerts, plays, and operas and collected dues from its members. Buch directed Calderón de la Barca's *La Dama del Duende* (The Ghost Lady) for this group. The very successful production received financial backing from the wealthy Cuban benefactor Nena Menocal

(Mrs. Andrew Goodman of Bergdorf-Goodman fame). Like other Spanish theatrical organizations that sprang up in the 1960s, Las Artes and the Greenwich Mews players expressed their intent to appeal to a broad audience, but they drew their most consistent support from a segment of the population with financial resources and familiarity with the classical tradition.

Buch and company left Greenwich Mews and in 1972 began operating from a building in Manhattan's Gramercy Park area, still a district with a cachet of status and wealth. Their first production was a Spanish-language version of Edward Albee's *Who's Afraid of Virginia Woolf?*

Over the years Repertorio Español has increasingly gained public attention with an inventory of productions that revolves around Spanish dramas, including plays by Lope de Vega, Calderón, and García Lorca. The repertoire has also included Spanish versions of English-language classics, including works by Shakespeare and Tennessee Williams. Modern dramas and comedies, musical theater, and productions of classical dance—especially flamenco—are important additions to this classic base. Repertorio Español has traveled throughout the United States and Latin America and has won numerous awards, including an Obie (Off-Broadway) Award (1981 and 1992) and the New York State Governor's Arts Award (1984). The money it received from the National Endowment for the Arts in 1987 enabled the company to operate from an additional location, the prestigious Equitable Life Building, with its theater located in midtown Manhattan.

When René Buch decided to add musical theater to the company's repertoire, he began with an American musical, *The Fantasticks,* which he presented in Spanish in 1980. This was soon followed by the company's first zarzuela, the comically irreverent *La Corte de Faraón,* which opened in January 1981. The success of this spicy production prompted the company to attempt another comic zarzuela, and in 1983 *Doña Francisquita* opened. Two years later the company offered its first serious zarzuela, the lushly harmonized melodrama *Luisa Fernanda* (see fig. 6). Repertorio Español revived this work in 1992 to take it on tour in the Midwest and to the Festival de la Zarzuela, at the Chamizal National Theater, in El Paso, Texas.

Buch's interest in musical theater was not limited to complete productions of single works. With the aid of his musical director, Pablo Zinger, Buch created two concert anthologies entitled *¡Habana!* (Havana, 1982) and *Puerto Rico: Encanto y Canción* (Puerto Rico: Charm and Song, 1984). The two anthologies (see figs. 7 and 8) present overviews of the songs of Cuba and Puerto Rico, respectively, and incorporate folkloric, popular, and classical material dating from the seventeenth century to modern times, including excerpts from native zarzuelas and operas. These productions reveal a keen awareness of the demographic characteristics of New York's

Figure 6. Scenes from Repertorio Español's production of *Luisa Fernanda.* From *Repertorio Español, Annual Report, 1984–85.* Photos by Gerry Goodstein.

Hispanic population, which is dominated by people of Caribbean ancestry, particularly Puerto Ricans, Cubans, and Dominicans. The anthology format allows the company to make a direct appeal to various national groups. At the same time the format remains attractive to a broad audience, including those who speak no Spanish, since there is no need to follow an extended plot.

The incredible success of these two productions (both ran for two years, and *Habana* was revised and revived for production in 1988) encouraged Repertorio Español's continued commitment to musical offerings. The anthology format so suited the resources of the company and the tastes of its audiences that Buch and Zinger created a third anthology, titled *La Revista de la Zarzuela,* that featured only zarzuela. Musical production at Repertorio Español surged in 1988, for in addition to staging *La Revista de la Zarzuela* and *¡Habana!* the company offered another comic zarzuela, *La Generala.*

Productions in the 1990s show renewed emphasis on capturing the attention

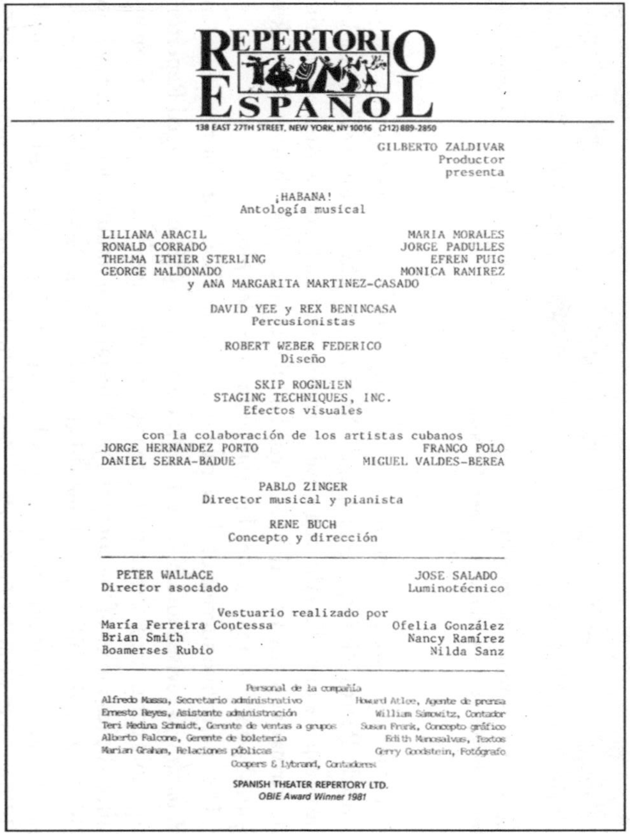

REPERTORIO ESPAÑOL

138 EAST 27TH STREET, NEW YORK, NY 10016 (212) 889-2850

GILBERTO ZALDIVAR
Productor
presenta

¡HABANA!
Antología musical

LILIANA ARACIL
RONALD CORRADO
THELMA ITHIER STERLING
GEORGE MALDONADO
MARIA MORALES
JORGE PADULLES
EFREN PUIG
MONICA RAMIREZ
y ANA MARGARITA MARTINEZ-CASADO

DAVID YEE y REX BENINCASA
Percusionistas

ROBERT WEBER FEDERICO
Diseño

SKIP ROGNLIEN
STAGING TECHNIQUES, INC.
Efectos visuales

con la colaboración de los artistas cubanos
JORGE HERNANDEZ PORTO
DANIEL SERRA-BADUE
FRANCO POLO
MIGUEL VALDES-BEREA

PABLO ZINGER
Director musical y pianista

RENE BUCH
Concepto y dirección

PETER WALLACE
Director asociado

JOSE SALADO
Luminotécnico

Vestuario realizado por
María Ferreira Contessa
Brian Smith
Boamerses Rubio
Ofelia González
Nancy Ramírez
Nilda Sanz

Personal de la compañía
Alfredo Massa, Secretario administrativo
Ernesto Reyes, Asistente administración
Teri Medina Schmidt, Gerente de ventas a grupos
Alberto Falcone, Gerente de boletería
Marian Graham, Relaciones públicas
Howard Atlee, Agente de prensa
William Simowitz, Contador
Susan Frank, Concepto gráfico
Edith Manosalvas, Textos
Gerry Goodstein, Fotógrafo
Coopers & Lybrand, Contadores

SPANISH THEATER REPERTORY LTD.
OBIE Award Winner 1981

Figure 7. Program for *¡Habana!* (1982 production), first page, Repertorio Español.

REPERTORIO ESPAÑOL

GILBERTO ZALDIVAR
Productor
RENE BUCH
Director Artístico

Ganador del Premio de las Artes del Gobernador de Nueva York 1984

presenta

PUERTO-RICO: ENCANTO Y CANCION

PABLO ZINGER
Director Musical y Pianista

La Compañía

ELIZABETH ACOSTA
RONALD CORRADO
DELIA D'CAMPOS
RENE DE LA GARZA
BRENDA FELICIANO
MYRA GARCIA-FERNANDEZ
THELMA ITHIER-STERLING
GEORGE MALDONADO
SALOME MARTINEZ
JORGE PADULLES
EFREN PUIG
ALBA QUEZADA
YOLANDA VADIZ
ROSENDO VILLAMIL

ROBERT WEBER FEDERICO
Diseñador de producción

DAVID YEE y REX BENINCASA
Percusionistas

ADOLFO VAZQUEZ
Coreógrafo

RENE BUCH
Concepto y dirección

PRIMERA PARTE

Danzas
"LA BORINQUEÑA" de Félix Astol*
"FELICES DIAS" de Juan Morel-Campos
"SARA" de Angel Mislán
"NO ME TOQUES" de Juan Morel-Campos*
"LA PONCEÑA" de Juan Morel-Campos*
"AMANECER" de Monsita Ferrer
"LA ALONDRA EN LOS BOSQUES" de Carlos Padilla*

Canciones infantiles y navideñas de Narciso Figueroa
"A LA LIMON / ALFONSO XII"
"ARROZ CON LECHE"
"HIJO DEL CONDE"
"LLEGAN LOS REYES"
"SOY UN POBRE JIBARITO"
"DE PUERTO RICO VENGO"*

Esta producción se estrenó en Nueva York el 17 de noviembre de 1984
y está auspiciada en parte por CITIBANK

GRAMERCY ARTS THEATRE
New York City

Figure 8. Program for *Puerto Rico: Encanto y Canción* (1987 production), first page, Repertorio Español.

of the larger, non-Hispanic audience. That year the company presented *La Viuda Alegre,* a Spanish version of Franz Lehar's operetta known in English as *The Merry Widow.* This work has always held a position in zarzuela repertoires and been popular with New York audiences in many formats (see chapter 7 for a fuller discussion). The company's 1990 production of Menotti's *El Cónsul* (The Consul) is especially remarkable, since Menotti himself has always claimed that he favored English as the language for operatic music. Despite these Spanish-language appropriations and the company's unwavering commitment to staging works only in Spanish, Repertorio Español accelerated its efforts to court non-Spanish-speaking patrons in 1992 when it initiated simultaneous English translation options for its (nonmusical) production of Gabriel García Marquéz's "La Cándida Eréndira" (Innocent Eréndira). From that date forth, translation has been available for all the company's musical productions, including *¡Y se Armó la Mojiganga!* (And the Carnival Erupted), a musical comedy using the seventeenth-century format of the *mojiganga* as a point of departure. The musical drama is based on a story by Tomás Carrasquilla and the comedy *A la Diestra de Dios Padre* (To the Right of God the Father), by Enrique Buenaventura. Directed by visiting Colombian artist Jorge Alí Triana, the play opened in 1994.

The latest musical enterprise of Repertorio Español, *Cuentos Afro-Caribeños* (Afro-Caribbean Tales), is a new anthology of music based on traditional songs and prayers connected with the *Cuentos Negros de Cuba* (Negro Stories from Cuba), collected by the legendary Cuban ethnographer and author on Afro-Cuban religions Lydia Cabrera. Although this anthology highlights Cuban retention of African practices, the extravaganza has been constructed around a theme that emphasizes a heritage shared by more than one Hispanic nationality. The theology and practices explored in *Cuentos Afro-Caribeños* were introduced to Cuba by enslaved Africans, a process that also occurred in other locales in the Americas. The program notes for the production highlight Brazil, Puerto Rico, and the Dominican Republic as examples. Promotional literature carefully defines the implications of this work regarding ethnic self-identification. It is described as "una obra musical que explora los elementos y las tradiciones folkloricas del pasado africano de nuestra cultura" (a work that explores elements and folkloric traditions of our culture's African past [ancestry]). The articulated identification with African ancestry is limited to past influences, although audiences are left to make their own connections.

In his assessment of contemporary Hispanic theaters, John C. Miller correctly recognizes the strong financial base supporting Repertorio Español, but he seems to have overlooked the production energies of Gilberto Zaldívar, also the company's president (see chapter 8), and the impact of the company's artistic

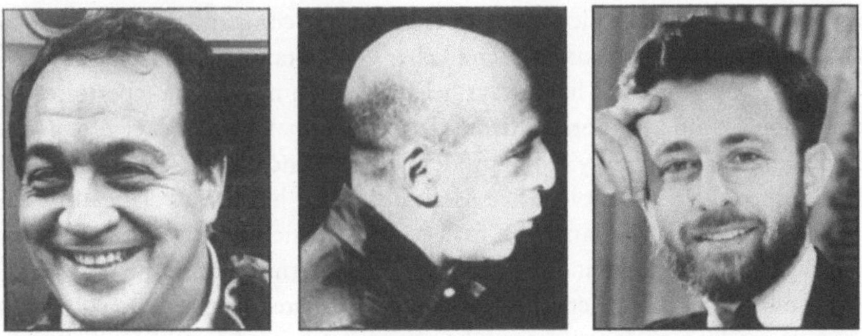

Figure 9. Photos of René Buch, Gilberto Zaldívar, and Pablo Zinger. From *Repertorio Español, Annual Report, 1985–86.* Photos by Gerry Goodstein.

director and vice-president, René Buch (see fig. 9). A man of strong convictions and a remarkably innovative director, Buch lends his lean, abstract vision of staging to all the company's shows. Buch's approach distinguishes Repertorio Español's productions, including the musical ones, from those of other companies.

Buch explains his view of zarzuela in this way: "I consider zarzuela part of theater. To me, opera, dance, ballet—it's all theater."[2] This view is clearly reflected in the company's programming policies; it also affects the manner in which Buch stages zarzuela. He continues:

> I think that all theater—and all musical theater—is an abstraction, because it cannot be realistic. No one sings in real life. So that immediately implies that it is a process in which you have to place the play at an aesthetic distance from real life. Because who wants to go and see real life?
>
> When I do a zarzuela, I go to the book; usually the books are very bad. So I cut the dialogue to the bone and I replenish the music.[3]

Buch adds that he feels completely free to alter the production traditions of zarzuela because "the genre was never sacred; composers turned out zarzuela after zarzuela to suit the circumstances and fashions of the age. It was like TV."

Despite the relative intimacy of its productions, Repertorio Español has, in the words of *Newsday* reviewer Paul D. Colford, "emerged as [Hispanic theater's] preeminent representative in New York."[4] Evidence of the company's increasing influence continues to mount, with new support rolling in from major foundations, including American Express and the Lila Wallace Reader's Digest Fund. Increasingly the larger public recognizes Repertorio Español as a showcase for Hispanic culture. Its productions, including the zarzuelas, are designed to appeal to a broad audience. It is precisely on these grounds that the company competes with other New York Spanish theaters, including the most devoted producer of zarzuelas (outside of the Sociedad Pro-Arte Grateli, in Miami): the Thalia Spanish Theatre.

A Profile of the Thalia Spanish Theatre

The Thalia Spanish Theatre owes its stability and success to the vision and energy of its director, Silvia Brito. Brito, a Cuban-born actress and, along with Herberto Dumé, a cofounder of the Dumé Spanish Theater, starred as Martha in Repertorio Español's production of Albee's *Who's Afraid of Virginia Woolf?* Her appearance in that production is a reminder of the close ties that unite New York's Hispanic theatrical artists. Although Brito is now, in many senses, in competition with René Buch and his group, she remains very supportive of his work.

In 1978, when Dumé made arrangements to move to Florida, Brito took over the theatrical company bearing his name, renamed it the Thalia Spanish Theatre, and relocated in Sunnyside, Queens, in a building set between a grocery store and a laundromat (see fig. 10). By moving Brito hoped to minimize competition with theaters in Manhattan and serve the growing Hispanic population in Queens.

Although Thalia has not received as much general attention or financial support as Repertorio Español, in its seventeen years of existence Brito's company has become one of the most celebrated Hispanic theaters in the United States, especially for its work with zarzuela. There are many similarities between Thalia and Repertorio Español. John C. Miller, a historian of Spanish-language theater in New York, notes that both companies are stable organizations operating from a traditional perspective.[5] Like Repertorio Español, Thalia also offers a range of both classic and modern plays augmented by traditional musicals. Thalia's productions represent more conservative programming choices and stagings.

Although Thalia produced *Zarzuela in Concert* in 1983 and shows called *Potpourri de Zarzuelas,* first in 1987 and others through the 1990s, the company has favored full zarzuela productions over the musical anthology format employed more extensively by Buch. Thalia also presents dance shows promoted in ways that make clear that translation is unnecessary for patrons who might not know Spanish. The first of these, called *Fiesta Española,* opened in 1983 and featured flamenco dancer Paco Montes. Beginning in 1988 the company initiated an annual series called *Tango and Folklore Argentino,* which became so popular that in some seasons (e.g., 1992–93) it offered the show for three different extended runs.[6]

Brito did not direct the zarzuelas at the Thalia between 1983 and 1987, but the

Figure 10. The Thalia Spanish Theatre, 41-17 Greenpoint Ave., Sunnyside, NY. Photo by Janet Sturman, 1989.

significance of her presence was undeniable, looming even larger than Buch's at Repertorio Español. Brito has single-handedly run the theater, working as administrator, artistic director, and producer, for most of its life. Along the way the company has won over fifty-six ACE awards, presented by the Association of Critics of Entertainment. Brito herself was honored by twice receiving the Arts and Business Council's ENCORE award (1989 and 1997) and by earning the prestigious New York State Governor's Arts Award in 1997 for her outstanding arts management (see fig. 11). She shared this honor with such legends as choreographer Jerome Robbins, actor Christopher Reeve, jazz great Billy Taylor, artist Chuck Close, and former chair of the New York State Council of the Arts Kitty Carlise Hart.

Brito does not identify Thalia as a repertory company. Actors and actresses work on a part-time basis, and although there is a faithful core group, casts change with each production. One of Thalia's earliest shows was a musical, a children's play entitled *El Globo Felíz* (The Happy Balloon). In 1985 Brito decided to try producing a complete zarzuela. She explains that it was a dream of hers long before Repertorio Español started to produce zarzuela, although Buch beat her by four years with *La Corte de Faraón.* Finally she decided it was a step Thalia "had to take." In 1985 she explained: "The thing is, a movement started three or four years

Figure 11. Silvia Brito accepts the 1997 New York State Governor's Arts Award. From the *Annual Report, The Thalia Spanish Theatre, 1998,* p. 11. Courtesy of the New York State Council on the Arts.

ago, and now every couple of months someone is producing a zarzuela. It has a place in Repertorio and other theaters, and we hope it stays here also. It's not that they have become popular, it's that people like zarzuela, and it's becoming more and more known. People like it because it has everything: some music, some dancing, comedy, drama—whatever you like, you are going to find it."[7]

Thalia relied on the renowned Miguel De Grandy to direct the company's first two efforts, *La Verbena de la Paloma,* in 1985 and *Los Gavilanes* in 1986 (see fig. 12). De Grandy is, to use his granddaughter's words, "the Plácido Domingo of Cuban zarzuela—he was that famous."[8] He starred in many Spanish zarzuelas in his native Cuba. He also premiered the leading roles in many Cuban zarzuelas written between 1927 and Castro's revolution, and most of those roles were written with him in mind. Among those works were *Cecilia Valdés, María la O, Rosa la China, La Hija del Sol* (Daughter of the Sun), *Soledad* (Solitude), *El Pirata* (The Pirate), *Guama, La Habana que Vuelve* (Havana Returns), *Lola Cruz, María Belén Chacón,* and *Amalia Batista.* After moving to Miami in 1969, De Grandy joined forces with the Sociedad Pro-Arte Grateli, Miami's oldest Span-

Figure 12. Program cover and scene from *La Verbena de la Paloma,* Thalia Spanish Theatre, April–June 1985. Performers, from left to right: Teresa Catoni, Gonzálo Madurga, Myrna Colon. Photo by Rafael Llerena.

ish-language theater and an organization that has specialized in zarzuela since 1969, when it opened with its first production, *La Verbena de la Paloma.*[9] He served as the company's artistic director until he retired in 1986 but continued to work as a zarzuela director until his death in 1988.

De Grandy's work provides a link between generations of zarzuela practitioners in the Americas and reinforces ties across states, linking Hispanic theatrical communities in New York and South Florida. He directed numerous zarzuelas in the 1970s, and before that his performances in zarzuelas and *revistas* delighted New York audiences during the 1930s.

Although Brito has directed Thalia's zarzuela productions since 1987, De Grandy's vision of the genre continues to shape the company's approach. Set designs are representational and elaborate, far more traditional than the abstract sets at Repertorio Español (see figs. 13 and 14). The musical component of each work is stressed, although most of the dialogue is retained. Casting favors the actor over the musician at Thalia, and although trained voices appear in the principal roles, the voices in the secondary roles are frequently less secure.

Every year since 1985 Thalia has offered a zarzuela. No company in New York is more dedicated to the preservation of the genre. In the past fourteen years the company has presented eleven different completely staged zarzuelas. This repertoire, to be discussed in more detail in chapter 7, embraces the most celebrated works of the tradition. Thalia has participated in the International Festival de la Zarzuela, held at Chamizal National Park in El Paso, since its inauguration in 1986 as an expansion of the annual Siglo de Oro festival of Spanish drama in El Paso–Ciudad Juarez (see fig. 15). Reviewers, especially in the local Spanish-language press, have praised Thalia for its energy and polish, regularly identifying the company's productions as the "best in the festival." These responses confirm the strong appeal of Thalia's traditional yet professional approach (see chapter 6).

Although praise for Thalia's work extends well beyond the Hispanic community, the company still has not attracted as much recognition from the larger English-language press in New York and elsewhere in the country as has Reper-

Figure 13. Stage set for the first act of *La Verbena de la Paloma,* Thalia Spanish Theatre, 1985. Photo by Rafael Llerena.

Figure 14. Scene from Repertorio Español's production of *Luisa Fernanda,* directed by René Buch. Performers, from left to right: Salomé Martínez, Angelo Cruz, René Torres, and Delia D'Campos. Courtesy of Repertorio Español.

torio Español. Thalia's success with enterprises such as the International Festival de la Zarzuela fuel Brito's hopes. In 1985 Brito explained how she expected zarzuela to expand the company's general recognition. "With zarzuela we can do what we cannot do with a regular play; we can bring in the American audience to see something in Spanish. Our goal is to show quality."[10] Brito's remarks indicate that she sees Thalia as a showcase for Hispanic culture and that its work with zarzuela, featuring "quality music," points to its level of cultivation.

Other Contemporary New York Approaches to Zarzuela

Other theaters in the New York area have at times included zarzuela, some producing lavish productions; one such group is the Asociación de Teatro Musical (ATM) in Union City, New Jersey. Union City is a thirty-minute car or bus trip across the Hudson River from Manhattan and boasts a majority of residents of Cuban descent, many of whom enthusiastically supported the ATM's produc-

Figure 15. Promotional brochure and membership application form for the International Festival de la Zarzuela, El Paso, Texas, summer 1995.

tions. The association ceased operation in 1987, but while it functioned, it enriched the availability of Spanish lyric drama in the New York metropolitan area. Unlike Thalia or Repertorio Español, the ATM offered only occasional productions, all of them musical. Its productions included not only zarzuelas but also American musicals such as *Fiddler on the Roof,* concerts of Italian opera arias, and most notably, Afro-Cuban music dramas. Before Repertorio Español's 1998 production of *Cuentos Afro-Caribeños,* the ATM was the only company in recent years to produce Cuban *costumbrista* works with full staging.

The ATM operated more like a club than a professional theater, and despite its lavish productions, it retained a grassroots character. The organization began in 1968 as an informal group associated with the Holy Family Church in Union City. In many regards the work of the ATM is reminiscent of the amateur and semiprofessional Hispanic theater groups that worked via the mutualist societies or churches in the 1930s and 1940s in New York. Under the name El Grupo Lírico Cultural, Raúl Cuervo and a team of actors produced *género chico* zarzuelas, such as *La Dolorosa* (The Lady of Sorrow). The organization changed its name to La Asociación de Teatro Musical in 1984 and soon thereafter began producing approximately three shows a year.

In the 1980s the ATM began staging its productions at the Park Theater, renting the civic theater in downtown Union City in a manner reminiscent of early New York practice. The group's policy of hiring a full orchestra for each production distinguished its zarzuelas from efforts elsewhere in the New York area. The expense of the orchestra, along with the elaborate costumes and sets and theater rental, was so high that each show ran for only one to two weekends (two to six performances). The short runs made the ATM's productions seem more like special events than regular theatrical offerings.

Like the Thalia Spanish Theatre and Repertorio Español, the ATM relied on the energies and vision of directors of Cuban heritage. Unlike those of the other two theaters, the ATM's productions were bound to the local Cuban community in Union City. Although the productions included New York city performers, especially instrumentalists, many of whom came from Juilliard and other Manhattan conservatories, most of the actors and singers represented the local community. The ATM was more concerned with appealing to this specific population than with attracting recognition from the larger public.

In keeping with its recognition of Union City residents, the ATM was the only theater to highlight Afro-Cuban zarzuela and lyric drama. Works such as *Ochún Mayéye,* a musical based on Afro-Cuban ritual, and the Cuban zarzuela *María la O* were proudly produced by the ATM. Despite its attentions to a large, working-class population, however, other efforts of the group allied it with opera and the classical music world. The latter connection was especially evident in the ATM's showcase concerts featuring operatic repertoire and classically trained singers.

During the 1980s patrons in the New York metropolitan area enjoyed the contributions of numerous independent presentations of zarzuela. Groups such as the Concertante Musical Society, founded in 1982, presented a single zarzuela, in this case the historic *El Barberillo de Lavapiés*. The intent, said Angélica Rosa, founder of the group, was to "capitalize on the current zarzuela craze."

Rosa, a soprano and voice teacher residing in New Jersey, organized the society primarily to produce concerts. Barbieri's *El Barberillo de Lavapiés* was its only effort to produce zarzuela. The production ran for six performances in November 1985 (Sunday afternoons and Wednesday evenings) at Rincón Taíno, a Puerto Rican club located at 113 East Twelfth Street (see fig. 16). It also ran for two performances at Festival Hola at the William Redfield Theatre, 354 West Fifty-fourth Street, between Eighth and Ninth Avenues. In December 1985 the company offered one more performance at El Museo del Barrio. All performances were well attended; the small halls were filled to 70–90 percent capacity (about 100 patrons per event).

The Concertante Musical Society is but one example of a group that used zarzuela to bolster its cultural status and tried to capitalize on the public's growing recognition of Spanish music.[11] From the turn of the century, Hispanic social organizations have delighted in presenting musical and theatrical works. Their small-scale concerts, patronized largely by friends and acquaintances, recall the salon concert, an important feature of cultivated society life in the Americas.

Working in the tradition of society concerts, Evaristo Corredor and Hernando Silva attempted in 1940 to organize a New York society entirely devoted to zarzuela. Recent examples of similar efforts include La Asociación Pro-Zarzuela en América (The Association for Zarzuela in America), founded in 1977; Los Amigos de la Zarzuela (Friends of Zarzuela), founded in 1985;[12] and the Friends of Spanish Opera, founded in 1980 (see figs. 17 and 18). These organizations collect dues from members and raise funds to sponsor recital performances of zarzuelas, usually in excerpt form. These concerts contrast with the staged zarzuelas offered by regional theater companies, but they too help to build audiences for Spanish and Latin American music.

Like the ethnically defined cultural clubs of the 1940s, these organizations tend to form around a core membership with strong ethnic affiliations. For example, musicians of Basque ancestry and origin, with names such as Valdivielso, Gallastegui, and Outeiral, steered the organization Los Amigos de la Zarzuela. Many of these musicians trained in Latin America, and the ethnic ancestry of board members varies; Mauricio Chacón, for example, was born in Colombia. The group's programs are open to the public but initially attracted limited attention from the general population.

Under the combined direction of Pablo Zinger and Victor Chacón, Los Amigos de la Zarzuela helped to sponsor a presentation of *Los de Aragón* (Those from

Figure 16. Program for *El Barberillo de Lavapiés,* Concertante Musical Society in conjunction with Rincón Taíno, November 1985. The cast includes artists who regularly appear with the Thalia Spanish Theatre and La Asociación de Teatro Musical.

Aragón) for the El Paso festival in 1995. The production included Spanish dancers and a group of onstage guitars and mandolins, features of many zarzuela scores that are often omitted from contemporary productions. Los Amigos operates as a philanthropic society and has helped to promote zarzuela across the nation, lending support, for example, to artists and companies wishing to participate in El Paso's international zarzuela festival.

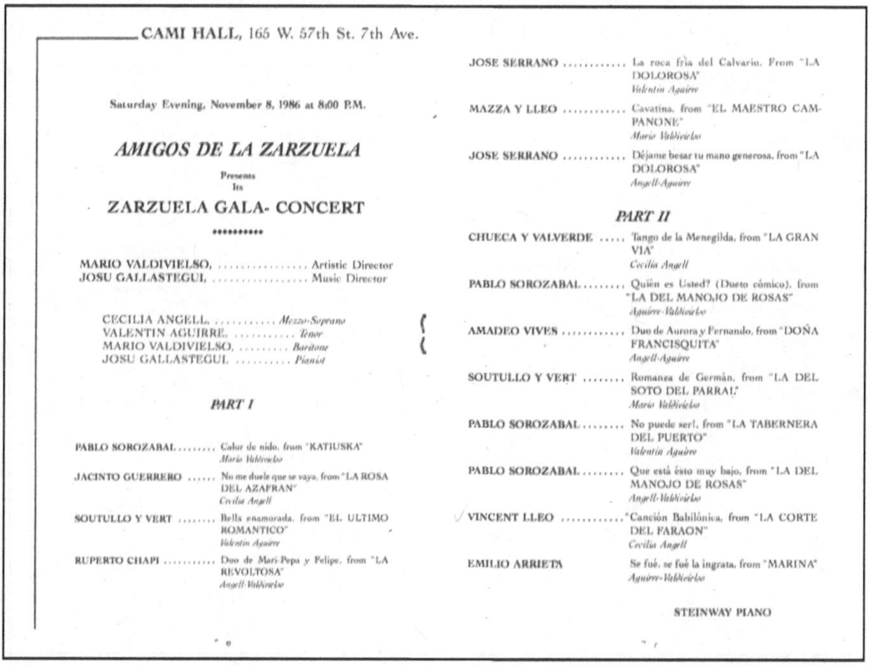

CAMI HALL, 165 W. 57th St. 7th Ave.

Saturday Evening, November 8, 1986 at 8:00 P.M.

AMIGOS DE LA ZARZUELA

Presents
Its

ZARZUELA GALA- CONCERT

••••••••••

MARIO VALDIVIELSO, ... Artistic Director
JOSU GALLASTEGUI, ... Music Director

CECILIA ANGELL, ... *Mezzo-Soprano*
VALENTIN AGUIRRE, ... *Tenor*
MARIO VALDIVIELSO, ... *Baritone*
JOSU GALLASTEGUI, ... *Pianist*

PART I

PABLO SOROZABAL .... Calor de nido, from "KATIUSKA"
Mario Valdivielso

JACINTO GUERRERO ...... No me duele que se vaya, from "LA ROSA DEL AZAFRAN"
Cecilia Angell

SOUTULLO Y VERT .... Bella enamorada, from "EL ULTIMO ROMANTICO"
Valentin Aguirre

RUPERTO CHAPI .... Duo de Mari-Pepa y Felipe, from "LA REVOLTOSA"
Angell-Valdivielso

JOSE SERRANO .... La roca fria del Calvario. From "LA DOLOROSA"
Valentin Aguirre

MAZZA Y LLEO .... Cavatina, from "EL MAESTRO CAMPANONE"
Mario Valdivielso

JOSE SERRANO .... Déjame besar tu mano generosa, from "LA DOLOROSA"
Angell-Aguirre

PART II

CHUECA Y VALVERDE ..... Tango de la Menegilda, from "LA GRAN VIA"
Cecilia Angell

PABLO SOROZABAL .... Quién es Usted? (Dueto cómico), from "LA DEL MANOJO DE ROSAS"
Aguirre-Valdivielso

AMADEO VIVES .... Duo de Aurora y Fernando, from "DOÑA FRANCISQUITA"
Angell-Aguirre

SOUTULLO Y VERT .... Romanza de Germán, from "LA DEL SOTO DEL PARRAL"
Mario Valdivielso

PABLO SOROZABAL .... No puede ser!, from "LA TABERNERA DEL PUERTO"
Valentin Aguirre

PABLO SOROZABAL .... Que está ésto muy bajo, from "LA DEL MANOJO DE ROSAS"
Angell-Valdivielso

VINCENT LLEO ...."Canción Babilónica, from "LA CORTE DEL FARAON"
Cecilia Angell

EMILIO ARRIETA Se fué, se fué la ingrata, from "MARINA"
Aguirre-Valdivielso

STEINWAY PIANO

Figure 17. Program for the Zarzuela Gala-Concert, by the Friends of Zarzuela (Los Amigos de la Zarzuela), CAMI Hall, New York, November 8, 1986. Many of the performers' names indicate Basque ancestry.

Some Initial Conclusions

The stories of these theatrical companies and organizations lead to this simple conclusion: although zarzuela is hardly new in New York, today's productions carry a status different from that of productions in the first decades of the twentieth century. In part, this status is tied to the growth and establishment of Hispanic theaters in New York. Another undeniable part of the attraction is the music, which some prefer to isolate as concert repertoire.

Zarzuela is no longer the bread-and butter repertoire of Spanish theater, but the repertoire, especially the peninsular zarzuelas, serves as a unifying force within New York's pan-Hispanic population. As in the past, the genre allows New York performing artists to expand their reach to diverse audiences. It is significant that although companies such as Repertorio Español rotate repertoire in patterns remarkably like the rotations that governed theatrical presentations in the 1930s at venues such as Variedades (see appendix B), most contemporary producers have

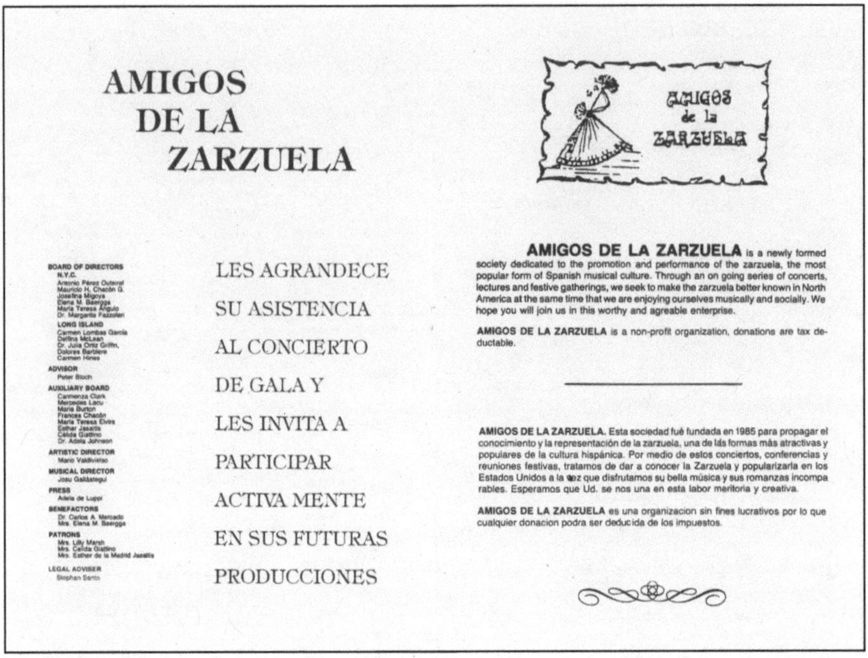

AMIGOS
DE LA
ZARZUELA

BOARD OF DIRECTORS
N.Y.C.
Antonio Pérez Outeiral
Mauricio H. Chacón G.
Josefina Migoya
Elena M. Baergga
María Teresa Angulo
Dr. Margarita Fazzolari
LONG ISLAND
Carmen Lombas García
Delfina McLean
Dr. Julia Ortiz Griffin,
Dolores Barbiere
Carmen Hines
ADVISOR
Peter Bloch
AUXILIARY BOARD
Carmenza Clark
Mercedes Lacu
María Burton
Frances Chacón
María Teresa Elvira
Esther Jasaitis
Célida Giattino
Dr. Adela Johnson
ARTISTIC DIRECTOR
Mario Valdivielso
MUSICAL DIRECTOR
Josu Gallástegui
PRESS
Adela de Luppi
BENEFACTORS
Dr. Carlos A. Mercado
Mrs. Elena M. Baergga
PATRONS
Mrs. Lilly Marsh
Mrs. Celida Giattino
Mrs. Esther de la Madrid Jasaitis
LEGAL ADVISER
Stephan Santo

LES AGRANDECE
SU ASISTENCIA
AL CONCIERTO
DE GALA Y
LES INVITA A
PARTICIPAR
ACTIVA MENTE
EN SUS FUTURAS
PRODUCCIONES

Amigos de la Zarzuela

AMIGOS DE LA ZARZUELA is a newly formed society dedicated to the promotion and performance of the zarzuela, the most popular form of Spanish musical culture. Through an on going series of concerts, lectures and festive gatherings, we seek to make the zarzuela better known in North America at the same time that we are enjoying ourselves musically and socially. We hope you will join us in this worthy and agreable enterprise.

AMIGOS DE LA ZARZUELA is a non-profit organization, donations are tax deductable.

AMIGOS DE LA ZARZUELA. Esta sociedad fué fundada en 1985 para propagar el conocimiento y la representación de la zarzuela, una de lás formas más atractivas y populares de la cultura hispánica. Por medio de estos conciertos, conferencias y reuniones festivas, tratamos de dar a conocer la Zarzuela y popularizarla en los Estados Unidos a la vez que disfrutamos su bella música y sus romanzas incomparables. Esperamos que Ud. se nos una en esta labor meritoria y creativa.

AMIGOS DE LA ZARZUELA es una organizacion sin fines lucrativos por lo que cualquier donacion podra ser deducida de los impuestos.

Figure 18. Inside cover of the Zarzuela Gala-Concert, presented by the Friends of Zarzuela, CAMI Hall, New York, November 8, 1986. The copy indicates the group's goals and identifies its board, directors, and advisers.

chosen to revive only the zarzuela and not the topical *revistas, bufo* comedies, or *costumbrista* works of this period. The zarzuela has emerged as the more prestigious choice. More important, the Spanish zarzuela allows presenters and audiences to invoke a peninsular identity, as remote or imaginary as that may be in reality. Zarzuela may still be classified as popular lyric drama or light opera, but the tradition is hardly popular in the way it was fifty years ago, when zarzuelas were the musical equivalent of television sitcoms.

Finally, professional production standards emerge as a critical concern of New York performers, past and present. New York standards of professionalism set the measure for theatrical production, as well as musical performance, across the United States. This rule of thumb holds for zarzuela productions, too. The goals of New York theatrical companies extend beyond presenting Spanish-language drama in ways that merely accommodate existing standards of professionalism. Many seek to establish new standards. In this regard, companies such as Teatro

Repertorio Español and the Thalia Spanish Theatre have goals rather like those of Marita Reid discussed in the previous chapter. Despite a historical reputation for weak production standards, zarzuela has advocates who take it seriously, who aim for the highest production standards, and who see in such skilled performances of zarzuela an avenue for establishing Hispanic perspectives as integral to mainstream culture.

6

Identity and Choice

Contemporary Zarzuela Audiences

In the first pages of his book *The Hispanic Condition: Reflections on Culture and Identity in America,* Mexican American author and cultural critic Ilan Stavans asks: "Who are we really? What do we want? Why are we here? And for how long will the *bodega* [neighborhood grocery store] be owned by somebody else?"[1] These same questions might be turned toward the audiences for contemporary zarzuela productions. Who attends and supports such productions and why? What does or might this group control? This chapter builds on previous historical observations and sharpens the focus on contemporary answers to these questions. The answers involve issues of ethnic identity, social status, prestige, and power. Zarzuela productions help to create and project a composite identity that does not exist outside the confines defined by these performance situations.

The previous chapter indicates that the distinctive composition of New York's Hispanic population played an important role in the character of theatrical offerings in various locales and during different periods of the city's history. This chapter will explore in greater detail the identity of the audiences for recent zarzuela productions (fig. 19). Data for this examination come from firsthand observation, follow-up interviews, and the results of a series of audience questionnaires. Three factors emerge from analysis of this material. First, the average zarzuela patron is not the average Hispanic American. Here, of course, I am comparing statistical constructs, but both constructs focus attention on general characteristics in proportion to a range of possibilities. Second, the commonly used designation *Hispanic* proves to be both problematic and desirable. The term embodies assumptions regarding language and heritage with connotations that vary according to who uses it and when and where it is used. Third, national origin frequently proves to be as unsatisfactory a referent for marking ethnicity as it is

Figure 19. Views of audiences who attend productions at Repertorio Español. From *Repertorio Español, Annual Report, 1985–86,* p. 11. Photos by Gerry Goodstein.

for choosing musical and theatrical repertoire. All these factors will be examined in more detail in the following discussion.

Language Choice and Identity

"Cervantes's tongue is the glue that keeps Hispanics together, the point of encounter for Latinos north of the border," claims Stavans.[2] Indeed, many would join him in arguing that this historical connection to language is one of the few factors that unites people with essentially different backgrounds into a group commonly called "Hispanic." The history of zarzuela in the United States reinforces this claim. With a few notable exceptions, such as the 1917 production of *The Land of Joy,* in New York zarzuela productions have been offered exclusively in Spanish.[3] Although it may seem obvious that, as a result of language choice, most zarzuela productions would attract patrons who know Spanish, this assumption is by no means justified in parallel cases. An American production of Italian opera does not typically attract audiences dominated by Italian speakers or those of Italian background. Despite the possibility that zarzuela productions *might* attract large non-Spanish-speaking audiences, however, the reality is that, in New York and elsewhere across the country, these productions primarily attract patrons who know Spanish and are of Hispanic descent. In New York the audiences for zarzuela at the Spanish theaters tend to be about 80 percent Hispanic and 20 percent non-Hispanic. Across the country audience proportions vary, depending on the language of the production and the venue. The Chicago Opera Factory offers zarzuela with the spoken dialogue in English and the songs in Spanish. The audiences for these productions are generally about 60 percent Hispanic and 40 percent non-Hispanic.[4]

My polls of audiences at the three principal theaters that regularly offer zarzuela in the New York area show that overall 50 percent of the respondents preferred seeing theatrical productions in Spanish.[5] This implies not a discomfort with English but merely a preference for Spanish when given a choice: 22 percent of this sample reported that they would be equally comfortable seeing a production in English, yet 86 percent of them responded using the Spanish side of the bilingual questionnaire.

In New York, as in most of the United States, Spanish speakers are generally of Hispanic descent, meaning that they can trace their ancestry to Latin American countries or to Spain. As I have already noted, not all Hispanics in New York, or elsewhere in the country, are interested in zarzuela, nor do *only* Hispanics attend productions of the genre. Before trying to determine who is interested in zarzuela and why, we should examine the implications of the ethnic label *Hispanic.*

Confronting the Label *Hispanic*

Although the term *Hispanic* is used throughout the United States, the populations to which it is applied differ greatly from one region of the country to another. For example, although slightly more than one-half of the 25 million Hispanics living in the United States today are of Mexican descent, this segment is concentrated in the Southwest. Mexicans constitute less than 4 percent of New York's Hispanic population (see table 2).[6] Although one-tenth of the Hispanics living in the United States are Puerto Rican, the vast majority of Puerto Ricans live in, or near, New York City and make up just under half of that city's entire Hispanic population.[7] Cubans represent the third-largest segment of the total

Table 2. A Comparative Analysis of Persons of Spanish/Hispanic Ancestry in the New York Metropolitan Area

Group	1980 Percentage	1990 Percentage
Argentine	1	< 1
Bolivian	< 1	< 1
Chilean	< 1	< 1
Cuban	**4–5**	**6**
Colombian	2.8	4
Costa Rican	< 1	< 1
Dominican	**8.5**	**14**
Guatemalan	< 1	1
Ecuadorian	2.8	4
Honduran	< 1	1
Mexican	2.0	4
Nicaraguan	< 1	< 1
Peruvian	1.3	1.5
Puerto Rican	**60**	**53**
Salvadoran	< 1	2
Spain	< 1	< 1
Uruguayan	< 1	< 1
Venezuela	< 1	< 1

Note: The three largest groups have been highlighted in boldface type. Information on persons of Spanish/Hispanic origin or descent from the 1980 census was derived from answers to census question 7: "Is this person of Spanish/Hispanic origin or descent?" Such persons are those who reported either Mexican, Puerto Rican, Cuban, or other Spanish/Hispanic origin in response to this question. Persons who chose the "other. . ." category were presumably individuals who came from Spain or the Spanish-speaking countries of Central or South America or who identified their origin or descent as Spanish, Spánish/American, Hispano, Latino, and so on. Origin or descent can be regarded as ancestry, nationality group, lineage, or country in which the person or person's parents or ancestors were born before their arrival in the United States. It is important to note that persons of Spanish origin may be of any race. See U.S. Department of Commerce, Bureau of the Census 1982, appendix B-5. These concepts continue to hold for the 1990 census.

New York Metropolitan Area here corresponds to the U.S. Census Bureau's Standard Metropolitan Statistical Area embracing New York City and environs. The Standard Metropolitan Statistical Area (SMSA) is a statistical construct devised and used by the U.S. Bureau of the Census to provide a common basis for the collection and presentation of statistics in areas of major population concentration. An SMSA almost always includes a major city (cities) and the county (counties) in which it is located. An SMSA may cross state lines. The New York, N.Y.–New Jersey SMSA includes New York City as well as Putnam, Rockland, Westchester, and Bergen (N.J.) Counties and is the statistical equivalent of the standard geographical expression "New York Metropolitan Area." See Nelson Rockefeller Institute, "Definitions and Abbreviations," *New York Statistical Yearbook* (Albany: New York State Division of the Budget, Office of Statistical Coordination, 1983–84), 7.

Totals do not tally to 100 percent because catchall categories such as "Other-Hispanic" have been omitted and because of rounding. The variation reflects the differences between self-reporting of ancestry and figures obtained from data on Hispanic foreign-born residents in the census tables on citizenship and year of immigration. See *Characteristics of the Population,* ch. D, pt. 34, "New York," vol. 1 of *1980 Census of the United States,* 2 vols. (Washington, D.C.: GPO, 1983). The 1990 census included more (and different) subcategories than did the 1980 census, making the comparative value of this chart useful only in general terms. For additional data and discussion of comparisons between the 1980 and 1990 censuses, see Louise L. Hornor, ed., *Hispanic Americans: A Statistical Sourcebook,* 4th ed. (Palo Alto, Calif.: Information Publications, 1994).

Hispanic population in the United States, but their numbers are considerably smaller, approximately 4 percent of the national total. Cubans are heavily concentrated in Miami and elsewhere in the states of Florida, New Jersey, and New York. The metropolitan area around New York City is also home to a strong concentration of Cubans, but they constitute less than 6 percent of the total Hispanic population, or approximately 15 percent of the non–Puerto Rican Hispanics in that region.[8]

The realities of self-identification and ethnic affiliation for Americans of Hispanic descent are complex. Although the larger society often treats the Hispanic population as a group with common characteristics and common problems, the differences among segments of this population are great. Each group became a part of the American population in a different manner. Each confronted different economic, political, environmental, and cultural circumstances.[9] Each group has a different sense of its own identity. The groups share a connection to the Spanish language, but speech and use patterns also vary by background, region of residence, and generation. Consequently, Hispanics in the American Southwest may share little with Hispanics in New York and New Jersey.

The label *Hispanic* is generally imposed by the larger English-speaking American society on Spanish-speaking immigrants and their children, regardless of national origin. Many individuals so labeled do not embrace this designation with its composite or pan-ethnic dimensions, even if this may be the term by which the rest of the nation identifies them. Some prefer to refer to themselves as *Latinos;* others shun such all-embracing terms entirely and instead elect to identify themselves according to their national identity or ancestry, as Cubans, Puerto Ricans, or Argentineans. The realities of living in Anglo-dominated America prompt others to emphasize their composite regional identities as well as their political postures by insisting on designations such as *Chicano* or *Nuyorican.* Still others, when racial features make it feasible and social situations invite it, prefer to identify themselves as black.[10]

In his exploration of various self-selected options, Stavans notes the different connotations of certain choices. He writes: "In mammoth urban centers (Los Angeles, Miami, New York), the Spanish language media—newspapers and television stations—address their constituency as *los hispanos,* but hardly ever as *los latinos.* The deformed adjective *hispano* is used instead of *hispánico,* which is the correct Spanish word; the reason: *hispánico* is too pedantic, too academic, too Iberian. When salsa, merengue, and other rhythms are referred to, *latino* is used."[11]

This last statement illustrates the utility of musical expression to signify the character of a group. The zarzuela proves equally potent in this regard, especially as it contrasts with salsa, merengue, and other popular musics born of a merger of Latin and African traditions. As I will show, despite claims made by those who advocate using the term *Latino* to refer to North Americans of Hispanic descent, choosing the term *Hispanic,* like choosing zarzuela, emphasizes a unity based on the European roots of shared historical ties. Although this implication of the term *Hispanic* may be largely unrecognized by the larger society, it is often a real issue for those of Spanish and Latin American ancestry who choose to identify themselves in ways that highlight European affinities and corresponding status.

Ethnic Composition of Sample Zarzuela Audiences

Only a small percentage (3 percent) of New York's Hispanic population hails from Spain, yet Spanish zarzuelas far outnumber the rare production of a Cuban zarzuela or any other New World derivative. Still, this overwhelming emphasis on Spanish zarzuela has never been made to the point of excluding musical theater expressing more specific regional ethnicities.

Just as New York's Hispanic population embraces a wide range of ethnic and national identities, the precise ethnic makeup of a typical zarzuela audience is complex. In the 1980s the largest group represented in the audience and on stage was likely to be Cuban, although other nationalities were also represented (see table 3). Patrons tended to be more ethnically diverse than the performers they came to see, and the samples polled indicated patrons hailing from Argentina, Bolivia, Chile, Colombia, Cuba, the Dominican Republic, Ecuador, Italy, Mexico, Peru, Puerto Rico, Spain, and Uruguay, as well as from the United States. Most patrons were immigrants. Patrons born in the United States, including Hispanics, constituted only 12 percent of those who responded.[12] To some extent these results are valid for audiences in the 1990s, although now many more patrons are born in the United States than were so in the past.

Questionnaire results also indicated the complex nature of ethnic self-identification. Despite the fact that 29 percent of the composite sample reported Cuba as their place of birth, only 4 percent of that same sample identified themselves as Cuban. In general, patrons did not choose to identify themselves by nation of birth when asked to describe their ethnicity. The consistent discrepancy between country of birth and ethnic self-identification indicates that patrons do not necessarily find the former to be the best way to clarify their identity.

The inadequacy of nation of birth as an ethnic marker is demonstrated most vividly by the responses made by the segment of the sample that reported being born in the United States (12 percent). Only 2 percent of the total sample identified themselves as "Americans." Many in this group demonstrated no concern

Table 3. Nationalities of Performers at Three New York Theaters in the 1980s

	Percentage of Artistic Personnel		
Nationality	Repertorio Español	Thalia Spanish Theatre	La Associación de Teatro Musical (ATM)
Argentinean	7	7	
Asian American	5		
Costa Rican	2		
Chilean		4	
Colombian			4
Cuban	**36**	**53**	**53**
Dominican	7		
Ecuadoran	2		
Italian/Italian American	2	4	4
Peruvian			4
Puerto Rican	21	11	9
Mexican American	7		
Nicaraguan	2		
North American	2	14	
Salvadoran	2		
Spanish	2		9
Uruguayan	2	4	
Venezuelan		4	

Note: The largest group has been highlighted in boldface type. Artistic Personnel includes cast, directors, and onstage musicians. Figures do not include the backgrounds of the hired orchestra for the ATM. Individuals can and do perform with more than one company; hence, personnel overlaps somewhat. Totals do not add up to 100 percent because of rounding and the relatively small sample sizes (twenty-eight persons total for Repertorio Español and Thalia; twenty-three for the ATM). The figures thus provide only a general, comparative sense of proportion and representation. Designations reflect information from artist biographies.

The strong Cuban dominance evident in the 1980s has diminished somewhat in the 1990s, although it persists. Repertorio Español reports that since 1990 there have been more American-born performers and more Colombians performing with the company. Thalia reports that in addition to American-born actors, more Mexican, Colombian, and Spanish performers have performed with the company since 1990 than in past years.

for ethnic identity in its traditional sociological sense and described their ethnic heritage as "great," "good," or "wonderful." Many, but by no means all, who responded in this fashion were students under twenty years of age who seem to have misunderstood the question. Others born in the United States preferred to identify themselves by retracing their immigration heritage and described themselves as "English-German" or "German-Dutch." Still others relied on specific locale to describe their ethnicity and identified themselves as "Native New Yorkers."

The shortcomings of nation of birth as an ethnic marker were equally evident for those born outside the United States. Respondents listed fourteen different countries to indicate place of birth but offered twenty-four different categories in response to the a query regarding ethnicity. Not all the data indicate greater distinction between ethnic categories; indeed, some suggest a merging of identities. For example, 6 percent of the overall sample chose *Hispanic* as a term of self-identification. The figure rises to 8 percent if one includes related pan-ethnic designations such as *Hispano-Américano* and *Latino.* Although only 4 percent of the total sample were born in Spain, 17 percent used the term *Spanish* to indicate their ethnic identity, suggesting that to them their Spanish heritage is more important, or more convenient, than a more circumscribed national indicator.

The convenient shortcut of labeling oneself "Spanish" frequently carries critical overtones regarding race. Many who emphasize ancestral links to Spain look European; they may lack physical traits revealing Afro-Hispanic lineage. Despite the fact that many Hispanics in New York elect to stress their ties to the African American community, few at zarzuela productions do so (less than 3 percent overall). This is especially interesting given the strong Dominican presence among the actors at Repertorio Español and the inclusion of full-scale Afro-Cuban productions at the ATM in the 1980s (see appendix C).

In New York zarzuela's peninsular origin, its Castilian traditions—in short, those characteristics that indicate its ties to European culture—are repeatedly stressed. Performers, directors, and even reviewers regularly contrast zarzuela music with salsa. For example, in his *New York Times* review of *Cecilia Valdés* at Carnegie Hall in April 1974, John Rockwell remarks, "This was definitely a show for the parents of those who turn out for the Latin 'salsa' festivals at Madison Square Garden."[13] Even as early as 1942, Evaristo Corredor explained his goals in presenting zarzuela in similar terms: "We would like to change the usual idea that *rumbas* and *sambas* are all we [Hispanics] care about for amusement."[14] Rumbas and sambas are not salsa, but they are popular dance styles with blended roots including African contributions.

Although the popularity of salsa also encourages a merging of ethnic boundaries, it is still generally considered to be "music of the street," and promoters tend to stress its Afro-Caribbean roots.[15] The style has a distinguished tradition, but neither promoters nor patrons consider or desire it to be akin to European art music.

This division along lines of ancestry, European versus Afro-Caribbean, is far from incidental in a society such as that of the United States, where ethnic distinctions are customarily framed in simple black-and-white terms.[16] Despite the enormous contribution of African tradition to American culture, the larger American society still emphasizes its European heritage over all others. Racial lines are less simplistically drawn in many Latin American countries, where economic status and educational level tend to carry more weight than overt racial characteristics. Nonetheless, the countries from which many U.S. Hispanics hail still carry the burden of colonialism, and European manners and ancestry retain the highest levels of status.

The wide range of responses from the audiences polled at zarzuela performances indicates that the musical genre's appeal is not limited to a single nationality or ethnic segment but is, to a large extent, tied to promotion of the Spanish language. Nevertheless, since less than a quarter of the respondents stress Hispanic heritage in identifying themselves, the attraction to zarzuela, although in some ways tied to its "Spanishness," cannot be limited to this aspect alone. It is clear that people who patronize zarzuelas share characteristics other than a facility with the Spanish language. Beyond satisfying the majority's stated preference for drama in the Spanish language, what else does zarzuela appear to offer its New York audiences? A closer look at the "average" zarzuela patron in the 1980s, when zarzuela productions rose in popularity, may provide some clues.

The "Average" Zarzuela Patron

By merging data obtained from the questionnaires mentioned previously with regular observations and conversations, it is possible to construct a profile of the average zarzuela patron (AZP) who attended the full productions mounted at Spanish theaters in the New York area during the late 1980s. This effort allows us to see some general patterns. The characteristics of the AZP, while not necessarily representative of any single individual, do highlight features of the audiences that supported zarzuela during this period and also help to explain trends that have developed since then.

Overall, this AZP is approximately forty-one years of age and attends with a family member (61 percent, with 33 percent coming with their spouses) or friends (25 percent). Only 3 percent of patrons attend alone. In addition, the audience is fairly evenly divided according to sex, with females constituting a slight majority (41 percent male, 44 percent female—15 percent left this question unanswered).

As noted before, the AZP is Spanish speaking and Hispanic and, if not born here, is most likely to have been born in Cuba, Colombia, or Spain. The AZP has some college education and holds a professional job, with an income falling between $20,000 and $40,000 per year. Educational background is an area where the AZP contrasts with the average Hispanic population both in New York and across the United States. By most measures Hispanics as a group lag behind other Americans in educational achievement, but the AZP has attended college.[17]

The median income of the AZP in 1986 was $30,000. although this certainly does not establish the AZP as wealthy, especially in the New York metropolitan area, the figure is considerably higher than the medians for all New York City ethnic or racial subgroups in 1980 ($16,058 for whites, $10,713 for blacks, $8,913 for Puerto Ricans, $14,727 for Colombians, $9,681 for Dominicans, and $12,400 for other Hispanic groups). In general financially secure, if not well off, the AZP considers the $10–15 ticket price to be moderate and fair.

The AZP lives in New York City (rather than any of the outlying the suburbs), most likely in Queens, and drives to the theater (instead of taking public transportation). The decision to see the show is based as much on the recommendations of friends as on the advertisements encountered on Spanish radio and television broadcasts. The AZP's favorite kind of music is "classical." Despite this preference, the AZP is more likely to have attended a Broadway show, especially a musical, than an opera in the past year. The AZP does enjoy opera, however, and many have attended at least one operatic production in New York.[18] Although musicals are in general the AZP's favorite kind of dramatic work, the typical patron is also fond of classic dramas and comedies. The typical patron has also attended other Spanish theatrical productions in the area, particularly at Repertorio Español, the Thalia Spanish Theatre, Casa España, and the Puerto Rican Traveling Theater. The AZP's interest in contemporary, Nuyorican, or political dramas appears minimal, and visits to less established, more experimental theaters are infrequent.

This profile contrasts with the larger American-Hispanic population in that the AZP is typically not Puerto Rican, the largest segment of the total Hispanic population in New York. Although Dominicans constitute the largest segment of the non–Puerto Rican Hispanic population in New York, the AZP is far more likely to be a Cuban, Colombian, or Spaniard. These results can be explained in part by New York demographics and in part by the history of zarzuela in these countries. The previous historical chapters showed the depth of support for zarzuela in Cuba. They also indicated that throughout Latin American the most active supporters of zarzuela were Spanish immigrants and white Creole intelligentsia living in major cities where colonial rules of status continued to hold sway. The first waves of Cuban and Colombian immigrants to the United States came largely from those same segments of the population. Thus with all factors combined, we find that the AZP is more likely to manifest a European outlook, if not European appearance or direct ancestry.

The prominent role of Cubans as patrons of zarzuela performances can also be explained in part because of the dominance of Cubans in theatrical direction

(Cubans presently direct all the New York theaters that regularly program zarzuela, and they directed a majority in the past). Cubans constitute practically a third of the composite audience (29 percent), but the readiness of this same audience to describe itself as "Spanish" may be equally revealing. A significant portion of the audience appears to feel a stronger affiliation with Spanish culture than with specific national, American, or African components that characterize individual Hispanic cultures and that are frequently stressed in ethnic identification.

The AZP is considerably older than twenty-two years of age, the median age for Hispanics in the United States.[19] This important characteristic is underscored by the proportion (37 percent) of patrons who are already familiar with the zarzuela programmed or with the zarzuela tradition in general.

In summary, the average zarzuela patron is not average overall, particularly not in terms of the statistical averages (obtained from census reports) for Hispanics residing in New York. The average zarzuela patron is well educated, enjoys a middle-class lifestyle, and exhibits middle-class tastes and aspirations. The profile of the AZP supports the conclusions of researchers who note ties between the middle class in general and the promotion of traditional theatrical genres.[20] In exploring the relationships among ethnicity, class, and traditional tastes, Joan Moore writes: "Traditionalism is also a function of class status. It is not clear just how this relationship works, although we know that in small towns middle-class Hispanics are likely to be upholders of the traditional. Urban middle-class Hispanics in the 1980s are usually children from poor families, but there are also many Hispanics, like the Cubans, who were middle class in their country of origin and imported middle-class versions of traditional Hispanic family values."[21]

Reyes Schramm, like Barthes, has argued that the maintenance of traditional forms in the immigrant context reflects much more than an ethnic group's attempt to preserve premigration culture. A similar case can be made regarding zarzuela productions. Zarzuelas are produced and supported in New York not simply because they preserve traditions that Hispanic patrons enjoyed prior to moving to the United States (which, as I have shown, differed considerably). An equally important reason for producing and supporting zarzuela is that the skillful manipulation of the genre enables a segment of New York's Hispanic population to foster desirable social and musical interactions among themselves and between themselves and the larger New York population. The traditional zarzuela symbolically defines alliances, goals, and values as a result of production processes that link it to prestigious artistic traditions associated with the most influential segments of the larger New York society.

The preceding profile of the average zarzuela fan at New York area theaters in the 1980s deemphasizes the variation one encounters among zarzuela audiences overall and from one venue to the next. For example, it would be wrong to conclude that Puerto Ricans do not attend zarzuela productions; they were represented at all three of the major theaters and constituted the third-largest group of the audience polled at Repertorio Español.[22] When the theaters are considered individually, a different audience profile emerges for each. Given the different strategies of each theatrical company, it is not surprising that the audiences also differ in significant ways.

Individual Audiences and Specific Goals

Although the average age for patrons at the three metropolitan theaters surveyed lies between thirty and forty-five, in general audiences at Repertorio Español tend to be younger, with as much as one-third of the audience falling under the age of twenty, most of them teenagers. Repertorio Español attracts more patrons from out of state and from beyond the metropolitan area, whereas the audiences at the other two theaters are dominated by patrons living nearby. Repertorio Español also seems to attract more first-time patrons with little prior exposure to Spanish theater.[23] Indeed, it actively courts new patrons, especially students. Student groups also attend performances at the Thalia theater, but until the 1990s that company had fewer regular outreach programs than did Repertorio Español. In 1995 Thalia began its annual Thalia Outdoors series with one of its express goals being to attract students.

To make it easier for classes to attend, Repertorio Español offers noontime performances of classic works such as Lope de Vega's play *Fuenteovejuna* and discounts for groups at other times. The company's simultaneous translation program, instituted in the 1990s, extends such outreach efforts well beyond student audiences. In commenting on his original goals for the company, Buch reveals an overt educational intention: "I wanted to do all the repertory that is never done. You know, I'm sick and tired of everyone knowing who Molière is and nobody knowing who Lope de Vega is. It's ridiculous. So we decided to do the classics; the classics were the backbone at the beginning and they still are."[24]

Music directors Pablo Zinger and Victor Chacón echo Buch's sentiments in a musical context. The apparent contradiction between repertoire that "is never done" and the emphasis on classic works is resolved when we recognize that Buch (like his colleagues) is not limiting his discussion to Hispanic audiences. Buch wants more than just a Spanish-speaking audience to recognize the value of Lope de Vega. In his vision, and with his efforts, the Spanish classics will someday take their rightful place among generally recognized theatrical repertoire. The zarzuela, with its distinguished Spanish genealogy, fits into Buch's emphasis on the classics.

Zarzuela also assists with the company's goal to reach as large an audience as possible. The audience need not be limited to any set population, insists Buch. "If you ask me what kind of theater I like, I say a theater that is full, because it is true."[25] A full theater is certainly a goal of the other directors, but presently their efforts principally attract patrons who are familiar with Spanish theater in general.

In short, Repertorio Español attracts a more diverse population than do the other theaters. Although only slightly older than the others, it is considerably wealthier and better connected. The company's programs are available for tourist packages, and its central location in Manhattan has garnered more attention from the press and other media. The company's status, however, is due to more than material conditions; there is no denying the power of Buch's daring conceptions. Although informal audience interviews reveal that some Thalia patrons view Repertorio Español's productions as "Americanized" or "too abstract," many others find the company's productions of the classics to be "strikingly contemporary." The nature of these productions will be more fully examined in chapter 7.

Music and the Projection of Social Status

The questionnaire data suggest that, unlike those who champion the African contributions to Hispanic culture, the majority of those who patronize zarzuela in New York are interested in reinforcing their ties to the European traditions openly admired in American society. The situation is reminiscent of that observed by Manuel Peña in his study of Texas-Mexican *conjuntos,* the accordion-driven ensembles specializing in popular dance songs and ballads. Peña notes the important role that social-class status and aspiration play in the patronage of traditional music among Mexican immigrants. Those who favored the style of music played by more formal dance orchestras, known as *orquesta,* over the *conjunto* style were keenly aware of the more cultivated status associated with the former compared to the working-class status of the latter.[26] Zarzuela, even more than *orquesta,* is also a kind of *música culta* (cultivated music). Its ties to the operatic tradition and classical Spanish drama offer symbols of upper-class status that hold the promise of connecting with the genteel domains of New York's performing arts scene. Both zarzuela and salsa reflect Hispanic identity, but zarzuela projects an image more in keeping with the notions of educated taste held by the dominant, and much larger, non-Hispanic society.

Examination of the audiences at zarzuela productions reveals their multinational, educated, middle-class, and aspiring character. For that group, especially in a city dominated by English speakers, the genre of zarzuela becomes a potent symbol for promoting Spanish culture in ways that serve a composite body of Hispanic residents. The candid remarks of Plácido Domingo in 1983 concerning Hispanic culture in a larger American context speak for those who champion zarzuela in New York and across the United States.

> It is my impression that this group's cultural roots are being ignored or forgotten in a shameful way. The Spanish-speaking population of the U.S. now numbers 19 million, and many of these people feel justifiably offended by what is presented to them and to the outside world as their cultural heritage: long running television soap operas, rhythmical music from the Caribbean, and not much else. This is hardly representative of such a rich multi-national culture. . . . I know that if I have been working all day in a language other than Spanish, I like to relax by speaking my language or hearing it spoken. If the only entertainment available to Spanish-speaking people in the U.S. is the sort of thing I have described, they may watch it for lack of anything better. . . . I'd like to carry the musical flag for these people. First of all, there is the zarzuela.[27]

Domingo's remarks are strikingly similar to sentiments expressed by directors of the Spanish theaters in New York. Although Domingo has had little direct involvement with the theaters discussed in this chapter, his promotion of zarzuela has helped to publicize productions in local venues.[28] Furthermore, like Domingo, Hispanic theatrical and concert directors see zarzuela as playing a role in the education of the general public. It is worth noting that Repertorio Español's productions of zarzuela and other lyric dramas were among the first to be fitted with simultaneous translation. At the same time, the fact that zarzuela is regularly featured by established Hispanic theaters acts as an endorsement of the genre and shows its viability in contemporary projections of Hispanic identity. The genre is especially valuable because it has traditionally been treated with great flexibility and because it proves to be popular with newcomers to the tradition as well as with those already acquainted with it.

As ensuing chapters will show, presenters such as Domingo, Buch, and Brito join hands with the audiences they court, the audiences that support zarzuela. Their work offers an answer to Ilan Stavans. In affirming ownership of the metaphorical *bodega,* these directors also let us know that its merchandise has a estimable market value well beyond the *barrio.* Although they might echo his call to the world, "Hey, hello, I am here," they would resist his claim that as "masters in the art of remembrance, [Hispanics] suffer from a traumatic past and refuse to inhabit the future." These artists, and their upper middle-class and seemingly nonrevolutionary supporters, may well be using striking traditional art to define themselves and their future. They refuse to be ignored and to have their culture ignored or reduced to a single vision. "Our stubbornness," they might say, again paraphrasing Stavans, "will force many non-Latinos to come to us, to adapt to our ways," beginning by recognizing our artistry.[29]

7

An Analysis of Performance Practices

The ways in which contemporary presenters treat zarzuela surely account for the genre's current appeal as much as does any other factor. At the same time, New York presenters are by no means agreed on the best way to stage productions. Although producers share some goals, such as a desire to promote pride and awareness of zarzuela and its European-influenced repertoire, their goals regarding specific aspects of production differ considerably. For example, the Thalia Spanish Theatre focuses on presenting familiar repertoire in ways that keep alive cherished performance traditions, whereas Repertorio Español emphasizes new interpretations of classic Spanish works and positions popular creole works as classic art. The rationales informing such diverging choices, coupled with the ways in which patrons respond to specific production decisions, help to explain the complex role zarzuela has played recently in New York and other U.S. cities.

The previous chapter addressed the relationship between presenter and audience. Performances of zarzuela in New York and across the United States attract a predictable core population of upper- and middle-class Hispanic patrons from venue to venue. As I have shown, however, audience profiles differ with respect to factors such as the proportion of non-Hispanics to Hispanics, the average age of patrons, and the location of a patron's residence. These differences correspond to variations in presentation approach, or what musicians often refer to as performance practice.

Comparing appendixes A through C makes it clear that the range of repertoire now being offered in New York and across the nation is more limited than has been the case in the past. The works presented recently are old chestnuts, largely from the *género chico,* and the same works appear from one stage to the next. The goal is less to provide variety than to build on a preexisting, albeit limited, familiarity with certain key works. As a result, these works must bear the burden of classical masterpieces: they represent an entire tradition, including the artistic talents of their creators and recreators. Not all works are up to the task, nor can all productions sustain the weight of representing not just a specific drama but an entire genre.

So far I have emphasized the theatrical stage, considering its productions as separate from those offered on the concert stage. In this chapter I will continue to focus on the theater as the most complete forum for the presentation of zarzuela and will illustrate the two most prominent approaches of presenting Spanish lyric drama. One approach builds on or establishes an intimate connection between audience and the work presented. The other challenges habits of thought and repositions the audience into new, more distanced, and possibly more objective positions vis-à-vis the repertoire and its performance. Each approach facilitates a different set of options for presenters and viewers alike, and neither is limited to the theatrical stage. Concert presentations also manipulate the distance between audience, work, and artist in ways that either question or affirm familiarity.[1]

The Contrasting Approaches toward Zarzuela of Two New York Theatrical Companies

In New York distinctive approaches to zarzuela are most evident in the two theaters most known for their work with the genre. Despite the convivial atmosphere in its home theater, Repertorio Español in many ways tends to formalize the relationship between its audiences and the works performed. In contrast, the producer and directors at the Thalia Spanish Theatre tend to assume familiarity and strive to minimize the separation between audience and the work.

Thalia's approach in its 1986 production of the *género chico* work *Los Gavilanes* offers a good example of the company's efforts to invite audience participation. At one point in the production the audience was handed sheets printed with the Spanish lyrics for Rosaura's song "No Hay que Gemir" (There's No Reason to Sigh), and the cast encouraged viewers to sing along with them on each chorus. Producer Silvia Brito explained that since the theater was not equipped with *telones* (curtain-like screens on which the words to various songs are projected for the audience), like many theaters in Cuba or Spain, these lyric sheets were the next best thing.

When participation was less overtly solicited, and emerged simply as a result of the action on stage, the company had even better luck getting viewers to sing along with the performers. One guest director, the former Cuban stage star Miguel De Grandy, cleverly repositioned "Siempre Amigos" (Friends Forever), another popular number in *Los Gavilanes,* so that it closed not just the second act but also the third, thereby serving as a familiar finale to the entire drama. Its memorable melody and catchy rhythms, frequently excerpted by touring companies offering medleys of zarzuela favorites, proved irresistible to many in the audience who joined the cast in song. When the number reappeared in the drama, more viewers chose to sing along. De Grandy himself led the dancing chorus in the reprise, which shifted into a *habanera* rhythm as he danced toward the audience.[2] This last move clinched the bond between the patrons, many of whom were Cuban and virtually all of whom, no matter what their heritage, recognized that Cuban rhythm and its associations with popular Latin dance music. Such comfortable immediacy characterized Thalia's productions of zarzuela throughout the 1980s.

Thalia's productions include many innovative approaches, but never at the expense of tradition. Brito explains that her goal is to "recapture the vitality of the traditional stagings."[3] The energy and integrity that the company brings to its productions demonstrate that goal. One reviewer's claim that Thalia's 1987 production of *La Revoltosa* (The Rabble Rouser) "could have been an 1890 import from Madrid" is a source of great pride to the company.[4]

Thalia's approach to zarzuela contrasts with that of Repertorio Español in many ways, but especially in terms of the formality and social distance established by presentation format. Repertorio Español's staging of *Doña Francisquita* in 1983 offers a striking example (see fig. 20). In this production René Buch retained the original music by Amadeo Vives but dispensed entirely with the book by Guillermo Fernandez Shaw and Federico Romero y Saráchaga. Instead he turned to the author's original source of inspiration, Lope de Vega's classic comedy *La Discreta Enamorada* (The Discreet Woman in Love), a work much less familiar to general audiences. Although less well known than Vives's lyric incarnation, Lope de Vega's story is undeniably the superior literary work.

Buch used a double cast for the production, letting the actors tell the story, following Lope de Vega's script, and letting the musicians sing Vives's divine songs in a concertlike manner, but with an actor's sensibility for projecting the essential meaning of the song. Francisquita of the zarzuela sings and stands on stage alongside her dramatic counterpart, Fenisa, who speaks but does not sing.[5] In addition to using this innovative double casting, Buch dispensed with elaborate scenery and stage sets and instead projected reproductions of paintings by the Spanish artist Goya onto a large screen behind the cast.

Taken as a whole, the production of *Doña Francisquita* offered attractive challenges to all who attended, for no one could claim complete familiarity with the new composite construction by Buch and his team. In some respects this approach positioned Hispanic patrons on equal footing with non-Hispanic viewers in that

REPERTORIO ESPAÑOL

GILBERTO ZALDIVAR
Productor
RENE BUCH
Director Artístico

Presenta

DOÑA FRANCISQUITA **LA DISCRETA ENAMORADA**

Música de Amadeo Vives con de Lope de Vega

YOLANDA VADIZ ó SALOME MARTINEZ (Francisquita) — MILLIE SANTIAGO (Fenisa)
EFREN PUIG ó ULISES ESPAILLAT (Fernando) — MATEO GOMEZ (Lucindo)
BRENDA FELICIANO ó ELIZABETH ACOSTA (Aurora La Beltrana) — ANA M. MARTINEZ-CASADO (Gerarda)
JORGE PADULLES (Cardona) — RICARDO BARBER (Hernando)
GEORGE MALDONADO ó RENE DE LA GARZA (Don Matías) — RENE SANCHEZ (Capitán)
ELISAVIETTA DE LA ROCHE (Doña Francisca) — OFELIA GONZALEZ (Belisa)
FELIPE GOROSTIZA ó FRANCISCO PEREZ ABREU (Lorenzo Perez) — RENE TORRES (Un Cofrade)

ANNA ALVAREZ EUGENIA CROSS LAURA DELANO MYRA GARCIA-FERNANDEZ
FELIPE GOROSTIZA CLARISSE OJEDA NORBERTO PETRELLO COOKIE RUFINO

Producción diseñada por ROBERT WEBER FEDERICO
Coreografía de ADOLFO VÁZQUEZ

Director musical y pianista
PABLO ZINGER

Producción concebida y dirigida por
RENÉ BUCH

Vestuario femenino realizado por
NANCY RAMIREZ, MARIA FERREIRA CONTESSA y BRIAN SMITH
Vestuario masculino realizado por BOAMERSES RUBIO
Efectos visuales por
D. GORDON ROGNLIEN, Jr.—STAGING TECHNIQUES
Pantalla de proyección construida por DICK SHEPARD
Proyecciones de Goya fotografiadas por SPINDLER PRODUCTIONS
Esta producción se estrenó en Nueva York el 27 de agosto de 1983

Figure 20. Program from Repertorio Español's production of *Doña Francisquita,* showing the innovative double casting used in this production merging Vives's zarzuela with Lope de Vega's drama. Courtesy of Repertorio Español.

all were newcomers. Everyone present was asked to consider classic tradition from new perspectives.

Although Repertorio Español's production of *Doña Francisquita* constitutes an extreme transformation of the original zarzuela, it also represents the general view at Repertorio Español that it is permissible to refashion classical conventions to project a modern vision. Repertorio Español is more willing than Thalia to jettison historical practice in favor of contemporary insight. This attitude permits the company to treat zarzuela with considerable freedom and makes each work a fresh experience (while at the same time less familiar) for viewers and listeners alike.

The contrasts of approaches bring to mind remarks the great Cuban musicologist Alejo Carpentier offered in 1955 when he was asked to comment on Havana's enthusiastic reception of an American production of Gershwin's *Porgy and Bess.* He compared this enthusiasm to the Cubans' indifferent response to the visit of the Spanish National Theater under the direction of Manuel Moreno Torroba and its program of unidentified zarzuelas. Carpentier applauded the modern stage techniques he saw in *Porgy and Bess* and lamented the comparably dated staging of the zarzuela production. He wrote:

> If I note an unfortunate contrast between the triumph of *Porgy and Bess* and the disaster of the National Theater Company, it is as a result of the difference in focus of production. . . . We know that the score alone is not responsible for the triumph of *Porgy and Bess;* on the contrary, it is as much a result of the show itself. And what was this show except a practical, active, and efficient application of all the theatrical techniques possible . . . ? Do you remember the extraordinary scenic movements throughout the popular opera? What was that? Simply modern theater as we've become accustomed to seeing in the cinema. . . . On the other hand, the Spanish zarzuela continues with its procedures from the era of our grandmothers. . . . It continues to be a show from 1900.[6]

I do not know whether Carpentier would like the zarzuela productions at Teatro Repertorio Español, but I imagine that he might applaud Buch's willingness to experiment with the boundaries between authenticity and ownership. René Buch at Repertorio Español clearly resists presenting zarzuela the way his grandmother knew it. His resistance signals claims to ownership, and here zarzuela is one item of property.

Ownership and Language: Issues of Pronunciation and Translation

Buch's attitude of ownership emerges when he discusses language and performance. He has no qualms about his performers delivering lines with Hispanic American rather than Castilian pronunciations. A little background on the nature of speech in zarzuela is necessary to understand his view.

Dialogic portions of zarzuela frequently feature speech patterns linked to specific regions and communities in Spain. In many cases the spoken text relies on conventions and expressions rarely heard in American Spanish practices. Depending on the director's decisions, these dialectic features, while appealing to some as colorfully exotic, might be interpreted by others in the audience as distancing features. In addition to regional and often historical pronunciation patterns—which may omit or transform letters or exchange vowels (such as *i* for *e*)—critical wordplay also challenges listeners. Certain expressions, such as those reflecting Madrilenian custom, may be lost on American listeners, Spanish speaking or not.

The issue of pronunciation colors decisions regarding personnel and mode of presentation. Although concert productions may occasionally feature singers who do not speak Spanish (an occurrence more common outside New York), most stage productions rely on performers who are fluent in the language, at least for the principal roles.

"Zarzuela with an American or any foreign accent is death!" says Metropolitan Opera tenor and Spanish diction coach Nico Castel, who was born in Portugal; studied in Caracas, Venezuela, and the United States; and is a great supporter of zarzuela and other forms of Hispanic music.[7] He is referring to non-Spanish-speaking singers who struggle with Spanish pronunciation, however, and not to the many patterns of Spanish pronunciation. His view is widely held, so much so that, as previously mentioned, some U.S. companies choose to translate an entire zarzuela into English or to sing in Spanish and speak in English. A recent example of a complete translation is Richard Traubner's 1999 Ohio Light Opera productions of *La Verbena de la Paloma* and *La Gran Vía* (Traubner calls his English version *Broadway* to evoke the status and impact of this great street in Madrid). There have been other complete presentations in English, but they are few and far between. The San Antonio Opera production of *La Verbena de la Paloma* in 1984 is another example.

Partial translations are more common. Tito Capobianco's multilanguage production of *La Verbena de la Paloma,* produced as *A Fiesta in Madrid,* offered the songs in Spanish and the dialogue in English. Two currently operating groups who prefer the multilanguage option are Chicago's Opera Factory, and Zarzuela at UTEP (University of Texas at El Paso). Using supertitles is a third, increasingly attractive, option. The Thalia Spanish Theatre has indicated that it plans to incorporate supertitles in future presentations.[8] To date, however, the option has been explored primarily by opera companies, especially large professional companies that have attempted zarzuela, such as the Washington Opera, as well as a few universities, notably the University of New Hampshire.[9] The expense of the projection equipment and the work required to prepare slides with sufficiently pithy, yet effective translations deter many.

Directors who translate do so primarily to accommodate audience members who cannot follow the dialogue in Spanish. That task frequently raises other issues, however, including the need to update dialogue and clarify obscure references. Hugh Cardon, director of the Hispanic Music Association at the University of Texas at El Paso, explains some of the linguistic accommodations he made in staging *La Tabernera del Puerto* (The Tavern Girl at the Port): "We present the dialogue in English and the songs in Spanish. We recognize that even our bilingual audience wouldn't catch all the dialogue, with its reliance upon regional idioms and jokes. We adjust the jokes and bring in local references. For example, we had the patrons at the tavern order a Coors Lite."[10]

These concerns and others guided Richard Traubner in his translations for the Ohio Light Opera. In the program notes he writes: "As might be expected, the dialogue in *La Gran Vía* is filled with very specific allusions to Madrid life and politics in the mid-1880s. These are now highly obscure, and even in Madrid today a new book is usually woven around the classic musical numbers."[11] In this case translation included reconceptualizing the work to make it a workable revue for modern audience and to preserve the original drama's "comic-lyric-fantastic-streetsmart" character.[12]

Traubner frankly states his reasons for staging his innovative productions in full translation: "I have a passion for these works, and I wanted to prove that they are accessible to modern American audiences."[13] Unlike audiences at most professional zarzuela productions, the one at Wooster, Ohio, home of the Ohio Light Opera, was not predominantly Hispanic. Patrons from the nearby Columbus and Cleveland areas attended the production, but even these cities do not feature large Hispanic populations, so few of these attendees were Hispanic. Furthermore, a survey of local promotion efforts indicates that little effort was made to attract Hispanic residents. Promoters clearly saw their job as introducing patrons to a "new" genre (the evening was advertised in the Ohio Light Opera's season brochure under the generic headline: "¡Zarzuela!" and not by the titles of individual dramas offered, as were all the other presentations in the annual series).

Traubner's decision to use full translation suits the Ohio locale, but Cardon's decision to blend Spanish and English is a more controversial one, especially in El Paso, a city with a sizable Spanish-speaking population. Cardon reports: "Some in the audience report that they wouldn't have come if they knew we were going to have the dialogue in English; others say they wouldn't have come if we didn't."[14] Given that most of those who attend the productions in El Paso are Hispanic (80 percent), many of them Mexicans from Ciudad Juárez, the so-called sister city across the border, the controversy is understandable, but it also serves as a reminder that American zarzuela presentations are rarely directed solely to those who know the tradition or those of Hispanic ancestry. For the festival in El Paso to earn its designation as international and for it to function on the national level, it needed to attract attention and support from non-Hispanic as well as Hispanic patrons.

New York companies may not agree on the most appropriate way to present zarzuela, but they agree on using Spanish and Hispanic performers to deliver lines in Spanish.[15] Each company handles translation concerns differently. Some presenters, such as the Thalia Spanish Theatre, offer detailed, printed synopses as part of their programs. Repertorio Español provides simultaneous translation using headphones and infrared transmission to bridge any language barriers. The headline in their monthly promotional brochure reads: "See them in Spanish, hear them in English!"

The actors at Thalia, virtually all Hispanic Americans, strive to adopt Castilian pronunciations during their performances, an approach favored by those who wish to emphasize the historical flavor of the dramas, including the companies from Mexico and Albuquerque that perform at the zarzuela festival in El Paso.[16] But this is not the case at Repertorio Español. In explaining his resistance, René Buch asserts his right to perform Spanish, even classical Spanish, with the inflections of America: "We will not take the zarzuelas to Spain. We found a great deal of resistance to our productions of the Spanish classics in Spain. For example, when we took Calderón to Almagro, Spain, critics asked us, 'Why do you speak the verse with an American accent?' I responded, 'You may have invented this language, and I know this is hard for you to believe, but it is our language too, and this is the way we speak it.'"[17]

Buch's claims do not stop with language; they extend to repertoire and rights of performance. Buch insists on the right to own Ilan Stavan's metaphorical store and influence the customers. His work celebrates an unquestionable pride in a distinguished Spanish heritage, but he shares Carpentier's concern for vital presentation. The classics, zarzuelas included, are not museum pieces for Buch. He sees his principal audience as American, not Spanish.

Despite Buch's clear emphasis on artistic vision, it is hard not to discern a political position. To many critics, zarzuelas seem almost antipolitical, displaying a neutral ethnicity (seen from the detachment of the modern American context) and revealing the dramatic and musical fascinations of by-gone times.[18] Nevertheless, whereas Carpentier directs our attention to features beyond the score and plot, to the show itself, others, including the linguist Dell Hymes, suggest that performance itself embraces social negotiations signaling social power. Hymes studies speech performance, but his concerns for style, manner, and context of delivery are equally valid for musical performance. He writes: "The central consideration is that speech styles reflect more than co-occurrences and correlations, but are subject to contrast and choices. Such choices are not merely appropriate or inappropriate, but meaningful."[19]

Hymes also draws our attention to points of disagreement in speech styles. Dissension is critical to understanding the social basis of performance. By further distinguishing between personal, situational, and generic language styles, he explores the ways those variations affect meaning and its perception. He adds that all members of the community may not agree on the use and meaning of a particular style: "Within its defined setting, a style may be prominent or obscured in relation to what else goes on. There may be clashes within the community as to the admissibility of certain linkages or as to the prominence or lack of it."[20]

Approaches to zarzuela in New York reveal the very tensions that Dell Hymes notes in speech communities. We can best sense these tensions, and the meanings behind them, by looking at several examples of the specific repertoire regularly chosen by contemporary presenters. By considering the features that attract contemporary performers and the different ways presenters choose to treat each work, we can gain an understanding of the genre's flexibility and its potential for helping individuals and larger groups project a satisfying image of Hispanic identity.

The Merry Widow Sings in Spanish

A surprise in the zarzuela repertoire, and one that underscores the importance of language choice, is *La Viuda Alegre* (The Merry Widow). A glance at appendixes A and C reveals that *La Viuda Alegre* was performed in New York as early as 1920, and major productions took place in 1974, 1982, and 1984. In 1990 the operetta joined the roster of works performed by Repertorio Español. Clearly this famous operetta, known in the original German as *Die lustige Witwe,* is not intrinsically a representation of Spanish identity, yet somehow performing it in Spanish suits the goals of Hispanic producers here in the United States.

After its premiere in Vienna in 1905, *The Merry Widow* was such a sensation that translated versions of it were performed around the world, and Spain was no exception. In Spain, Franz Léhar's music was fitted with a Spanish book prepared by Manuel Linares and Federico Reparaz, men who knew well the Spanish lyric tradition, and *La Viuda Alegre* quickly assumed a special place, rather like an adopted zarzuela, in the repertoire of Spanish companies specializing in lyric drama. The resounding popularity of *The Merry Widow* with major opera companies around the world, many of which rarely venture into the realm of operetta apart from this work, conveys a special status on Lehar's musical gem. The associative value of near-operatic status surely made a zarzuela version of *The Merry Widow* additionally attractive to Spanish-speaking fans.

Like zarzuela, *La Viuda Alegre* balances spoken dialogue with artistic song. Also like zarzuela, the work embodies European manners and cultivated bourgeois perspectives captured as light-hearted entertainment. An important structural difference between *La Viuda Alegre* and many original zarzuelas is that Léhar's music more than balances the dramatic dialogue and is abundant enough to require no supplementation. This feature alone, coupled with the decision to employ the Spanish translation, makes it a fine vehicle for talented singers performing in Spanish. We get some idea of the importance of a Spanish version of *The Merry*

Widow from the remarks of Cuban singer and director Miguel De Grandy, who states: "I am proud to be the first director to present a staged production of lyric theater delivered completely in Spanish, on Broadway: *La Viuda Alegre,* which was staged at the City Center in the month of June in 1974."[21]

The City Center, known more as a concert hall than a regular stage for drama, is indeed one of New York's major halls, although in recent years it has operated in the shadow of the halls at Lincoln Center. De Grandy is correct in noting how unusual it was for a lyric drama to be offered completely in Spanish in such a central venue. Here the notions of distance and familiarity surface yet again. Although the principal supporters of this project were of Cuban ancestry, the audiences included non-Hispanics, many of whom could count on their recognition of Lehar's popular melodies and their knowledge of the story, even if they did not follow the dialogue in Spanish. Few original zarzuelas are as widely familiar to non-Hispanics as is *La Viuda Alegre.* The work presented in Spanish highlights a Spanish perspective and invites viewers to note the similarities between Continental operetta and the Spanish lyric tradition.

Luisa Fernanda: "A Spanish *Aïda*"

Federico Moreno Torroba's 1932 zarzuela *Luisa Fernanda* has recently enjoyed popularity with companies in New York and elsewhere across the country, a trend that reveals the desire to promote a drama with international appeal and rich in musical numbers that might easily stand alone without the plot. The result is a combination of approaches ranging from concert performances to lavishly arrayed stagings.

Unlike many zarzuelas, *Luisa Fernanda* features a well-written book.[22] In the New York Metropolitan area two theatrical companies, La Asociación de Teatro Musical (ATM) and Repertorio Español, have offered complete productions of *Luisa Fernanda* (see fig. 21), and in 1989 the Bronx Arts Ensemble, directed by Pablo Zinger, presented a concert version. All productions retained the story of a young woman torn by her feelings for two men; she loves one, a soldier who hopes to gain fame and fortune by supporting loyalist causes, but not the other, a noble, kind-hearted landowner who supports the revolution and who, unlike the soldier, genuinely loves Luisa.

The plot may be partly responsible for the popularity of *Luisa Fernanda* both in the United States and Spain.[23] Pablo Zinger, former musical director for Repertorio Español, who has directed the work repeatedly in New York, Texas (El Paso), California (Napa), and his native Uruguay, speculates on the potentially universal appeal of *Luisa Fernanda:* "[It is popular] because it has to do with the clash of the personal world with the large world. It is a little like *Aïda* [with its]

Figure 21. Poster and program cover for the 1983 production of *Luisa Fernanda* by La Asociación de Teatro Musical, Union City, New Jersey. Artwork by Eliana Ivíricu.

clash of love, politics, fidelity to a cause, faithfulness to love, and the clash between ambition and love."[24]

Turning to *Aïda* for comparison is particularly apt. The staging of *Luisa Fernanda* by La Asociación de Teatro Musical, unlike those offered by Repertorio Español, embodied more of the grandiose production conceptions typically associated with *Aïda,* a work that many American companies treat as grand opera with all the spectacle the term implies. The ATM's productions belong to that spectacle tradition and featured elaborate stage sets and numerous props, including a live horse. As was the custom with all its performances, the ATM hired a small orchestra.

ATM director Raúl Cuervo faithfully employed the original libretto (he even prepared a six-page program insert detailing the intricacies of the plot, with the additional goal of assisting those who might not understand the Spanish), but not all American productions follow suit. The version at Repertorio Español was so abstract that one patron remarked, "If I didn't already know this work, I wouldn't have known it was *Luisa Fernanda.*" Such a strong opinion was not shared by all patrons, but director René Buch did substantially trim the libretto. His decision to minimize the dialogue pushed the music to the foreground.

Rather than try to recreate traditional presentations, Buch and Zinger again opted for modernizing the work. Their decisions, along with virtually all the directorial decisions at Repertorio Español regarding format, highlight what truly appears to be the principal attraction of the genre—its music. *Luisa Fernanda* is typical of the early twentieth-century, late romantic zarzuelas favored in New York productions: its score reflects standard nineteenth-century harmonic practice, more akin to Puccini than Wagner, and the vocal lines are considerably more important than the rather sparse orchestral accompaniment.

Chestnut of the Repertoire: *La Verbena de la Paloma*

Another work popular in contemporary settings is Tomás Bretón's *La Verbena de la Paloma,* first seen in Madrid in 1894. Once again, the work is technically not a zarzuela but a *sainete* (see chapter 2), but this distinction has little bearing on the way it has been treated in New York and elsewhere in the United States. Like many other works also classified as *género chico,* the drama does not include many solo or duet numbers that can be excerpted for solo concerts. The most memorable songs are for chorus, and the *seguidilla* "Un Mantón de Manila" (A Shawl from Manila) is the most frequently anthologized in concerts and revues in the United States. The song is considered so symbolic of Madrid that visitors to the Web site "Madrid Villa y Corte" (Madrid: Town and Court, a traditional epithet for Madrid) can hear it as background music in a recorded arrangement for barrel organ.[25]

The story, by Ricardo de la Vega, is a traditional farce of Madrilenian customs. A pretty working-class woman, a *chulapa,* hopes to ensure her fiancé's attentions and incite his jealousy by playfully returning the attentions of a wealthy old gentleman who escorts her and her equally lovely sister to the street fair in honor of Our Lady of the Dove. Her ploy results in a public standoff between the fiancé and the old man. The entire neighborhood joins the brawl, turning the festival into a lively fracas. The confusion resolves with the proverbial happy ending as the lovers make amends.

The evocation of historic Madrid surely accounts for some of the drama's incredible popularity over the years. Others would point to the integrity of the work as the reason. Carpentier considers it "one of the few masterpieces of the zarzuela."[26] Although modern presenters may agree with Carpentier's assessment of the work, critics argue that the balance between song and dialogue is less than masterful and that the plot is simply silly. Patrick Smith, in a review of Tito Capobianco's *Fiesta in Madrid,* a version of *La Verbena de la Paloma,* criticized the story as "slight" and merely "an excuse for song and color."[27] In fairness to Bretón, we must remember that Capobianco tampered with the dialogue and storyline by adding dances, jokes, and musical selections from other zarzuelas. Still, even devoted fans of *La Verbena,* such as Richard Traubner, admit to finding the plot to be far less compelling than the sparkling music.

Two New York productions of *La Verbena de la Paloma,* one in 1974 and another in 1985, were directed by Miguel De Grandy. His production for Thalia aimed for realism over abstraction and invited viewers to savor the exotic appeal of historic Madrid. Stage sets displayed recognizable shops and cobblestone streets, and costumes portrayed period dress (see fig. 14). This approach to staging highlighted the "slice-of-life" quality of *La Verbena* and is favored in all Thalia's productions of zarzuela, including the company's warmly received 1990 production of Jiménez's *El Barbero de Sevilla* (The Barber of Seville).

The musical components of the show were treated respectfully, given the company's resources. Lead roles were cast with trained singers, and the musical director supplied the orchestral parts via piano reduction. Despite the reputed balance of the work, the directors felt justified in enriching the musical component of the drama by inserting two arias. The first, "De España Vengo" (I Come from Spain), from *El Niño Judío* (The Little Jewish Boy), composed in 1918 by Pablo Luna, provided an opportunity to present a captivating flamenco dancer. The second addition, the duet of Mari-Pepa and Felípe from *La Revoltosa,* composed in 1897 by Ruperto Chapí, permitted the two central characters of *La Verbena* an additional opportunity to express their fidelity and gave the two singers another opportunity to display their bel canto technique.

Both additions served multiple purposes. They expanded the reach of the original drama, pointing it toward other zarzuelas, toward classic Spanish dance, and indirectly toward opera. *La Revoltosa* is a zarzuela with overt operatic pretensions, including references to Wagner. With such additions the directors engaged patrons' expectations and, in a limited way, challenged their familiarity with zarzuela repertoire.

Enriching the musical material of the zarzuela, especially the *género chico* works, is common practice here and abroad, but one that always seems to provoke debate. Some, like Traubner, argue that only works by the same composer should be added to a zarzuela in order to maintain stylistic integrity;[28] others argue that additions need only represent a similar style of composition. Still another view is that a much wider range of sources may be tapped as long as each addition can be dramatically and stylistically incorporated into the plot. For example, "De España Vengo" can be justified as a song suitable for the Andalusian Gypsy in *La Verbena* who performs at the local café, even though the music itself was composed well after the premiere of *La Verbena.* Thus Thalia's productions make use of several options to help it meet specific goals: they show how zarzuela can fill a void in the repertoire of light classical music available in contemporary New York, and they also promote the genre as a vehicle suitable for serious performers.

Another goal indicated by production choices is implicit in the variation that Thalia introduced in the closing of *La Verbena.* Here the directors emphasized the Cuban roots in the *habanera* that precedes the finale, where the number was choreographed as a *cha-cha-chá* for the entire company. There was no mistaking the audience appreciation of this gesture. People swayed in their seats and clapped as they softly hummed along with tenor, Gonzalo Madurga, who portrayed the lead character, Don Hilarion, and who led the entire company lined up across the stage.[29] Here a recognition of the Caribbean dominance among New York Hispanics, and especially among Thalia's regular patrons, was articulated musically in a work ostensibly emphasizing the music, dances, and customs of Madrid.

Zarzuela on the Edge: *La Corte de Faraón*

Repertorio Español's *La Corte de Faraón* in 1981 was the first local production of this comic zarzuela and the one that launched the New York revival of the genre. The book, written by the celebrated team of writers Perrín and Palacios (Miguel de Palacios Brugeras [1863–1920] and Guillermo Perrín y Vico [1857–1923]), is an irreverent account of the biblical story of Joseph and the pharaoh, full of racy *doble entendidos* (double entendres). The satirical tone of the work, which originally premiered in Spain in 1910, prompted government censors to suppress performances in Spain after Franco's rise to power. The textual parodies have their parallels in the music by Vicente Lleó (1870–1922), whose score pokes fun at opera in general, specifically targeting Verdi's *Aïda.*

Although *La Corte de Faraón,* has not been performed frequently in the United States, its most popular number, the "Canción Babilónica" (Babylonian Song) sung by the drama's principal character, the young Theban maiden Lota, finds its way onto numerous zarzuela recital programs. In addition to offering a soprano a chance to display vocal technique, the "Canción Babilónica" lets her exhibit sultry body language as she invites those in attendance to follow her to the land where the women are irresistible. The dramatic context of the song concerns Lota's sexual frustrations. Although she has recently married the pharaoh's general, Putifar, they have not consummated their union because he was castrated while in battle. He has returned to war, and Lota sings this song to entertain herself in his absence. Her thinly veiled lyrics are clearly designed to arouse the men of the court.

Repertorio Español's production stressed both the racy and the vaudeville-like nature of the drama and enriched the score with additional musical numbers. For example, a particularly memorable moment in the production occurs when the wife of the pharaoh attempts to seduce the chaste Joseph (José), known in the drama as "José el Casto." In Repertorio Español's version, the temptress sings the complete *habanera* from Bizet's *Carmen*—not in the original French, but in Spanish. This touch was applauded by the *New York Times* critic Theodore W. Libby Jr., who wrote, "Would that more Carmens could sing it the way she did!"[30]

Pablo Zinger, Repertorio Español's musical director at the time, explained some of the other changes: "Now, *La Corte de Faraón* is a takeoff on opera in general, not just a parody of *Aïda.* So we took the opportunity to create a very funny parody of our own, and at the same time we tried to introduce people to zarzuela. . . . [Since] the original work is very short, we kept all the original music, but we added things to make a full evening's entertainment."[31]

The additions Zinger mentioned include the aria "Caballero de Gracia" (The Graceful Gentleman), from *La Gran Vía,* Paloma's aria from Barbieri's *zarzuela grande El Barberillo de Lavapiés,* the polonaise from Jiménez's *El Barbero de Sevilla,* and instrumental quotations from Edvard Grieg's *Peer Gynt Suite* and Tchaikovsky's *Swan Lake.* To start the evening, Zinger prepared an overture consisting of pieces from all the numbers in the production and arranged it for piano with percussion accompaniment. This collective approach anticipated Repertorio Español's predilection for musical anthologies and also highlighted the freedom with which the company treated the zarzuela. The company's anthologies have either included or featured zarzuela in concert format and will be examined in more detail later.

Repertorio Español revived its production of *La Corte de Faraón* in 1987 and again in the early 1990s. The company's hilarious twist on this parody of sexual and social obsessions and its worldly approach to the musical score once again shocked, delighted, and baffled audiences.

The drama itself appears to invite such flexible treatment. In 1986 the Spanish film director José Luis García Sánchez created a contemporary cinematic version of *La Corte de Faraón* in which the operetta was used to mock government censors. This film was warmly received by New York audiences.[32]

Although most American presenters are content to raid *La Corte de Faraón* for individual songs, Repertorio Español turned the work into a rollicking introduction to zarzuela that reminds audiences of its contemporary entertainment value while at the same time proving the genre's adaptability as a springboard for artistic performance.

Accommodating Diversity: "Zarzuela with More Music Than Theater"

Critic Jim Braden's assessment of Repertorio Español's approach to *Luisa Fernanda* as "more music than theater" is even more appropriately applied to the company's musical anthologies.[33] Teatro Repertorio Español is not alone in highlighting music and dance. The Thalia Spanish Theatre on occasion presents a zarzuela anthology and every year since 1987 has hosted performances of at least one show spotlighting a particular dimension of Hispanic experience, such as the Tango y Tango series or the Sonidos de las Americas (Sounds of the Americas) series celebrating a different culture each year: Mexico in 1994, Venezuela in 1995, Brazil in 1996, and Puerto Rico in 1997. Most of these concertlike offerings are produced in cooperation with guest artists.[34] Despite these shows, full-scale productions of zarzuela have become the signature of Thalia, alongside classic and modern drama aimed at the larger Hispanic population. The company accommodates diversity by focusing on historically inspired treatments of the classic repertoire, spiced with an occasional nod toward local or contemporary experience.

In contrast, since the early 1980s Repertorio Español has specialized in anthologies that profile segments of the larger Hispanic community. Its first two anthologies focused on musical repertoire from Puerto Rico and Cuba. Both were so popular that they have been revised several times and continued to be included in the group's repertoire throughout the 1990s.[35] A closer look at these productions reveals some important choices.

A merger of popular, classical, and folkloric songs characterizes the company's first anthology, *¡Habana!* The three-part program opens with a set of compositions featuring popular and semiclassical songs by composers such as Eduardo Sánchez de Fuentes, Ernesto Lecuona, Jorge Anckermann, and F. Villoch arranged as solos, duos, quartets, and choruses. Part 1 of *¡Habana!* also includes popular Afro-Cuban songs such as "El Manicero" (The Peanut Vendor) and "¡Ay, Mamá Inés," by Moisés Simons (1889–1945). The second part illustrates Cuban folklore's influence on twentieth-century art music compositions by Eduardo Sánchez de Fuentes, Joaquín Nin-Culmell, Gonzálo Roig, and Alejandro García Caturla. The program notes highlight the inclusion here of Nin-Culmell's modern choral setting of "La Ma Teodora," one of the earliest known songs from seventeenth-century Cuba. Selections from twentieth-century Cuban zarzuelas and opera are highlighted in part 3 of the program, including "La Comparsa," by Ernesto Lecuona; duets from *María la O* and *Rosa la China;* and the entrance of

Cecilia Valdés from the zarzuela of the same name by Gonzálo Roig (see chapter 3 for a discussion of Cuban zarzuela and related lyric drama). Much more than a concert, *¡Habana!* offers an introduction to the development of Cuban music and its impact on the formal world of classical music. The program notes for the 1982 show summarize that goal by stating: "Cuban music has inspired not only Cubans and Spaniards since the end of the seventeenth century, but also people all over the world."

Equally important, the singers combine the voices of trained concert performers with the sensibilities of actors. The performers have clearly been directed to project the essence of each song. This approach, too often absent in concert recitals, is a signature of Repertorio Español's musical productions.

For *Puerto Rico: Encanto y Canción,* Buch and Zinger worked together to compile a program that represents the rich musical contributions of the island. As they wrote in the program notes to the 1984 version, they uncovered enough music for several programs and found that their struggle was to organize their selections so that a series of songs could become a "piece of theater in its own right." They decided against a chronological presentation and organized the program into two parts, each focused on revealing the qualities of the songs themselves by highlighting their contrasts and similarities. Part 1 features dance songs of the nineteenth century, including numbers by Félix Astol and Juan Morel-Campos, followed by a set of traditional *aguinaldos* (Christmas songs) and children's songs and closing with a set of popular duets from lyric dramas by Bobby Capó and Rafael Hernández, whose zarzuelas representing Puerto Rican perspectives are yet another example of creole appropriations of the peninsular genre. Part 2 focuses on works by living composers, including arias from the zarzuelas and operas of Manuel González, a Puerto Rican composer now living in New York, and contemporary songs and romantic ballads by composers including Jack Délano, Sylvia Rexach, and Ernesto Cordero. It also includes nostalgic favorites such "En Mi Viejo San Juan" (In My Old San Juan) and "De la Tierra Lejana" (From the Land Faraway).

The company's 1987 anthology *La Zarzuela* (see fig. 22) departs from the ecumenical mix of popular and classic forms. It too offers a wider vision of the genre than customarily provided in concerts, but the focus remains on traditional Spanish favorites; no New World contributions are included here. The program opens with the widely anthologized number "De España Vengo." The highly ornamented, Andalusian-inspired melody serves as a symbolic introduction to the genre that also came from Spain. The anthology also includes selections from lesser-known works by familiar composers such as Moreno Torroba, turning to *La Chulapona* rather than *Luisa Fernanda,* and features selections from several works

REPERTORIO ESPAÑOL

Gilberto Zaldívar
Producer

René Buch
Artistic Director

Ganador del Premio de las Artes del Gobernador de Nueva York 1984

presenta

La Zarzuela

MEJOR PRODUCCION PREMIO ACE 1988

PABLO ZINGER *Dirección Musical*
ROBERT WEBER FEDERICO *Diseño de la Producción*
RENE BUCH *Dirección*

REPARTO

Deborah Berruete · **Ana Gloria Vázquez** · **Verónica Villarroel**
Delia D'Campos · **Yamila Constantino** · **Ulises Espaillat**
Brenda Feliciano · **Héctor López** · **George Maldonado**
Salomé Martínez · **Jorge Padullés**

PABLO ZINGER, *Pianista y Arreglos Musicales*
REX BENINCASA y DAVID YEE, *percusionistas*
ADOLFO VAZQUEZ, *Coreografía*

DE ESPAÑA VENGO
El Niño Judío (Luna)
ESTE PAÑUELITO BLANCO
La Chulapona (Moreno Torroba)
LA MAZURCA DE LOS PARAGUAS
El Año Pasado Por Agua (Chueca)
MUJERES
Los Claveles (Serrano)
TE QUIERO MORENA
El Trust De Los Tenorios (Serrano)
MI ALDEA
Los Gavilanes (J. Guerrero)
NO ME DUELE QUE SE VAYA
La Rosa Del Azafrán (J. Guerrero)

LA TARANTULA
La Tempranica (Giménez)
EL SOMBRERO HASTA LOS OJOS
El Barbarillo De Lavapiés (Barbieri)
COMO NACI EN LA CALLE DE LA PALOMA
El Barberillo de Lavapiés (Barbieri)
TANGO DE MENEGILDA
La Gran Via (Valverde/Chueca)
DONDE VAS CON MANTON DE MANILA
La Verbena de La Paloma (Breton)
CABALLERO DE GRACIA
La Gran Via (Valverde/Chueca)
LOS NARDOS
Las Leandras (Alonso)

INTERMEDIO

LOS ROMANTICOS
Doña Francisquita (Vives)
UN TIEMPO FUE QUE EN DULCE CALMA
Jugar Con Fuego (Barbieri)
LAS CARCELERAS
Las Hijas Del Zebedeo (Chapi)
NIÑAS QUE A VENDER FLORES VAIS A GRANADA
Los Diamantes De La Corona (Barbieri)
TRIO
La Tabernera Del Puerto (Sorozábal)
MIRANDOME EN TUS PUPILAS
La Parranda (Alonso)
PICHI
Las Leandras (Alonso)
LAS MUJERES DE 15 A 20
La Tabernera Del Puerto (Sorozábal)
QUE ME IMPORTA QUE NO VENGA
Los Claveles (Serrano)
NO CANTES MAS LA AFRICANA
Dúo De La Africana (Caballero)
LA ROCA FRIA DEL CALVARIO
La Dolorosa (Serrano)
BOLERO
Pan y Toros (Barbieri)
PASACALLE DE LOS CHISPEROS
La Calesera (Alonso)

Programa supeditado a cambios

Esta producción se estrenó en Nueva York en el Gramercy Arts Theatre el 20 de Junio de 1987, auspiciada por Citicorp/Citibank USA

Las presentaciones de Repertorio Español en el Equitable Tower son posibles gracias a la ayuda de The Equitable Life Assurance Society of the United States.

STEINWAY PIANO

Figure 22. Program for Repertorio Español's *La Zarzuela* (1987 version). Courtesy of Repertorio Español.

by the nineteenth-century zarzuela master Barbieri, including *Los Diamantes de la Corona, Jugar con Fuego,* and *El Barberillo de Lavapiés.* The directors offered a dignified collection of solos, duets, and ensemble songs with the belief that listeners would find this music attractive and inspiring regardless of background. At the 1988 performance I attended in the Equitable Theater, the company emphasized this point by closing with their own zarzuela "commercial," singing new words to the finale of Bretón's *La Verbena de la Paloma* extolling the pan-Hispanic appeal of zarzuela; whether "*Cubano, Dominicano, Mexicano, Colombiano, a todos les gusta la zarzuela*"—everyone likes zarzuela.

Contrasting Approaches: A Summary

Whether Repertorio Español produces a complete, fully staged zarzuela or a musical anthology, René Buch insists that the work command respect as a contemporary drama. He does not rely on historical appeal. He refuses to stage an inferior book; instead, he might borrow a number (or several) from the score of another zarzuela.

At a rehearsal for *Luisa Fernanda,* Buch once cut off Pablo Zinger, who was working to get a specific sound from the tenor: "¡En este momento la voz no importa [Right now the voice isn't important]!" he called out. He then explained his view that when a performer has the acting down, the voice will come.[36] Buch's emphasis on dramatic integrity should in no way imply that he tolerates haphazard musical performances. Both he and Zinger will cast only singers who can handle the demands of the score, and the seamless flow of the company's musical anthologies is further testimony to the goal of absolute professionalism.

A commitment to the classics of the repertoire links the theaters that offer zarzuela, despite their differences. This focus on favorite repertoire intersects in several ways with the star mentality that dominates all domains of the performing arts. Public obsession with identifying star performers is not new, but the development of the recording industry has sharpened its effects so that classical audiences have grown accustomed to comparing performances. Composers and critics have long lamented the self-restricted repertoire featured on the concert stage. Carpentier speaks for many when he writes, "We're reduced to repetitions of the same twenty operas," and the public is loath to welcome new compositions.[37] Presenters of classical Spanish vocal music must face this conflict whether in the theater or on the concert stage. Audiences for classical fare have traditionally had limited interest in new repertoire, but they are readily interested in star performers and their interpretations. Those interested in the future of zarzuela in the United States might thus ask the following questions: Can zarzuela help make stars? If that is what audiences want, is it what producers want?

While Thalia focuses on presenting familiar repertoire, its emphasis is more on keeping the tradition alive than on presenting new insights into classic works. Repertorio Español, on the other hand, emphasizes new interpretations—a posture that matches the focus of the contemporary professional stage and attracts more attention from the non-Hispanic press. Repertorio Español, however, does not single out individual performers as stars. "I subscribe more to the approach of Balanchine," Buch explains, referring to the late director of the New York City Ballet. "He worked to earn recognition for the company as a unit, not as a collection of independent stars."[38] Buch invites the audience to focus on the quality of the production overall, as well as the quality of the repertoire, rather than on individual performers.

At the Thalia Spanish Theatre, Brito's approach is slightly different. Every program booklet features biographies on each performer in the cast. Although lead roles are often double cast to keep productions fresh during long runs, there is no sense among performers that individuals are anonymous or interchangeable.

In general, and certainly in the United States, zarzuelas' musical segments (rather than the spoken parts) present the greatest opportunity to display talent and gain public recognition. Curiously, some of the most ambitious productions have had surprisingly limited impact compared to the modest but tightly controlled productions of Repertorio Español and Thalia. The New Jersey–based La Asociación de Teatro Musical, for example, tried valiantly to offer luxurious productions with elaborate stage sets and full orchestra—unfortunately without allowing adequate rehearsal time. Hence, their productions, while exciting events for the local community, never attracted much attention from those not affiliated in some way with the company. ATM shows remained grassroots efforts despite considerable investments of time and money.

Strict concert productions represent another dimension of contemporary performance practice. Events and recordings that feature well-known musicians interpreting zarzuela attract considerable public attention, although they may or may not establish new audiences for the genre. Established stars such as Plácido Domingo, Alfredo Kraus, and José Carreras incorporate zarzuela excerpts into their concert programs with the same stated intentions as those of the theaters that stage zarzuelas: "to introduce audiences to the repertoire." These artists choose zarzuela because they can sing it to some advantage, and interpretation is only a part of the advantage. Choosing zarzuela also highlights the match between the repertoire and the singer's Hispanic ancestry. Carreras and his producer even elected to title his Avery Fisher Hall appearance "Concierto para la Hispanidad" (see fig. 23). The educational goals of individual artists such as Carreras have return benefits. As the public gains a general recognition of Spanish repertoire, this recognition prompts greater respect for those artists who perform it well and, in turn, for the cultures they represent. In this cycle of recognition, zarzuela performance functions more as a stepping stone than as a point of destination.

Zarzuela as Stepping Stone

Developments in the career of Pablo Zinger, former musical director for Repertorio Español (1983–94),[39] show zarzuela's potential to launch a career. In the 1990s Zinger is developing an international reputation as a conductor. His work as musical director at Repertorio Español led to a concert production of *Luisa Fernanda* with the Bronx Arts Ensemble Orchestra, among other engagements, and two recording projects. He was the musical director and orchestral conductor for El Paso's zarzuela festival and Zarzuela at UTEP (the University of Texas

Avery Fisher Hall
Home of the New York Philharmonic
Lincoln Center for the Performing Arts

Sunday Evening, October 12, 1986, at 5:00

AQUILES TUERO
presents and produces

Concierto para la Hispanidad
JOSÉ CARRERAS
Tenor
with
Members of the Metropolitan Opera Orchestra
JESÚS LÓPEZ-COBOS, *Conductor*

RUPERTO CHAPI	El Tambor de Granaderos (Prelude)
JACINTO GUERRERO	El Huesped del Sevillano (Raquel)
FEDERICO CHUECA	El Bateo (Prelude)
JOSE SERRANO	La Alegría del Batallón (Canción Guajira)
TOMAS BRETON	La Dolores (Jota)
SERRANO	La Dolorosa (Relato de Rafael)
	Intermission
CHAPI	La Revoltosa (Prelude)
PABLO LUNA	La pícara Molinera (Paxarin, tú que Vuelas)
REVERIANO SOUTULLO-JUAN VERT	La Leyenda del Beso (Intermezzo)
GUERRERO	Los Gavilanes (Flor Roja)
JERONIMO GIMENEZ	La Boda de Luis Alonso (Intermezzo)
PABLO SOROZABAL	La Taberna del Puerto (Romanza de Leandro)

Sponsored by: National Quinticentennial Commission
Spain 1992, Banco Exterior de Expaña, Compañia Telefónica Nacional de Expaña.

José A. Piñas, *Assistant Producer*

In consideration of the performing artists and members of the audience, those who must leave before the end of the performance are asked to do so between numbers, not during the performance.
The taking of photographs and the use of recording equipment are not allowed in this building.

17

Figure 23. The opening page from José Carreras's program for his *Concierto para la Hispanidad*, Avery Fisher Hall, Lincoln Center, New York.

at El Paso). A brilliant pianist, he concertizes and records Latin American and Spanish chamber music and has accompanied internationally known artists such as the late composer and *bandoneón* (accordion) genius Astor Piazzolla, soprano Angelina Réaux, and clarinetist Paquito D'Rivera.[40] Zinger and D'Rivera currently perform with the Brazilian cellist Gustavo Tavares as the chamber ensemble Triángulo.

One effort that emerged from Zinger's work with the opera department at Rutgers University in the early 1990s was called "Nuestra Opera" (Our Opera). This series of programs featured selections from Latin American opera and zarzuela, as well as works by European composers who have used Latin American themes. The program included Cuban zarzuela and selections from *Marta Gruni,* a Uruguayan tango opera. This work, supported by the Center for Latino Arts and Culture in New York, reveals Zinger's larger aspirations. His goals extend beyond merely achieving recognition for his own talents; he is committed to developing an audience for the best in Hispanic music, whether classical or popular. More than in the 1980s, when he first began working with zarzuela in New York, today Zinger works toward bridging the boundaries separating the repertoires of classical and popular music and their respective audiences.

In 1995 Zinger expressed his belief that the popularity of zarzuela in the 1980s resulted from a series of broader efforts to position Hispanic music on the American concert stage. He explains: "[The integration of Hispanic music into major concert series] is happening all over the place. That is, I think, a real difference between the 1980s and today. At that time there were a lot of people saying, 'We must do this.' At this time I am not saying that we have achieved our goal, but I can say that at this point lots of people *are* doing it. You know, it's happening."[41]

Zinger's observations extend well beyond New York City. His views remind us that establishing a core audience is only one step; another step is obtaining mainstream recognition of the value of Hispanic arts in general. This is a goal shared by all those presenting zarzuela. Once Hispanic contributions to lyric theater are recognized, there may be both desire and means to expand the repertoire performed.

Rescuing zarzuela from obscurity may have been the goal of a few New York–area organizations such as La Asociación Pro-Zarzuela or even the more philanthropic Amigos de la Zarzuela, both groups that sponsor concerts and theatrical presentations. Those involved with regular production today, however, seem much more interested in offering zarzuela as a introductory step toward a greater appreciation of Hispanic music and drama.

For Silvia Brito, a sign that zarzuela has brought the Thalia Spanish Theatre national and international recognition was the company's standing invitation to participate in El Paso's International Festival de la Zarzuela. The festival operated from 1984 until 1995, and Brito and company were invited each year. Thalia's interpretations garnered effusive praise from critics in El Paso and Ciudad Juárez. The singing in Thalia's productions was not always even across the cast (much of the musical burden rested on the artistry of the principal performers), but the acting skills and pace of the show always kept audiences engaged, laughing and crying.

Writing about Thalia's production of *La Revoltosa,* one appreciative El Paso patron (born in Valencia, Spain) wrote: "The most important element in a zarzuela is '*la chispa,*' or that special spark necessary in the actors to ignite the action. Without a doubt this group has the *chispa.* They could compete easily in a zarzuela festival in Madrid and come away the winners."[42] In the late 1990s, after ten years of experience and continually wider exposure, the musical performances of Thalia's productions continue to compare quite favorably to the standards of the classical concert world, but again, it is the integrity of the complete production that distinguishes this company.

Expanding Efforts

As Thalia's experience suggests, New York may not provide sufficient opportunity for recognition. Here is where the international zarzuela festival in El Paso played a major role. Until the mid-1990s there was hope that it would be a major national showcase for the genre. Even after the festival ceased operation, there was hope that El Paso would continue to be a site of serious zarzuela production under the banner of a new program at the university there called Zarzuela at UTEP.

Victor Chacón, hired by the university to direct its opera workshop, became the producer of El Paso's zarzuela festival and began working with Pablo Zinger in 1995. Together they developed ambitious plans for expanding the festival to include instructional efforts, touring, and collaboration with major opera companies. Both men hoped to see operations grow beyond the geographic boundaries of El Paso. Chacón, for example, hoped that the Houston Grand Opera would cosponsor zarzuela productions in the next couple years. He planned to work with contacts at Opera America and to invite other major opera companies across the United States to assume similar cosponsor roles. He was especially optimistic about such goals once Plácido Domingo was named artistic director of the Washington Opera.[43]

In addition, both Chacón and Zinger had planned to establish a series of master classes in the late spring that would train American artists to perform Spanish lyric drama. These classes were visualized as opportunities for developing the Zarzuela at UTEP program and for establishing a Hispanic music institute at the University of Texas at El Paso. Both men hoped that the master classes would involve internationally recognized artists who have displayed a commitment to zarzuela and Spanish classical music.

A third expansion goal involved taking the El Paso program on the road to major cities such as Los Angeles, Houston, and San Antonio. "I'd like to see something like the six-city tour that Houston prepared for *Porgy and Bess,*" said Chacón in 1995.[44] Chacón's projected itinerary reflects a recognition that cities with a strong Hispanic presence and a longtime commitment to opera and professional lyric theater are the most promising sites for the development of zarzuela production.

These ambitious plans never came to fruition. The International Festival de la Zarzuela ceased operation, and the replacement program, Zarzuela at UTEP, has became more of an annual college workshop than the site for professional training and interaction that Chacón and Zinger visualized. With the unflagging guidance of Professor Hugh Cardon and a series of temporary directors, Zarzuela at UTEP staged one zarzuela each summer since Chacón left in 1998, but the productions are no longer presented in the distinguished public theater of the Chamizal National Park, nor do they attract as much international and national attention or local support as they once did.

Given such dashed expectations, it is hard to fault the decision of Repertorio Español to devote less energy to zarzuela production in the 1990s. Rather than expand its commitment to zarzuela, Repertorio Español moved to new musical efforts. The company presented a Spanish version of Menotti's work *The Consul* in 1991. The fine production did not attract as much attention as its producers would have liked. Pablo Zinger speculates why: "It was a very good production, directed by René Buch, if I may say so myself. But it generated much less interest than the zarzuelas. Most people would probably prefer to see it in the original English, just as they would prefer to see *Rigoletto* in Italian. At the same time, most people prefer to see zarzuela and other forms of Hispanic musical theater in the original language as well."[45]

Zinger's observations make sense. A production of *Rigoletto* in Spanish would probably not draw much of an audience today. One can only speculate why a work like *La Viuda Alegre,* also a translation, regularly attracts solid audiences while *The Consul* was less popular. One answer is that the latter has no tradition of performance among Spanish and Latin American patrons, and such customs matter. Hispanic music dramas, however beautiful the music or entertaining the plot, are also valued as representing cultural customs and perspectives. On the other hand, cultural perspective might have aided reception of *The Consul.* The cold war plot of Menotti's opera centers on the uncertain and agonizing process of trying to obtain an exit visa. The story may seem of limited relevance to many contemporary Americans, but it promised to resonate in a powerful ways with viewers who have faced such circumstances, such as those who define themselves as Cuban exiles.[46]

From 1993 to 1995 Repertorio Español appeared to be courting an entirely different crowd with its production of *¡Y se Armó la Mojiganga!* a dramatic tale of a shrewd card player outwitting death. The show incorporates a wide array of popular dance music ranging from rock to salsa (see fig. 24). Recordings of electronically generated music support the singing of the fantastically garbed actors on stage, including death personified as a beautiful woman on stilts. Despite the sixteenth-century origins of the *mojiganga* as a dramatic genre, at first glance the production seems to be a surprising departure from the company's previous

¡Vamos al Carnaval!

¡Y se armó la mojiganga!

El éxito de la temporada

MIE	MAY	10	11 AM
DOM	MAY	14	3 PM
LUN	MAY	15	11 AM
LUN	MAY	15	2:30 PM
VIE	MAY	19	8 PM
DOM	MAY	21	7 PM
LUN	MAY	22	11 AM
SAB	JUN	3	8 PM
DOM	JUN	4	3 PM
DOM	JUN	4	7 PM
VIE	JUN	9	11 AM
VIE	JUN	9	8 PM
SAB	JUN	24	8 PM
DOM	JUN	25	3 PM

The New York Times

Friday, August 26, 1994

THEATER REVIEW

A Gambling Peasant Stumps Jesus and Satan

By D. J. R. BRUCKNER

"Y se Armó la Mojiganga" ("And The Carnival Erupted") is an apt title for a new musical at the Gramercy Arts Theater, the most spectacular production ever by Repertorio Español. Adapted by the Colombian director Jorge Alí Triana from a popular Colombian play that is itself derived from a classic 19th-century story, this "Carnival" starts on earth, falls into hell, ends in heaven, and makes all those places ring with laughter.

In 90 minutes throbbing with music that might be called rock salsa, it shows a miraculous cosmos: flights of gossiping angels and pits of lewd devils; cured cripples, wily bishops, jobless grave diggers, souls floating in the air; a fat, gartered king who is a real back-room politician; and Jesus, Peter and Satan all flummoxed by a peasant who gambles without pause and gives all his winnings to the poor.

Jesus and St. Peter come to earth to reward this generous peasant with five wishes. His apparently simple requests bring him irresistible power. His gambling becomes so faultless it reorganizes the world's economy.

He banishes Death (who hovers almost voluptuously over everyone on incredibly nimble stilts) up a tree and the fear of it from people's minds. And he does much more, until the rulers of heaven, hell and earth are clamoring for a return to the old ways.

He them cons a bored Satan into a card game in which he wins the freedom of everyone ever sent to hell, which creates a theological so exquisite problem that a solution can be imagined only by God. He uses his final wish, that he become as tiny as an ant, to produce an ending so touching and funny that it draws rolling volleys of applause from the audience.

Fifteen actors take 38 roles, and their movements are choreographed to produce a vision of tumult or of celebration in a world of captivating magic. And the spell of the magic never fails.

Performances are in Spanish, with simultaneous translation that becomes through with admirable clarity even during the musical numbers. "Y se Armó la Mojiganga" remains part of the company's regular repertory at least through the end of the year.

Figure 24. Promotional copy and photo for Repertorio Español's 1994 production of *¡Y se Armó la Mojiganga!* produced in Spanish with simultaneous translation. Courtesy of Repertorio Español; photo by Gerry Goodstein.

musical efforts and its focus on classic repertoire. Not only was *La Mojiganga* a tremendous success with New York audiences, but Repertorio Español took the production to El Paso, where it was included on the program of the zarzuela festival there. For patrons who viewed zarzuela as a natural extension of the Siglo de Oro festival (the annual festival of Golden Age Spanish drama), this production stretched the festival in a new direction.

The apparent incongruities separating opera, or even classic Spanish drama, from a fairy tale set to pop music cannot overshadow shared performance concerns. With both *El Cónsul* and *La Mojiganga,* Repertorio Español's directors continued to insist on an innovative approach to staging, on professional acting and singing, on emphasizing a distinguished heritage, and on performing only in Spanish. All these conditions match the company's approach to zarzuela. Indeed, Repertorio Español's anthologies, which merge popular and classical works into a single presentation, foreshadowed the company's refusal to be limited by the conventional boundaries defining any genre, popular or classical.

Performance Styles and Meaningful Choices

Whether they court newcomers or nostalgic fans, American producers of zarzuela engage the inherent flexibility of the genre in ways that promote connections among their Hispanic supporters and between them and the larger performing arts scene. To date, the most successful presenters have established guidelines (sometimes ones that challenge old boundaries) that allow them to express their vision of Hispanic culture via lyric drama. Individual presentations involve different performance approaches and different conceptions of the "distance" between the audience, the performers, and the work being presented. The ultimate goal, however, that of enlarging the group that supports and appreciates zarzuela and all it represents, is the same. In particular, New York presentations of zarzuela and related lyric drama invite recognition of a collective Hispanic identity that aligns with the genre's influential connections to history, the world of opera, the classical stage, regional or popular expression, and a language that will not be silenced.

The impact of the presentations previously described is due to more than choices involving the selection and performance of repertoire. The following chapter shows how a network of supportive activity, including advertising and promotion, underlies performance practice and affects the ability of promoters to project their intentions to specific audiences.

8

Support Networks for Artistic Production

In the 1980s when I first wrote about zarzuela, I examined financial backing and publicity as supporting activities crucial to any understanding of the role that this kind of musical theater plays in the projection of identity. These supporting activities remain important, but as I write now in 1999, two additional issues stand out. First, I have come to realize the power of personal networking, an aspect I had virtually ignored in my earlier studies. Financial backing and publicity are rooted in a system of interpersonal networks that help producers of zarzuelas in countless activities: finding performers, scores, and other material; sharing perspectives and expertise regarding performance operations; securing performance opportunities; obtaining financial resources; attracting publicity; and winning recognition. Much more than I initially realized, the support systems for zarzuela in New York are connected to the support systems for classical Spanish music and theater across the United States, and they have developed with surprisingly little assistance from broadcast media and recording, arguably the two most potent forces in contemporary music worldwide.[1]

The second issue concerns that relatively small role that the recording industry plays in supporting American presentations of zarzuela. Although a serious fan should find no difficulty in obtaining recordings of zarzuelas,[2] mass-marketed recordings rarely feature American performers or productions. A notable exception is the recording of the Jarvis Conservatory's (Napa, California) production of *Luisa Fernanda,* released in 1997.[3] The recording is especially remarkable because it documents a live performance sung in Spanish with spoken dialogue delivered in English. Unlike the majority of productions offered in the New York metropolitan area (or in Miami), most of the American performers do not have Latin American or Spanish backgrounds.[4] The CD is accompanied by a handsome booklet displaying the original Spanish lyrics printed alongside the English translation. It is, however, a self-produced CD, with limited distribution.

The majority of commercial recordings of zarzuela feature Spanish productions, and the ones most frequently mentioned by American performers feature internationally known opera stars such as José Carreras, Teresa Berganza, Alfredo Kraus, and most especially Plácido Domingo. Although the cover art for these recordings typically highlights the genre over the work, and the work over the artist, clearly these outstanding interpreters are an important attraction. Indeed, these artists might also be defined as "zarzuela stars," although such a designation might be a contradiction in terms since, as previous chapters have shown, zarzuela performance *alone* rarely catapults an artist to fame.[5]

Against the backdrop of high-profile stars and widely recognized music, supporters of zarzuela in the United States have developed a range of grassroots networks of people who share backgrounds, experiences, or interests to secure opportunities. Local mutual aid organizations and their influence on Hispanic theater have been well documented by Nicolás Kanellos.[6] Historically such organizations have supported the production of zarzuela as well. Recall that the Calpe Americano (see chapter 4), responsible for the production of many zarzuelas in the 1920s, was initially a mutual aid society.

The network I now see as most important extends beyond local efforts and organizations. This larger network links operations from city to city, state to state, and country to country. Nodal points form around intersections shaped by location, individual influence, material resources, and conceptual treatment. To highlight these intersections, I widen the focus in this chapter to consider in more detail the activities of American zarzuela producers and supporters outside the New York area.

Personal Connections and Access to Materials

People working with zarzuela in different U.S. cities tend to know one another and support one another's efforts. William Jarvis explains that Marta Domingo (wife of the famous tenor) first recommended that he produce *Luisa Fernanda.* Jarvis, owner of the vineyards and wine label bearing his name, along with his Mexican-born wife, Leticia, started the Jarvis Conservatory in 1995 to train singers and prepare zarzuela productions. After the company opened, Blanche Lewis, the director of the Chicago Opera Factory, called him to welcome him to the small group of U.S. companies producing zarzuela and to offer her support. By that time Lewis was a veteran producer. Her company began producing zarzuela in 1985 after Plácido Domingo appeared with José Tamayo's touring *Antología de la*

Zarzuela (see fig. 25). Lewis supplied local artist support and assisted with promotion for the Chicago leg of that tour. Today, long after the media blitz surrounding Domingo's appearance has subsided, zarzuela is a regular feature of the Chicago Opera Factory's annual programming. Both Jarvis and Lewis have established ties with the New York directors. Pablo Zinger and Lewis met in El Paso and have continued contact between New York and Chicago. Jarvis brought Zinger to California in 1997 to direct the orchestra for *Luisa Fernanda,* and their contact also continues.

Material support emerges from these relationships. Hugh Cardon, conductor and director of the Hispanic Music Association, housed at the University of Texas at El Paso, exchanges scores with the directors of La Zarzuela Alburquerque [*sic*] in New Mexico. He owes his earliest involvement with the genre to such personal connections. Cardon reminisces: "Just after completing my dissertation on Mexican music, I met an elderly El Paso citizen, Abel Gombra, who had amassed a personal collection of Mexican and Spanish vocal music. Just before he passed away he sold his collection of zarzuela scores to me. Sr. Gombra sang in the choruses, and even

Figure 25. Program cover (1991) and promotional brochure (1999); the Opera Factory of Chicago, 6161 North Hamilton Ave., Chicago, IL.

some lead roles, in zarzuelas produced in the 1930s in El Paso's Liberty Hall with companies from around the world, but particularly from Mexico City. Perhaps he worked with Domingo's parents."[7] Not only did Cardon begin his collection of zarzuela scores as a result of personal connections, but the collection grew as a result of new contacts. Whenever he came across a work not in his collection, he found a way of obtaining a copy of the piano score for study. Today, as in the past, when he elects to produce a complete work, he rents the orchestra parts from the Spanish equivalent of ASCAP, SGAE (Sociedad General de Autores y Editores).

Others working with zarzuela report equally serendipitous beginnings. Mary Montaño, cofounder of Albuquerque's El Teatro de la Zarzuela (later called "¡Viva Zarzuela!"), began her interest in the genre when she was charged with cataloguing the collection of manuscripts once belonging to Manuel Areu (whose activities are discussed in chapter 2) as part of the work for her master's thesis. These manuscripts were originally obtained from a town dump in Jerome, Arizona. Montaño tells this story of the remarkable find:

> The original collector, Manuel Areu, who lived from 1845 to 1943, came from a family of performers from Madrid who migrated to Havana, Cuba, where they sang and performed. He also played violin and acted. He took the piano-vocal scores he had brought from Spain and prepared performance parts for his company in Cuba. He even wrote some of his own zarzuelas there. In 1900 he moved to Mexico. He worked with talking pictures, worked in El Paso, and later moved to Jerome, Arizona. He stored his zarzuela scores in eight large trunks. Later he moved to Los Angeles, where he died. He left the scores with his children, who evidently lost care of them, and that is how they ended in the town dump.[8]

Montaño and three collaborators interested in performing works from this collection—Sally Bissell Quintana (scholar and soprano), José Apodaca (a baritone from a distinguished family of New Mexican musicians), and Carmen Acosta (soprano)—engaged a friend to recreate orchestral scores from the dusty, hundred-year-old handwritten, piano/vocal scores and generated parts using notation software. Although they did pay performance royalties to the Unión Musical de España, this monumental effort (not atypical of Americans interested in producing zarzuela) bypassed the music industry.[9] One of her accounts notes the lack of support she received from Spanish music distributors in the early 1980s: "One of our singers went to Spain and tried to buy the score for a very famous zarzuela. The proprietor told him the score was out of stock. His Spaniard friend went in immediately after him and was able to purchase the score. I find that Spaniards can be very ethnocentric about zarzuela. They don't care if Americans produce it."[10] Montaño's conclusions concern individual experience, not institutional policy, but they are also reminiscent of René Buch's sense that his versions of Spanish classics were sometimes not fully appreciated by Spanish audiences (see chapter 7).

Formal support from Spain for zarzuela productions in the United States seems to have been more forthcoming in recent years. In 1999 Richard Traubner was able to obtain substantial financial backing from the Ministerio de Cultura, Instituto Nacional de las Artes Escénicas y la Música, the branch of Spain's Ministry of Culture dedicated to promoting art and theater, and from the SGAE for his English-language production of *La Verbena de la Paloma* and *La Gran Vía* with the Ohio Light Opera Company. He notes that this support came about, in part, because of his good relationship with professional theaters in Madrid, especially the Teatro de la Zarzuela, which he regularly patronizes.[11]

Whatever the attitude of Spaniards toward American zarzuela performances, contemporary producers all note how difficult it can be to obtain scores, parts, and performing rights for Spanish zarzuela. Again, this situation has eased somewhat in recent years, for today one may contact the SGAE's New York office (SGAE-USA) for rental of scores and orchestral parts and permission to perform.[12]

Although more than two thousand zarzuelas have been written, only about one hundred are available through SGAE-USA. For individuals interested in examining a wider spectrum, archival holdings in the United States are an option. Once again, however, ease of access and photocopying privileges vary. The more than four hundred items cataloged in the Columbia University zarzuela collection include few complete scores; in some cases only a single part exists or just the libretto. Even when a full piano score is available, borrowing is rarely permitted, and photocopying is discouraged, making the archive of limited use for performers. Other zarzuela collections are archived at the Library of Congress, the New York Public Library, the New York Hispanic Society, the Center for Southwest Research at the University of New Mexico, and the library at Oberlin College.

University Links

University connections in the network of support for zarzuela should not be underestimated. Even companies operating outside college music departments have previous ties to such institutions and frequently draw on student performers to bolster their casts. Mary Montaño's companies in Albuquerque, with their links to the University of New Mexico, offer an example. Although Montaño's productions in the 1980s profited from her connections to the university, her company's directors aspired to professional performance standards. ¡Viva Zarzuela!

performed at El Paso's international zarzuela festival alongside professional companies hailing from New York, Chicago, and San Antonio, as well as Mexico and Spain,[13] underscoring Montaño's goals to present zarzuela as "an art form rather than as a cultural tool."[14] She stressed this distinction to clarify that her company set production standards to match those of the professional concert world.

The commitment of ¡Viva Zarzuela! to professional quality did not preclude an interest in educating audiences. Montaño said that many of the company's local presentations were for schoolchildren in northern New Mexico. She explained, "We wanted the students to know that their musical heritage included more than folk music. We also wanted them to hear that everyone did not speak Spanish the way they did" (recall the discussion of accent and delivery in chapter 7).[15] Her goals embraced some of the same educational and historical goals of New York presenters, as well as their concern for professional standards, and her productions were not primarily directed toward or limited to college, or even urban, audiences.

In contrast, the summer zarzuela program under the direction of Karen E. Breiner-Sanders at Middlebury College in Middlebury, Vermont, is largely an academic enterprise where students in the Spanish School present *María la O* in a kind of lip-synched version. Players speak the dialogue, but most do not sing without recorded assistance.

University connections can be a source of strength, but they may also impose limitations. In El Paso, university support initially strengthened professional zarzuela production. Although the International Festival de la Zarzuela began in 1989 as an outgrowth of the El Paso's Siglo de Oro Festival of Drama, it did not retain the civic and national support behind the parent festival, nor did it enjoy the same independence. The University of Texas at El Paso (UTEP) supplied personnel and funding to the zarzuela festival from its inception. Under the direction of Professor Hugh Cardon, studies in Hispanic music had long included zarzuela production, originally under the auspices of his Hispanic Music Association, a university-based organization. The festival repositioned university performers in a new public arena, alongside visiting professional companies.

When Victor Chacón was made director of opera at UTEP, the festival's board of directors soon tapped his skills as a director of zarzuela. Chacón sat on the board for several years and served as president for a year. In addition to offering this public service, he devoted considerable energy to developing a program at the university called "Zarzuela at UTEP."

In 1995 the board of the International Festival de la Zarzuela voted to reduce the scope of the festival and make it largely a local enterprise. Invitations to companies from Mexico, Spain, New York, and elsewhere in the United States ceased.

The board hoped that the more limited focus would reduce the costs of hosting visiting companies and allow programs at the university (Zarzuela at UTEP and a hispanic music institute) to develop. Pablo Zinger and Victor Chacón worked together to build Zarzuela at UTEP into a nationally recognized center for the art form. These goals, with their ethnically defined emphasis, proved to be too focused (some would say "limited") to generate wide support from the school of music, and by 1998 university support had declined precipitously. Advocates for making UTEP into a national center for the training and production of zarzuela claimed that the school was willing to support a limited summer program but was uneasy about "being known for zarzuela."[16] Within the year Chacón left El Paso and the university.

As of 1999 Zarzuela at UTEP continues to present an annual summer production, but community attention and attendance have declined. The tensions between civic and university concerns have stalled operations, at least temporarily. As outreach diminished in the late 1990s, professional production became subject to local and even departmental politics. The university connection, once so promising, seems to have reduced the impact of the promising zarzuela festival.

In New York university links have less impact on zarzuela production. Although Columbia University houses a collection of zarzuelas compiled decades ago by local enthusiasts, academic influence has been relatively absent in professional productions.[17] The majority of contemporary New York zarzuela presentations are not supported by university affiliation, despite a history of productions sponsored by Columbia's Spanish Institute in the 1930s (see chronology in appendix A) and the recent concert productions featuring the Boricua College Chorus and the Bronx Arts Ensemble (connected with Hostos Community College) conducted by Pablo Zinger. The groups presenting these recent examples function more like resident professional companies, operating somewhat similarly to the Ohio Light Opera, housed on the College of Wooster campus. These companies combine college performers with local and visiting professionals. They compete against the highest arts standards and commercial pressures in the country. These pressures have forced producers either to accommodate professional concert expectations or to content themselves with niche audiences.

Travel Linking New Yorkers to Other Zarzuela Presenters

New York directors, individual singers and actors, and full theatrical companies travel widely across the United States and beyond. Their travels broaden their support base and link audiences across geographic divides. Most important, these New York performers bring their production values along with them.

Operations at the Thalia Spanish Theatre illustrate the travel connections. The company's first zarzuela production linked New York and other Hispanic music centers when Thalia's Silvia Brito invited the director and star of the Cuban zarzuela stage Miguel De Grandy to come to New York from his home in Miami and direct the group's first two zarzuelas.

Individual artists associated with New York companies have expanded their careers as a result of such networking. Conductor and pianist Pablo Zinger, introduced in the previous chapter, built a reputation on his earlier work as musical director with Repertorio Español. In 1995 he conducted the orchestra for *La del Soto del Parral* (The Girl from the Grape Arbor) and *Los de Aragón* for the International Festival de la Zarzuela. In 1996 he conducted *La Verbena de la Paloma* for the newly formed Zarzuela at UTEP. The production was filmed and broadcast by El Paso television station KCOS.[18]

Zinger's influence is sweeping the country. His travels with *Luisa Fernanda* have led to work as a conductor for New York City's Bronx Arts Ensemble, a group that he later conducted in a concert series featuring other types of music by Spanish and Latin American composers. The concerts included a production of the Argentine tango opera *Marta Gruni* and the Cuban zarzuela *María la O* (1997). He returned to his native Uruguay in 1992 to conduct *Luisa Fernanda* and later traveled to California, where he conducted Daniel Helfgot's production of that same romantic masterpiece at the Jarvis Conservatory in Napa, California, in 1997. That same year Zinger wrote feature articles on zarzuela for *Opera News*.[19] Zinger enjoyed a banner year in 1998, for in addition to conducting *El Barberillo de Lavapiés* for the Santa Barbara Grand Opera and a concert version of *La Verbena de la Paloma* for the Boricua College Chorus in New York City, he served as the assistant conductor for Plácido Domingo's Washington Opera production of *Doña Francisquita*.

Zinger's work is an important example of the overlapping influence of people, locale, and conception in contemporary American approaches to zarzuela. In 1998 he reinforced those links and zarzuela's presence on the Internet by posting a personal Web page to provide information regarding his career and links to resources on zarzuela and Latin American music (including excerpts from his articles).[20]

Apart from conductors or directors, singers circulate the most freely within the zarzuela network. The cast of every production features a local core, but when guest stars are featured, they are frequently artists with wide-reaching reputations. In 1995 the Puerto Rican baritone and former Metropolitan Opera star Pablo Elvira performed the lead role of the 1995 production of *La del Soto del Parral* at El Paso's zarzuela festival. Elvira's appearance drew greater public attention (media coverage was excellent) and more attendees than a local artist would have. Like the opera stars who record zarzuela, Elvira's fame does not rest on his association with the genre. Nonetheless, the directors in El Paso counted on his skills and reputation to boost interest in zarzuela, as well as to enhance the specific performance and boost the overall reputation of the annual series of productions.

Increasingly, zarzuela singers also move from one locale to another. For example, soprano Donna Sadlicka performs regularly both with the Chicago Opera Factory and in the Jarvis Conservatory productions of zarzuela in Napa, California. Several New York singers who have worked at Thalia and Repertorio Español have sung in Miami for the Grateli company and for the ¡Viva Zarzuela! concert productions organized by Gonzálo Madurga (an activity separate from the Albuquerque company performing as ¡Viva Zarzuela!).

Repertorio Español stands out for eschewing the practice of highlighting individual performers, preferring instead to invite attention to the combined effort of the company over individual members of the cast and production team (see previous chapter). All the same, individual performers from the repertory company's cast have created national reputations for themselves via their skills in performing Spanish classical music, including zarzuela. Examples include soprano Brenda Feliciano, who was invited to star in the 1995 El Paso production of *La del Soto del Parral*,[21] and the Dominican-born tenor Ulises Espaillat, who released a CD recording of Argentine art song in 1994.[22]

A crucial result of interpersonal networking is that in the long run a New York production, even when it does not directly share material or personal resources, can trade on the status and recognition acquired by other productions across the country. The following discussion of publicity and advertising is designed to show how the promotion of zarzuela contributes to the public perception of the genre's role in American contexts and its connections to social status and ethnic identity.

Networks of (Nonprofit) Promotion

The behind-the-scenes interpersonal network feeds the more visible realms of publicity and funding, which also affect the nature of zarzuela productions in the United States. Promotional activities include advertising, publicizing, and perhaps other undertakings designed to engage public interest.

Advertisements may be considered in two categories: purchased advertisements, which are shaped by the presenters; and unpurchased, information-oriented promotion, often shaped by outside reviewers. I refer to the first as advertisement and the second as publicity. The differences between promotion generated by those responsible for the productions and promotion generated by individuals or groups outside such operations reveal a great deal about the relationship between performance and the projection of identity.

Apart from the international touring presentations such as Tamayo's anthology, the vast majority of zarzuela concerts and shows produced in the United States are offered by nonprofit organizations. These organizations differ from commercial enterprises, even though they must compete with them. Noncommercial advertising leans more toward providing information than toward convincing a consumer to make a buying decision.

Scholarly analyses of advertising have generally asked how advertising works, not whether it works. The communications researcher and sociologist Michael Schudson suggests that asking how advertising works is akin to asking how culture works.[23] Schudson claims that advertising, like culture, works by "taking things we know and making them actionable."[24] Schudson views culture largely as "the markers that create our social world." This, he says, "is a fairly primitive view of culture, but is an important beginning because it strongly suggests that symbols do not 'merely' remind us. They re-*mind* us. They make us focus—and on some things rather than on others. Ads do not merely reinforce existing social trends: they re-*enforce* them, and some trends and not others."[25]

Schudson's remarks emphasize action: ads do more than encourage the selection of a product or a course of action—if they have that effect at all. According to Schudson, advertisements operate indirectly to reinforce and shape people's ideas of their world. Although Schudson focuses on the way patrons respond to the *content* of ads, we might fruitfully consider also the format, delivery, and placement of both ads and publicity, in keeping with the emphasis on performance practice established in previous chapters.

Promotional methods employed by New York presenters of zarzuela use many of the same public and personal strategies employed by other similar companies across the United States. There are of course the more or less broadly targeted print ads, announcements, and preperformance feature articles; radio commercials or announcements; and television spots (including the occasional interview when broadcasters take notice of a specific production and consider it newsworthy). In addition, each group maintains its own list of supportive individuals to whom direct-mail announcements, flyers, or invitations are sent. The various media invite different approaches (including choices concerning language, photographs, descriptive text, and the size, placement, and content of message), depending on the audience that the promoters are targeting.

The power of direct mail should not be underestimated. The closure of the New Jersey–based company La Asociación de Teatro Musical may be due in part to its limited promotional efforts. The ATM sent flyers infrequently and did not systematically maintain its mailing list, at times neglecting even its regular patrons. Since the company relied almost exclusively on the labors of the founding director and his wife, it never enjoyed the benefits of the year-round staffs that serve Repertorio Español and the Thalia Spanish Theatre. In contrast, Repertorio Español's monthly mailings arrive so promptly and predictably that patrons frequently refer to the newsprint brochures as "newspapers" rather than as flyers or advertisements. These brochures list performance dates and times and offer engaging photos and brief synopses of the individual productions. These references highlight the informational tone of Repertorio Español's mailings, a tone for which the company strives despite the practical and obvious goal of encouraging ticket sales.

Like direct mail (see fig. 26), posters tend to be aimed at specific audiences. Posters advertising zarzuela in New York take different forms. They may feature an enlarged photo of the production's central performers, text-dominated announcements in an attention-grabbing layout, or an artist's renderings of scenes or visual imagery in some way associated with the production. Thalia favors the first option, in keeping with the production approaches that define the company and the image it seeks to present. These ads promote the appearance of individual artists and the theater's traditional stage sets as much as the individual production. Clearly the target audience is viewed as likely to recognize the venue and the artists. The assumption is that these viewers might be as interested in supporting the latest endeavor of familiar performers, or the theatrical company itself, by seeing the latest zarzuela.

The second, more abstract approach has been favored by Repertorio Español and the ATM. Particularly with posters for Repertorio Español, the emphasis remains on the show and the company's dramatic conception even when performers are pictured. Large art posters of the kind promoting major arts events across the country, such as the Mostly Mozart Festival in New York, are less commonly used by Thalia and Repertorio Español. El Paso's international zarzuela festival, however, sometimes used handsome art posters to advertise and raise funds. After each performance and during intermissions, patrons could buy posters for various productions (see fig. 27), including signed prints and original models. Such efforts combine publicity with fundraising and offer a high-status souvenir for patrons.

Posters tend to be placed in sites where those likely to know the performers, the company, or the featured drama congregate. In New York, promoters place posters for independent concerts at Casa España, Casa Galicia, the Center for

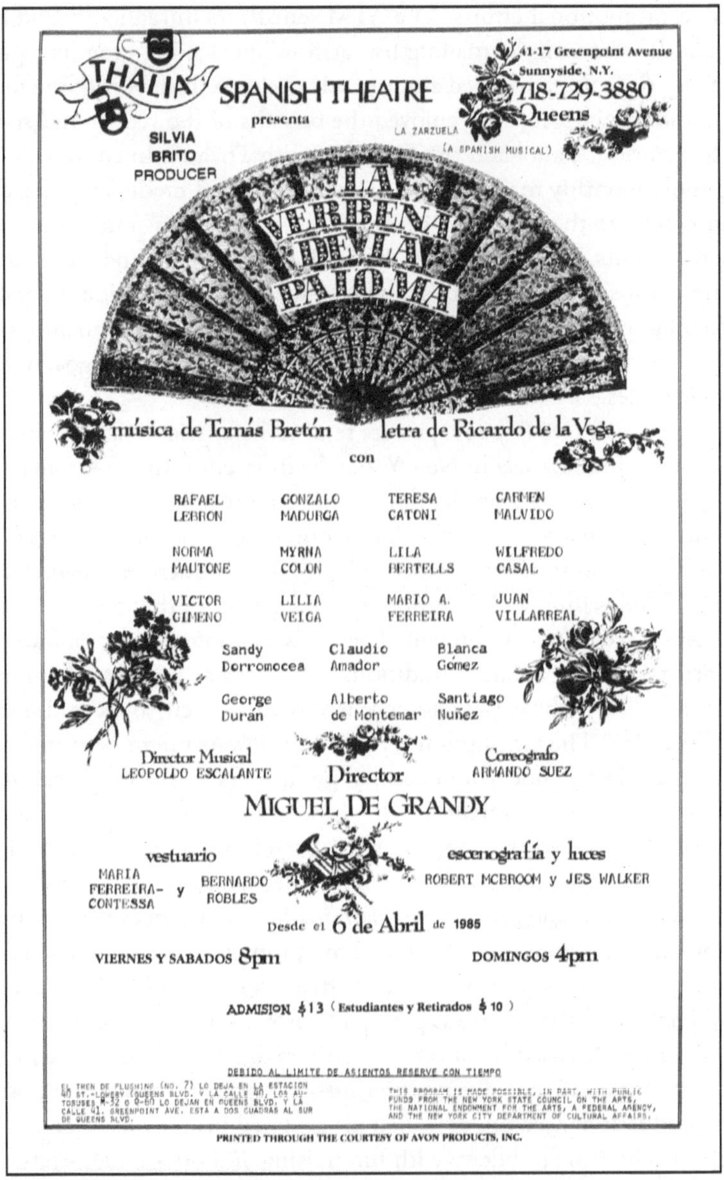

Figure 26. Poster for Thalia Spanish Theatre's 1985 production of *La Verbena de la Paloma.* Courtesy of the Thalia Spanish Theatre.

Figure 27. Poster/cover for the 1995 International Festival de la Zarzuela in El Paso–Ciudad Juárez. The painting, by Alberto Escamilla, depicts the final scene in the zarzuela *La del Soto del Parral,* here shown taking place by a farmhouse in Segovia overlooking the Alcázar. This is the fourth in a series of seven zarzuela prints Alberto Escamilla created for the festival.

Inter-American Relations, and similar social clubs. Other sites include the walls and windows of schools, local churches, and restaurants featuring Spanish or Latin American food. Posters for the larger theatrical productions frequently appear on public bulletin boards or on lampposts in neighborhoods surrounding the theaters. Posters for Plácido Domingo's appearance with the visiting production of *Antología de la Zarzuela* in August 1985 appeared in the New York City buses and subways and were plastered on the walls surrounding construction sites in midtown Manhattan—a favorite New York advertising technique, and one intended to reach a large cross-section of the general population.

Most zarzuela posters are positioned to attract a local clientele, but in recent years New York presenters have found city buses and subways to be an appealing venue for advertising to a wider public. The Thalia Spanish Theatre advertised both its Tango and Tango show and its 1997 production of the zarzuela *La del Soto del Parral* on over four hundred city buses in Queens and Manhattan in the month of June. In such cases the musical and dance features of the productions are emphasized, clearly conveying that such productions are accessible to the non-Spanish-speaking public. This recent effort indicates Thalia's growing desire to expand its regular clientele beyond the many loyal Spanish-speaking supporters and Queens residents who constitute its core audience.

All New York zarzuela presenters rely on the free promotion available via the local media. Local newspapers and some magazines, both English and Spanish, will list cultural events without charge. In addition, specialized publications such as *AHA,* the monthly journal of the Association for Hispanic Arts, regularly list events of interest to the Hispanic community. Similarly, the Spanish-language radio stations WADO and WJIT have been especially generous in promoting Hispanic cultural events. Silvia Brito, director of the Thalia Spanish Theatre, stresses how crucial she considers the support of these stations to be and graciously acknowledges their assistance with a printed *"gracias"* in the program booklets distributed at each Thalia production.

In many cases the Spanish-language media directly support the efforts of local theaters. Both Thalia and Repertorio Español include sponsors from the press, radio, and television in their list of patrons. The "thank you" section that appears in each newsletter distributed by Repertorio Español organizes contributors into sections, including one titled "Corporaciones Latinas" (Latino businesses). Included in that section are Frank Robles Communications, *Latina Magazine,* Lectorum Publications, Telemundo, WNJU (channel 47), and WXTV (channel 41).

The English-language press and broadcast media are not as consistent in promoting, or even listing, Spanish-language productions, but zarzuela productions fare better than most. Most of Repertorio Español's productions, musical or not, appear in these performance listings. Thalia's productions sometimes appear in the theater listings under "Other Boroughs." Significantly, both companies' zarzuela productions (like their dance shows and concerts) are consistently listed in the main "Musical Offerings" section. In the 1980s English-language radio stations occasionally announced New York productions of zarzuelas, and every so often public awareness of the genre was enhanced by special programming unaffiliated with any of the regional theaters. In 1984, for example, WQXR, one of New York's classical radio stations, presented a ninety-minute program entitled "An Introduction to the Zarzuela." The program featured selected arias sung by great opera singers throughout the twentieth century, including Caruso. Such programs appear sporadically and rarely feature the work of American presenters.

Although radio contributes little to creating new audiences for zarzuelas produced in the United States, the situation has improved in the 1990s. A notable departure from the generic introductions offered in the 1980s occurred in 1997 when WQXR featured the Thalia Spanish Theatre's production of *La del Soto del Parral.*

A Closer Look at Purchased Advertisements and Related Activity

Paid advertising is another story entirely. Repertorio Español regularly buys advertising space in the *New York Times,* as it did with the *Village Voice* and the *New York Daily News* while they were in print (see fig. 28), but neither it nor the Thalia has ever matched the 1985 and 1986 media blitz launched by the promoters of Tamayo's *Antología de la Zarzuela.* Whenever possible, local producers piggybacked on the promotional efforts associated with Tamayo's celebrated tour. Both Repertorio Español and Thalia advertised their zarzuela productions in the printed program for the performances of *Antología de la Zarzuela* at Madison Square Garden. Both ads clearly emphasized their central message: "If you like the zarzuela you see here, you can see more in our theaters" (see figure 29). To a lesser extent, these regional companies also piggyback on one another's advertising and promotional efforts. An ad for Repertorio Español might appear in a Thalia program even though the two theaters also compete for the same audience.

The promotional managers for Tamayo's *Antología* ran advertisements in all the relevant major newspapers, English and Spanish. They also ran television ads for several weeks prior to the show on both English- and Spanish-language stations. In the 1980s few local theaters, let alone independent zarzuela producers, could afford to advertise on TV, although the Spanish-language stations have been the most supportive of their efforts.

In the 1970s Spanish-language channels occasionally broadcast zarzuelas performed by Spanish or Mexican companies, but not by American companies. Only in recent years have regional companies turned to television performance and promotion. Although special programs featuring zarzuela are far from commercial advertisements in the usual sense, they certainly result in promoting the genre overall, for they focus public attention on a specific company's performance. Full-length shows, such as the PBS broadcast based on Tamayo's

Figure 28. Newspaper (*Village Voice*) ad for Thalia Spanish Theatre's productions, including the zarzuela *La del Manojo del Rosas,* June 1989. Dance is commonly emphasized in theatrical promotion. Photo of tango dancers by Rafael Llerena.

production, are rare, although this seems to be changing. Public television seems to be the most willing to present local productions, although New York City companies have attracted relatively little attention compared to the feature broadcasts of Zarzuela at UTEP's *La Verbena de la Paloma* that El Paso's KCOS-TV ran in 1996 and the Chicago-area television broadcasts of the Opera Factory (channels 66, 44, and cable).

Figure 29. Advertisements for local zarzuela productions placed in the program for José Tamayo's *Antología de la Zarzuela* (1986). Used with the permission of Mel Howard Enterprises. Photos by Rafael Llerena (Thalia) and Gerry Goodstein (Repertorio Español).

Evaluating the Effect of Advertisement and Promotion

The effectiveness of these advertising and promotional strategies is difficult to discern. Michael Schudson argues that the most powerful effects of advertising are likely to be indirect: "People attend to messages they already agree with, perceive primarily those parts of the complex or ambiguous messages that fit their preconceived ideas, and rely on trusted friends and relatives to develop opinions about the world."[26] This thesis helps to explain how American audiences respond not only to presenters' efforts to promote their productions but to the productions themselves.

The fact that local theatrical companies rely heavily on individual contacts (via their mailing lists) matches Schudson's assessment and indicates again the importance of networking. Responses to audience questionnaires also confirm this conclusion. In 1987, 51 percent of all respondents at selected New York zarzuela productions indicated that they heard of the production from friends or family. Only 21 percent elected to come because they were familiar with the work presented and liked it, and 15 percent reported coming simply because they like zarzuela in general. Moreover, 12 percent came because they were invited, and 9 percent came with a group; 25 percent came with friends, and 66 percent attended with a family member. These figures indicate that even though New York audiences for zarzuela are predominantly of Spanish or Latin American ancestry (generally around 80 percent, as discussed in chapter 6), many are seeing the specific work for the first time and are doing so because someone they know has encouraged them to attend.[27]

These figures correlate with Schudson's theory that most promotional attempts serve more to help consumers choose from among available choices than to convince them to pursue a completely new course of action. While not ignoring the larger public, zarzuela producers are well aware that selling zarzuela to those unfamiliar with the genre, Spanish music or theater, or operatic music will not fill the house. They also know that "a theater that is full," as René Buch puts it (see chapter 6), especially one that is regularly full, attracts interest and further consideration from the larger public.

The tendency of both major companies to promote their musical offerings in connection with special dance appearances is clearly designed to attract the attention of potential patrons who do not speak or understand Spanish. Individuals unfamiliar with zarzuela are more likely to have heard of tango or flamenco, and these productions do indeed attract more non-Hispanic patrons.

The issue of public interest prompts another examination of the role of media in the promotion of zarzuela and the associated goals of producers. Critical reviews of performances also serve as means of promotion. Research conducted by the Newspaper Advertising Bureau notes that people are much more likely to be influenced to see a show as a result of a positive review than they are to decide against attending because of a negative review.[28] The real value of a review, in Schudson's opinion, is that it is informative; it introduces the public to locales as well as presenters and their presentations.

Apart from reviews, feature and human interest articles offer additional information on various productions. As might be expected, the larger the show and the better known its performers, the more likely it is to receive such attention. The *New York Times* devoted two full pages of the Sunday edition to José Tamayo's *Antología de la Zarzuela.*[29] Similarly, *New York* magazine ran a full-page story on the show.[30] Furthermore, both articles were written by respected authors in the field of classical music.

In this case the newsworthy event was Plácido Domingo's appearance with the touring group, an occurrence that sparked general interest in the "unknown" genre of the zarzuela. Articles on zarzuela continued to appear long after the show left town. In April 1986 *Dial* magazine, the program guide for New York's public television station, ran an article entitled "Viva Spanish Opera" to draw attention to the station's upcoming broadcast of a videotape of Domingo with *Antología.* Interestingly, the article focused less on the special characteristics of zarzuela than on the features that it shares with opera, the genre more liable to be familiar to public television supporters. The article also celebrated Domingo's involvement with the show, again indicating that for newcomers, the star, not the genre or the production, is most likely to be the primary attraction.

In the press, as in self-generated promotion, local producers benefited from the attention given to the allied production of Domingo and Tamayo. In both the *New York Times* article and the *New York* magazine review mentioned previously, Repertorio Español's productions of zarzuela were noted. Indeed, *New York* writer Peter Davis clearly preferred Repertorio Español's work to that of the Spanish touring company, noting: "For those who may still be curious about zarzuela and were not automatically turned off by this tacky affair, I recommend a visit to the Repertorio Español's production of *Luisa Fernanda.*"[31] Every theater might wish for such an open endorsement.

Any coverage from the *New York Times* would suit Thalia's Silvia Brito. Thalia's productions are regularly reviewed and lauded in the Spanish-language press, and New York's *Newsday,* the former newspaper known for its strong commitment to covering the boroughs outside Manhattan, featured Thalia in its two-page spread "And You Don't Have to Speak Spanish,"[32] but Brito speaks from experience when she notes, "*Times* reporters refuse to take the subway ride to

Queens to review our productions."[33] The open endorsement of Repertorio Español in the most prestigious English-language publications (those with a national circulation) may help to explain the larger non-Spanish-speaking audiences at Repertorio Español.

Outside New York Thalia often gets more positive attention from the press, especially the Spanish-language press, than does Repertorio Español. In El Paso critics lauded Thalia's productions for their historical accuracy, noting of one that "it could well have been an 1890 import from Madrid";[34] another reviewer labeled Brito's 1987 production of *La Revoltosa* "without a doubt, the best of the festival."[35] In contrast, Repertorio Español's *Luisa Fernanda* was evaluated as thoroughly professional and "more of a musical treat than a theatrical treat."[36]

Prestigious Support: Foundations, Grants, and Independent Awards

Publicity in its many guises bears an important relationship to the funding zarzuela producers are able to obtain. At various points during the past fifteen years, producing zarzuelas, and the publicity they generate, appears to have enhanced the ability of local theaters to obtain certain funds. Certainly zarzuela is like theater in general and musical theater in particular in that it is not possible to produce shows without funding that supplements box office revenues. Consequently the rise of Hispanic theater in New York parallels the development of governmental subsidy for the arts.

The New York State Council on the Arts (NYSCA) was founded in 1961, and in 1965 the federal government instituted the National Endowment for the Arts (NEA). American arts activity grew at an unprecedented rate during this decade, precisely the decade that witnessed the birth of the Hispanic theatrical companies: INTAR, the Puerto Rican Traveling Theatre, Nuestro Teatro, and Las Artes (the predecessor to Repertorio Español; see chapter 4). In 1971 the NEA turned its attention to neighborhood and community programs with the implementation of the Expansion Arts Program.

The NEA states its objectives as follows: "to make the arts more widely available to millions of Americans; to preserve our cultural heritage for present and future generations; to strengthen cultural organizations; and to encourage the creative development of talented individuals." The endowment seeks to achieve these objectives through grants to official arts agencies of the states (and overseas U.S. territories); to nonprofit, tax-exempt arts organizations; and to individuals "of exceptional talent."[37]

To obtain these government grants, an organization must demonstrate that it meets the criteria noted previously. Because the award process is highly selective, recipients take great pride in obtaining this support and use such government "endorsement" to obtain additional funding. For example, theatrical companies such as La Asociación de Teatro Musical, the New Jersey–based organization that specialized in zarzuela production, have received little support from government agencies and thus have come up short elsewhere, too. Director Raúl Cuervo noted that "without NEA support, it is very difficult for us to get other grants."[38] Financial woes definitely contributed to the demise of the organization in the late 1980s.

Silvia Brito, director of the Thalia Spanish Theatre, is quick to credit local arts agencies, such as NYSCA, as well as the NEA for supporting her theater and others like it through the 1980s. As the ATM case implies, it would be difficult to overestimate the importance of obtaining such funds on a regular basis. In 1985 Brito remarked: "Most of my funds come from NYSCA, NEA and the city's Department of Cultural Affairs." In April 1995, with all these agencies struggling under budget reductions of 50 percent, Brito voiced concerns: "[The zarzuela *La Dolorosa*] may be our last; we'll do the tour [to El Paso], but without support we can't keep our doors open."[39] Happily, the company not only survived the rest of the 1990s but thrived. The annual report for 1998 celebrated Thalia's twenty-year anniversary and looked optimistically toward continued success in the new millennium.

Beginning in the 1980s, theatrical companies found it prudent to solicit funds for specific productions. Repertorio Español has been especially successful at this process. In 1985–86 the Andrew W. Mellon Foundation awarded a grant to Repertorio Español to support the production of "theater classics not ordinarily affordable." This grant enabled the company to produce *Luisa Fernanda*. The Mellon Foundation tries to limit its grants to the development of national programs for major organizations in the visual and performing arts, only occasionally awarding funds to New York City organizations.[40] Repertorio Español's fine reputation for performances of Spanish classics across the country, its projection of *Luisa Fernanda* as a classic work, and the producers' savvy anticipation of the national attention Domingo's appearance with *Antología* would bring all contributed to the company's appeal to the Mellon Foundation.

In the absence of support from large foundations, producers rely heavily on individual contributions, many of which are earmarked for a specific production. Individuals who have contributed are listed in the program booklet under designations such as *patron, sponsor, friend,* or *benefactor.*

Local merchants also provide critical funding, and the program booklets of all the New York theaters, especially Thalia, acknowledge contributions or feature advertisements purchased from local merchants. Many of these commercial contributors have Hispanic ownership or feature products aimed at the Hispanic population, such as Goya Foods or the Cuban restaurant Victor's Café.

The ethnic component of zarzuela has played an important part in securing production funding. Los Amigos de la Zarzuela, organized by Antonia and Carmina Outeiral Pérez in Long Island, has contributed financial support to Thalia and Repertorio Español to assist their participation in the international zarzuela festival in El Paso. Both theatrical presentations and concerts, such as La Asociación Pro Zarzuela en América's *Viva Zarzuela,* frequently receive support from national sources earmarked for minority development. The Avon Foundation's long-standing support of Thalia's productions is a powerful example of such support. Funding from Avon made it possible for Thalia to present its Tango and Tango show at Lincoln Center's Alice Tully Hall, further enhancing the company's general visibility.

Similarly, the Spanish government—through offices such as the Ministry of Culture, the General Consulate, and the U.S.-Spanish Chamber of Commerce—supports concert programs featuring zarzuela when performed by at least one Iberian artist. In New York most of these funds go to performances in major concert halls, although local theaters have benefited at least from receptions hosted in honor of their zarzuela productions and from funding that facilitated travel. The lines are drawn less clearly in El Paso, where the Chamizal Theater does not compete against halls with the status of Lincoln Center. Spanish governmental agencies clearly emphasize the classic aspects of Spanish culture, and zarzuela performances seem to fit into this vision. Funds from the Spanish consulate have supported both Thalia and Repertorio Español and have helped both companies to take their zarzuelas and classic Spanish plays on tours in the United States and abroad.

Even before the budget crises of the 1990s, companies such as Repertorio Español and Thalia had to be creative in the ways they obtained funding. Funds are available for tours, educational efforts, community outreach, and expansion, and both companies have skillful development or production directors who know how to take advantage of these opportunities. As a result, both Thalia and Repertorio Español have taken their productions to cities and states across the United States with assistance from Citibank. By scheduling productions during weekdays (so that schoolchildren could attend as classes), Repertorio Español has been able to obtain funds from the New York Community Trust and the Lila Wallace Reader's Digest Funds for educational efforts.

Few companies have a development director as able as producer Gilberto Zaldívar at Repertorio Español. In 1985 his efforts propelled the small theatrical company into a new league by securing funds from the Ford Foundation and the Equitable Assurance Society. Equitable offered Repertorio Español the chance to use the 500-seat auditorium in the company's corporate headquarters in midtown Manhattan, and Ford Foundation money helped to pay for the preparations necessary to transform productions to accommodate the larger stage.

The transformation proved especially valuable for the company's musical productions, which frequently filled the large hall, and Repertorio Español was able to demonstrate the need for additional space by citing the popularity and general appeal of its musical productions. Well into the 1990s Repertorio Español continued to operate from two homes and enjoyed growing attention from some of New York's most wealthy and powerful residents. In the last years of the decade, Equitable stopped providing space for concert and stage productions, but Repertorio Español to some degree compensated for the loss by acquiring additional space in the building from which it has long operated in New York.

Another of Zaldívar's skills is coordinating a prestigious board of directors, a roster of individuals whose status and connections assist the company with obtaining funding and opportunities. Significantly, beginning in 1987, Raymond Colotti, executive vice president of the Equitable Life Assurance Company, sat on the theater's board. Other members include several lawyers, physicians (presidents and partners of their firms), the CEO of Citicorp/Citibank, and the advertising director of *El Diario–La Prensa,* the largest Spanish-language newspaper in the city.

The success of organizations such as Repertorio Español and the Thalia Spanish Theatre is certainly due in part to the roles their respective boards play in fundraising and promotion. Companies outside New York face special challenges when it comes to such fundraising. Victor Chacón, in El Paso, noted that "the problems with production start with funding, and in smaller cities like El Paso, there is a danger of many worthy organizations tapping the same limited resources and exhausting local supporters."[41] For either enterprise to grow, each required additional funding. Each operation had separate but linked goals. A greater awareness of those links might have helped the respective boards to bolster the relations between the International Festival de la Zarzuela and the music program at the University of Texas at El Paso.

For New York's professional theatrical companies, the high visibility and popularity of zarzuela productions, often strengthened by musical anthologies, appear to have been an important stepping stone to growth, prestige, and stability in an era when the very survival of theaters, and arts organizations in general, was constantly threatened. The decisions of the Thalia Spanish Theatre and Teatro Repertorio Español to embrace lyric drama, particularly zarzuela, enabled these companies to attract financial support from a much wider range of corporate and institutional contributors. The ever-growing list of individual supporters makes it clear that success with higher-level funding spurred additional support from within the local community.

Funding Realities: Concluding Realizations

Although many features of the zarzuela—its ties to European classical music, its combination of music and drama, and its "Spanishness"—attract donor support, the genre itself is not sufficiently powerful to garner funding. As we are likely to find with many musical genres, the context in which zarzuela is presented is critical. Highly visible productions, those that take place in major concert halls or feature internationally recognized stars in single or limited performances, often receive substantial support from special-interest donors. Whereas the Hispanic community and other such supporters, including the Spanish government, seek to foster public awareness of Spanish artistic genres, such as zarzuela, many private American foundations espouse the larger goal of fostering general cultural development. Productions that appear to promote the interests of a particular ethnic group (however broadly defined) are not excluded, but many foundations are less likely to award priority funding to such efforts. Only when zarzuela is promoted as a genre of universal appeal, representative of and contributing to the diverse array of American arts options, does it garner wide support from both Hispanic and non-Hispanic sources. Repertorio Español has effectively projected such an identity, and Thalia Spanish Theater has increasingly benefited from its own strategies for wider appeal.

The realities of financing help to explain how zarzuela presentations in the United States connect to much broader strategies on the part of the presenters than simply reviving old repertoire. Producing zarzuelas provides an entry point into an enlarged network of connections; realizing the larger potential of such productions is up to the individual presenter. Keeping the needs of local patrons and supporters in the foreground is the first step. Making productions accessible to non-Spanish-speaking patrons is a second step in the New York context, whereas elsewhere in the country it may be the first. The most dedicated and reliable supporters are those in the local Hispanic community. Networking, personal interaction, and word-of-mouth promotion have been essential to the health of presenters, big and small. Although support from outside the local and ethnic community is absolutely fundamental to survival, growth, and increased prestige, it cannot be courted at the expense of the values and needs of the company's primary customers.

9

Ends and Means

Projecting Status, Ability, and Ethnicity

"Nos Hablamos Después": Reflections on Change

It is 4:00 on a Tuesday afternoon in the summer of 1999; once again I have come to take up René Buch's invitation to "talk later" (see the introduction). Too early in the day and week for actors or patrons to begin gathering, the lobby of the Teatro Repertorio Español is quiet. There is plenty of activity a couple flights above, however, in the spacious offices taking up the third floor. The rooms gleam from the remodeling completed after the company acquired both sides of the handsome brownstone building where it has rented theater space since 1979. René Buch sits across from me, framed in the yellow light of the afternoon sun streaming through the window behind his desk. Gazing at the old programs I handed him, he draws a deep breath as he wistfully remembers several actors who have passed away and others who have left the country. The poignant impact of so many departures startles us both. He flips through a few more programs: "Ah, *La Generala,*" he remarks, "I loved that show." Later, he tells me, "We no longer do zarzuela; it has become too expensive to produce."[1] I cannot help but wonder whether a change in priorities, too, rather than expense alone, explains the company's hiatus in zarzuela production.

Despite the many changes and the many financial battles the company has weathered, Repertorio Español is thriving; gaining more building space is evidence of the company's solidity and comfortable footing in New York's theatrical scene. Proudly, Buch invites me to the newest production: *Crónica de una Muerte Anunciada* (Chronicle of a Death Foretold), a drama conceived and directed by Jorge Alí Triana (responsible for *¡Y se Armó la Mojiganga!*) and based on a work by Gabriel García Márquez. Although there may no longer be plans for new productions of fully staged zarzuelas, there can be no question that earlier productions of zarzuelas enhanced the company's visibility and brought its work to the attention of a wider public, permitting continued innovation and the greater specialization seen in recent productions such as *Cuentos Afro-Caribeños* (Afro-Caribbean Tales).

That same week I visited Silvia Brito. As I arrived at the playhouse I noted that the windows of the "Cathedral of Zarzuela," as one critic dubbed the Thalia Spanish Theatre, are still only plate glass in dented aluminum frames. Beyond the stark exterior storefront, however, the lobby—featuring crimson carpet, upholstered furniture, and walls covered with framed photos, reviews, and awards—beckons visitors with a comforting warmth. There Brito and I sat and talked about the company's latest productions. "We are the only company in New York still presenting fully staged zarzuelas," she reminded me.[2] Producing zarzuelas has helped to define the company, but even the steady and persistent Thalia has changed. Brito told me that she plans to retire in 2000. I find it difficult to imagine this dynamo of a woman in retirement and even harder to imagine the Thalia Theater able to continue without her at the helm. Brito's recipe for success over the years has been a combination of brilliant financial management, skilled artistic direction, and a keen focus on the company's priority: serving the local Spanish-speaking community. This commitment has brought her recognition ranging far beyond a local clientele. I glanced at the stage photo hanging on the wall behind me (see fig. 30), where I saw fresh evidence of Brito's commitment to local development in the smiling faces of the little children who performed in the 1997 production of *Agua, Azucarillos, y Aguardiente* (Water, Sweets, and Brandy, or The Beverage Vendor). It remains to be seen whether a new director can sustain Brito's commitment to zarzuela with such a combination of familial and professional zest.

On the long subway ride back to Manhattan, I realized that zarzuelas were opening across the country at that very moment. Closing my eyes, I placed imaginary pins in a map and noted that they outline the perimeter of the United States (New York, Miami, El Paso, Napa, Chicago, Wooster). Outside New York and Miami the productions feature English translations. In each locale producers are building on a base of dedicated followers to create new audiences and to convince Americans performers to begin to think of zarzuela as material that belongs to them, no matter what their heritage. The invitation is to embrace these Spanish works with the sense of ownership that non-Italians feel regarding the operas of Puccini or non-Austrians feel for operettas by Franz Lehár. Zarzuela thus perceived would remain ethnically defined but be more universally valued.

Glitzy claims for ethnically identifiable universal appeal bombarded me as I exited the subway and found myself facing the exterior wall of a large record store

Figure 30. The cast and chorus of *Agua, Azucarillos y Aguardiente,* taken from the *Annual Report, The Thalia Spanish Theatre, 1997,* p. 14. Photo by Anthony Ruiz.

plastered with larger-than-life posters of Ricky Martin, the year's superstar of Latin pop music. The overwhelming success of his Grammy Award–winning song "Livin' la Vida Loca" (Living the Crazy Life) may hold a lesson for proponents of more classically oriented Spanish music such as zarzuela. Martin's hit features English lyrics set to a salsa beat modified by rock- and Caribbean-influenced pop textures. Martin has been criticized for diluting aspects of traditional Latin dance music, but in his bid for crossover appeal, he preserves enough salsa-influenced dance rhythms and Spanish lyrics (in the English version; a version solely in Spanish also exists) for the selection to be clearly identified as Latin. The song's "universal" appeal retains an ethnically defined component. Although zarzuela is not likely to appeal to the same broad audience that thrills to "Livin' la Vida Loca," the analogous goal of convincing an audience that music and drama with Spanish or Latin American characteristics are accessible to non-Spanish-speaking clients still unites those who present zarzuelas in the United States today.

One important difference between the modern commercial pop music of Ricky Martin and the popular music of zarzuela is the latter's connection to the worlds of classical music and theater. Another difference, one that follows from the first, is that in zarzuela the repertoire, the product rather than the individual artist, is conventionally acknowledged as the principal focus. With notable exceptions (discussed later), entire companies, not individual stars, earn recognition. Although individuals can and do earn recognition performing zarzuelas, overall the status earned by these productions is collective status, status for the presenting group and for the repertoire presented. The issue of collective representation plays an important role in the revival of zarzuela production by New York's Spanish theaters. That same issue may limit the genre's appeal when produced in other venues.

Particularly in New York, zarzuela serves as a powerful symbol of ethnicity by reinforcing links among Hispanics as a group and between them and an elite, influential segment of the larger society. Present-day realizations of the genre's flexibility account for much of the renewed interest in the zarzuela. Contemporary American producers stress the pan-Hispanic options of individual works, all the while ensuring that audiences of various backgrounds and tastes, including non-Spanish-speaking ones, can identify with some aspect of the zarzuela. The genre's broad appeal, its historical pedigree, and the many options for adaptation make zarzuela an attractive way to promote greater public recognition of Hispanic contributions in the domains of theater and concert music. At the same time, the genre frequently serves as a stepping stone for greater recognition of the abilities of individual performers and presenters.

Zarzuela and the Eth-Class

"Is ethnicity a relevant issue?" asks Pablo Zinger in an article he wrote for *Opera News* magazine.[3] My answer is a qualified yes. Ethnicity has played a powerful role in the way zarzuela is and has been received in the United States. Nevertheless, the musical and theatrical circles where American presenters position zarzuela are today as likely to be defined by social-class status as they are by ethnicity. This reality helps to explain the limits that have characterized zarzuela production in the United States. Zarzuela may have been street theater in eighteenth-century Spain, and the performances in the early twentieth century may have filled the popular entertainment role now covered by television and films, but today, especially in the United States, the genre is performed by serious artists who position their work as high culture and as entertainment recognizing the demands of an informed and influential segment of the population, largely of middle- to upper-class status.

The intersection of ethnic affiliation and social-class status projected by many zarzuela presentations brings to mind Milton Gordon's discussions in his book *Assimilation in American Life*. Although not new, Gordon's views call attention to the all too frequently ignored complexities of ethnic identity. He proposes that intersections of social class and ethnicity call for conceptualizing social identity as a combination of multiple affiliations. Social class—and all the conditions that accumulate to determine and temper it, such as age, economic assets, educational level, lineage, and racial ancestry—is as important as nationality. The resulting group might be generically described as an "eth-class." What this term omits is any reference to its larger frame, in this case the intersecting domains and tensions of American life. Any such group ultimately positions itself as American. Hence upwardly mobile Hispanic Americans constitute the eth-class that zarzuela both attracts and helps to define in the United States.

Rarely do people of any background identify themselves in such abstract compound terms. Instead they let their behavior and their cultural practices indicate the complexities of their identities. Music and stage performance offer particularly potent arenas for projecting the complexities of identity, and zarzuela is no exception. American treatments of the zarzuela exemplify how music and associated behavior may serve to project not just ethnicity but also class status and accomplishment. In this study I have tried to illuminate the complexity of ethnic identity as defined by performance in the United States. The striking conclusion is that zarzuela productions do much more than *project* identity. They actually *create* a composite identity that does not exist outside the confines defined by performance situations such as zarzuela concerts and shows.

There never existed, and still does not exist, a single cohesive Hispanic group waiting to be represented. The discussion of ethnicity in chapter 6 emphasizes the wide range of identities of Spanish-speaking Americans. Puerto Ricans do not naturally see themselves as aligned with Cubans, Dominicans, or Mexicans. Such alliances are more often contextually defined. Even those who share nationality by birth do not necessarily see themselves as a group; backgrounds vary, especially with regard to economic and educational opportunity. The genre of zarzuela allows presenters to bridge some of those gaps, specifically those of natal nationality, and reinforce others, particularly those shaped by economic status, educational background, cosmopolitan status, and personal aspiration.

American zarzuela presentations also indicate how musical symbols change and how those changes are closely related to the social conditions in which they originate. Most striking is the sense that American productions of zarzuela tie into much higher conceptions of social status here in the United States than was typically the case in Spain or Latin America after the eighteenth century. In the United States the zarzuela does not carry the ambivalent status it held in Latin American countries that chaffed under the yoke of Spanish colonialism. This study of zarzuela shows that political realities have always shaped the creation and presentation of musical repertoire, especially if we define politics as the negotiation of power relations.[4] Discussions in chapters 5, 6, and 7 note many of the ways that zarzuela producers and supporters in the United States have interpreted the genre's history to serve contemporary needs. These activities help to explain recent patterns in the choice of repertoire and in the manner of presentation.

Concluding Reflections

From the perspective of the 1990s, we can see that the zarzuela revival of the 1980s was subject to definite limits. Only certain works have garnered regular attention. Overall, creole genres and new compositions in the genre are presented rarely and have enjoyed limited notice. This neglect can be explained in part by production expense. The scores for these non-Iberian works are less available and frequently subject to more burdensome copyright restrictions. In addition, *costumbrista* treatments of racial issues may leave contemporary supporters of Afro-Hispanic identity uncomfortable, and in any event, the identity issues evoked in many creole dramas do not match the concerns of current zarzuela sponsors, whose efforts more frequently reinforce ties to white European ancestry. When it comes to newly created zarzuelas, other issues emerge. New zarzuelas do not prompt nostalgic memories and devotion, nor do they necessarily tap into the existing support network for familiar repertoire. These links have practical as well as philosophical consequences ranging from the availability of performance materials to concerns regarding the breadth of appeal.

By focusing on zarzuela productions in New York, I have been able to illustrate how producers work to serve their audiences. It is telling that both major theatrical companies in New York began by presenting English-language dramas in Spanish (including popular American musicals such as the *Fantasticks*) but quickly turned to presenting classic plays and musicals by Spanish and Latin American writers. The heart of their work has been to promote Spanish-language theater by making classic dramas available to audiences who will appreciate them. Educating a larger public about the richness of Spanish culture was, and remains, a secondary goal. Each company developed its own approach and refused to compromise on the integrity of a work to please newcomers.

American treatments of zarzuela do not simply effect transformations of imported repertoire; they constitute examples of forthright appropriation. Overall, American zarzuela productions are rarely offered as "foreign fare," even if reviewers in the English-language press sometimes approach zarzuela as exotica or worse.[5] These productions are New York productions, El Paso productions, Brooklyn concerts—in short, *American* productions of repertoire offered as part of the fabric of America's music. Indeed, such appropriation is much stronger with the musical components of zarzuela than with its theatrical aspects. Concert productions and the regular custom of detaching musical numbers from their theatrical frame tend to lessen the affiliation of individual songs with any particular constituency or circumstance and broaden their appeal. The musical numbers are the truly portable features of any zarzuela. They are what people hum or sing informally (or enjoy in arrangements for media other than voice).

The presentation of zarzuela in the United States is more than a musical issue; it is a political issue as well. The genre's continued existence here is based on affirmations of power and the social status that accompanies power. Such claims are often voiced as aesthetic evaluations coupled with statements indicating pride and ownership, such as "Our music deserves recognition; it should not be ignored"; "Our musical theater has something for everyone"; "When produced professionally, our material can compete very well with the standard repertoire."[6]

As Americans characterized by a shared colonial history with Spain and ties to the Spanish language, both presenters and supporters of zarzuela share an interest in seeing themselves as a group defined, in part, by maintaining their distinction from the larger U.S. population. At the same time, artists of Hispanic ancestry want the dominant society to recognize that what they have to offer is as good, if not better, than what currently receives the most attention. As I have shown, these powerful claims have all been voiced by the directors and performers associated with zarzuela production in the United States.

For the Hispanic American group "created" by zarzuela (and similar) productions, the negotiation of the elements that constitute "our music" and "our theater" is ceaseless. The relative rarity of creole forms in contemporary American zarzuela performance indicates how individual claims to identity are often set aside in the face of competing demands or made more universal, as in the formal concert anthologies featured by Repertorio Español and the dance and music programs featured by Thalia.

A more general identity offers the promise of achieving a wider constituency with greater power, recognition, and financial backing. Cuba's Ministry of Culture offers no subsidies for the presentation of Cuban zarzuela abroad, whereas Spain's does. Yet local producers find ways to accommodate and recognize the principal backgrounds of their primary audiences. Cuban zarzuelas are represented in musical anthologies and concert programs and have even been used to enrich scenes of works with peninsular origins. Popular dance music with Cuban, Colombian, and Puerto Rican rhythms finds expression in new musical dramas presented alongside traditional zarzuelas.[7]

In no way is zarzuela the only or even the most representative music for any Latino group. Much of the genre's power and commercial viability stems from the way current productions are positioned as alternatives to the wide array of social dance music marketed internationally as *música latina* (including salsa and even the commercial mix featuring popular stars such as Ricky Martin). Correspondingly, the pan-Hispanic identity promoted by zarzuela differs from the pan-Latino identity promoted in other circumstances.[8] In New York zarzuela has enjoyed an independent (semicommercial) status unparalleled elsewhere in the United States. Although the New York companies, with their reliance on grants, are a long way from absolute commercial status, they still enjoy an independence remarkable in contrast to companies working in other cities. Nonetheless, the sense that zarzuela has the potential to be commercially viable makes it an especially attractive symbol of ethnicity and power.

The negotiations that shape performance of zarzuela in the United States remind us that a community of any kind, be it a community of music lovers or an ethnic community, is a created phenomenon. The emergence of a community cannot be assumed from temporal or physical (geographic) proximity.[9] Similarly, conceptions of musical genres and practices do not travel wholesale from one location to another but instead are shaped by the values and aspirations of those who sustain them. This may well explain why we can find performances of zarzuela in major cities across the United States that meet two basic criteria: a large Hispanic population and a tradition of supporting opera, usually coupled with a tradition of supporting classical Spanish theater as well.

As I have discussed, the approach to zarzuela varies from one presenter to the next. Many of the Cuban Americans who support zarzuela in New York and Florida identify themselves as refugees and stress their inability to return to their country of birth, a perspective that differs from that of many Mexican or Puerto Rican patrons. Cuban Americans do not see themselves as having any options for two homes and often display antagonism toward new art (musical or otherwise) emerging from Cuba. With the changes in Cuban politics in the 1990s, this is softening somewhat.

For many Cuban patrons, zarzuela represents the practices of a Cuba remembered, and Spanish zarzuelas (although still performed in Castro's Cuba) carry idealistic connections to the old republic shaped by an assumed acceptance of the international dominance of European order, capitalism, and class distinction.[10] As noted before, zarzuelas provide music and drama with popular appeal and elite aspirations. Creole variants question the social order established by Spain in its colonies. Some even celebrate the non-European heritage and native-born concerns that distinguish local territories. These perspectives challenge the legitimacy of the very circles of power to which many presenters in America aspire. Creole plots tackle issues of racism and social discrimination. The realities these works address touch on concerns Hispanic Americans in the United States confront on a daily basis. Unlike the Spanish zarzuela, Cuban zarzuelas, like the creole variants found in Argentina, Uruguay, and elsewhere in Latin America, cannot be presented as distant, escapist (and often amusing) morality tales. In the hands of an innovative director such as René Buch or Pablo Zinger, however, they can be reshaped to address modern concerns. Repertorio Español's new productions such as *Cuentos Afro-Caribeños* and *Serenata Dominicana* (Dominican Serenade) meet this challenge. Some argue that such restructuring is akin to new composition in the genre, but these works make zarzuela and related lyric theater into contemporary fare. They also respond to demographic realities in the United States and across the nation, where Hispanics of Afro-Caribbean ancestry are a large portion of the population. Still, these responses make no attempt to recreate original contexts for African-influenced practice but instead are cast in the comfortable frame of the formal theatrical or concert stage.[11]

Physical interaction as well as ideological perspectives shapes presentation efforts and the resulting implications for ethnic identification. Producers outside New York more frequently encourage interactions between resident and international artists. This is especially the case in the American Southwest, where producers profit from their location near the border between Mexico and the United States. Recall that in El Paso, for example, American companies shared the stage with Mexican performers, both individual artists and entire troupes.

In contrast, only recently has Repertorio Español had direct contact with artists in Cuba (although guest directors and collaborators from elsewhere in Latin America have worked with the New York company). When the company's executive producer, Gilberto Zaldívar, traveled to Cuba in 1995, he risked incurring the ire of many of the theater's loyal patrons. He nonetheless reported that he did not regret the trip and returned to New York inspired.[12] This inspiration found voice in several new projects. In 1998 Repertorio Español won an extended collaboration grant from the Theatre Communications Group and Metropolitan Life Foundation to bring noted Cuban playwright Abelardo Estorino and four actors from Cuba's innovative Hubert de Blanc Theatre to New York City for a month-long residency to work on a stage adaptation of the classic nineteenth-century Cuban novel *Cecilia Valdés.* These opportunities have contributed to a shift in Repertorio Español's programming and a new definition of itself as a Latino theater.

From the vantage point of the late 1990s, there appear to be several directions in zarzuela programming, each with different implications regarding the projection of identity. There are the revivalists; New York's Thalia Spanish Theater is one of the best at this effort. There are those who wish to find a place for zarzuela alongside standard operatic repertoire; Plácido Domingo is the most visible spokesperson for this effort, but the activities of Pablo Zinger and Victor Chacón are more consistent, if more ecumenical. Zinger sees zarzuela as one way to merge interest and support for popular music with involvement in classical musical in the United States. Finally, there are the innovators with more daring views regarding theater and identity, those who are not content to see zarzuela as historical repertoire: René Buch and those working at Repertorio Español are the obvious examples.

At times these visions overlap, and presenters adopt a combination of several basic positions. In general promoters seek to gain recognition for the cultural genius of Hispanic artists. All seek to represent a larger Hispanic population, not limited by natal ancestry. All are interested in the finest cultural representation, if not in Domingo's concern for the "elevation" of public taste.

In the final analysis, Gordon's concept of eth-class may be insufficient. The intersection of ethnicity and social status within the boundaries of a broadly defined ethnic group, such as Hispanic, may be less important than efforts to redefine social status (and artistic status) across large ethnic boundaries. The decision of the editors of *Opera News* to devote an entire issue to zarzuela suggests that the revival efforts are working at some level. Although such efforts reinforce American perceptions of the links between European and Latin America culture, others are reviving Creole concerns for self-identification. *Cecilia Valdés,* like *Cuentos Afro-Caribeños,* may speak to those of Caribbean ancestry no matter what their specific nationality. Likewise, these productions might foster new alliances among patrons whose ancestries include some dimension of African heritage. The secret of the New York Spanish theaters seems to lie in their ability to satisfy specific home audiences while gaining wider attention. If presented in ways that address the tensions between African and European ancestry in formats that accommodate classical concert and stage traditions, these works also promise to bring together patrons from diverse backgrounds, bridging divisions between social classes and ethnic groups.

The conclusion that makes sense of so many diverse developments and approaches is this: the potency of zarzuela and related Spanish lyric theater lies as much in the ways that Americans produce and receive these dramas as in their musical and textual content. New York producers have always been among the most willing to interpret the old traditions. The visions and the backgrounds of those who produce zarzuelas have contributed to this attitude. Zarzuela offers entertainment and a stepping stone toward recognition and opportunity. The future of zarzuela in this country will depend on how well its presenters continue to find flexible ways to treat the genre so that it both builds and serves its supporting constituency.

Appendix A

A Chronological Compilation of a Century of Zarzuela and Related Lyric Theater Presented in New York

Date of Production	Title/Description of Production	Director/Company/ Sponsor	Location
Dec. 1895	Zarzuelas: *Niña Pancha, Don Segismundo, Tragarse la Píladora*	Luis Baralt and Co. (Cuban-born director)[a]	Berkeley Lyceum
Feb. 5, 1898	*La Gallega Ciega* (J. M. Bermejo), *Robo en Despoblado* (R. Carrión and V. Arza)	Club Lírico Dramático Cubano (Luis Baralt, dir.)	Carnegie Lyceum
Mar. 19, 1898	*Su Excelencia, Con la Música de Otra Parte* (Vital Arza)	"	"
June 1898	*Los Hugonotes* (J. Echegaray)	"	"
Jan. 16, 1899	*No lo Quiero Saber* (listed as a *jugete*)	"	Central Opera House
1905	(Repertoire unavailable)	Manuel García and Co.	unavailable
1916–17	Zarzuelas and *sainetes* by Vital Arza, Angel Guimará, and the Alvarez Quintero brothers	Manuel Noriega and the Compañía Dramática Española	Teatro Leslie Amsterdam Opera House Carnegie Hall
1917	*La Tierra Alegre,* a bilingual production	Quinito Valverde with a company of fifty Spanish artists	Park Theater
Oct.–Dec. 1918	Zarzuelas and *entremeses* including *El Contrabando, Ya Somos Tres, Los Chorros de Oro, El Terrible Pérez, La Guerra*	Quinito Valverde and Co.	Amsterdam Opera House

Date of Production	Title/Description of Production	Director/Company/ Sponsor	Location
	Capitana, Los Tientos, Los Granujas, Fea con Gracia, El Puñao de Rosas, Eden Concert (a *revista*), *La Macarena, Los Chicos de la Escuela, San Juan de Luz, La Gatita Blanca, El Amor Asusta, Los Guapos, La Alegría de la Huerta, Tony o la Risa del Payaso, La Reja de Dolores, La Borrica*		
1919	*San Juan de Luz, Las Campanadas, El Caperucito, Películas Callejeras, La Real Gana, Mala Hembra, Apaga y Vámanos*	"	"
Mar. 1919	*Maruxa, Marina, Los Bohemios, La Corte de Faraón*	Manuel Noriega and his Grand Opera and Zarzuela Company	Park Theater under the name of El Teatro Español
July–Oct. 1919	*La Viejecita* (operetta) *Musas Latinas, Marina, Molinos de Viento* (zarzuelas)	"	Cort Theatre
1920	*El Gato Montés*	unavailable	Park Theater
1920s	*Los Gavilanes, La Princesa de Dólar, El Conde de Luxemburgo, Carceleras, La Viuda Alegre*	unavailable	Casa Galicia
1921	*El Terrible Pérez, La Mala Sombra* (Serrano), *Tío . . . Yo No He Sido* (Pérez y González and A. Rubio), *El Lucero del Alba* (M. Pina), *Ruido de Campanas* (A. Viergol)	Pilar Arcos and the Compañía de Zarzuela Española Arcos-Sardina	63d St. Theatre
1921	*Bufos cubanos: Pobre Papá Montero, Las Mulatas de Bombay*	Arquímedes Pous and the Compañía de Bufos Cubanos	14th St. Bramhall and Olympic Theatres
	La Bandera (a *bufo cubano*) *Del Puerto a la Gloria* (*revista*)	Compañía Narcisín	Park Palace Theatre

Date of Production	Title/Description of Production	Director/Company/ Sponsor	Location
1922	Unidentified set of comedies, Spanish zarzuelas, and *revistas*	Compañía de Marita Ríos; Compañía de Pilar Arcos	Dalys Theater
1925	Zarzuelas, Cuban *bufos,* and Italian operas including *Cavalleria Rusticana,* and *Pagliacci*	La Compañia de Zarzuela Española Antonio Trujillo with Marita Reid, appearing alongside the Compagnia de Opera Italiana Verdi	
1925–26	unavailable	Compañía de Zarzuelas, directed by Pilar Arcos and Fortunato Bonanova	Dalys Theater
	Comedies, melodramas, zarzuelas, vaudeville, variety acts	La Compañía Teatro Lírico Española, directed by Manuel Aparicio with Marita Ríos	"
1927	Various zarzuelas and *bufos cubanos* such as *Tres para Una, La Herencia del Amigo, En la Calle 116*	Compañía Lírica Española	Teatro Alhambra
1928	*Bufos cubanos: Cubita Bella, Si Papá lo Mandó*	Compañía Hispana de Nueva York with Alberto O'Farrill	"
1929	Zarzuela: *El Hombre de las Tres Mujeres*	Compañía Artistas Unidos	
1930	Puerto Rican zarzuela: *Día de Reyes*	"	
1930	Zarzuela version of Vicente Blasco Ibáñez's *Sangre y Arena* and Ruperto Fernández's Cuban zarzuela *Un Toque en el Trigémino (o las Curas del Dr. Asuero)*	Gran Compañía de Zarzuela Española, Gran Compañía de Zarzuelas Cubanas	Teatro Español (Apollo)
	unavailable	Compañía de Bufos Cubanos, Gran Compañía de Zarzuela Española, starring Alberto O'Farrill	"
1930–41	Various zarzuelas (titles unavailable)	Cuadro Declamación	Casa Galicia

Date of Production	Title/Description of Production	Director/Company/ Sponsor	Location
1931	*Los Sin Trabajo* (Cuban zarzuela)	unavailable	Teatro San José
1932	Puerto Rican zarzuela: *Día de los Reyes* (Rafael Hernández)	Compañía de Fernando Luis and Francisco Gomez	Teatro Variedades
Apr. 23, 1933	*Gigantes y Cabezudos*	Ateneo Hispano	Hamilton House
Mar. 1935	*La Dolorosa*	A week-long run by unidentified artists	5th Avenue Theater
May 1935	*El Puñao de Rosas*	A week-long run by unidentified artists	Mansfield
Jan. 1936	*Los Claveles*	A week-long run by unidentified artists	Campoamor
Apr. 4, 1936	*La Viejecita*	Spanish Institute of Columbia University	McMillan Theater
Oct.–Dec. 1936	*Los Africanistas, Fea con Gracia, Los Chicos de las Escuelas, El Pobre Valbuena*		El Calpe Americano
1937	*La Gatita Blanca*	Mexican comic soprano María Luisa Crespo, Puerto Rican comic tenor Jaime Estrella, Puerto Rican soprano Raquel Abella, and Venezuelan actor and later director Luis Mandret	unavailable
Sept. 26 and Oct. 9, 1937	*De Padre, Muy Señor Mío, La Trapera*	Marita Reid, dir., and Cuadro Artístico del Calpe Americano	El Calpe Americano
Jan. 15, 1938	*Las Estrellas*	"	"
Sept. 27, 1938	*Agua, Azucarillos, y*	"	"
Oct. 11, 1938	*Aguardiente, La Señora*		
Nov. 24, 1941	*Capitana, El Amor Ciego*		
Nov. 1941 (week)	*La Condesa María*	Marita Reid	Radio Teatro Teatro Hispano
Mar. 28, 1942	*La Buena Sombra*	Marita Reid, dir., and Cuadro Artístico del Calpe	El Calpe Americano
Nov. 15, 1942	*La Leyenda del Beso,* concert version with full orchestra	unavailable	Cosmopolitan
Jan. 1, 1946	*Maruxa*	unavailable	Centro Español
Feb. 17, 1946	*Maruxa*	unavailable	Central Opera House
Oct. 16, 1948	*Las Leandras* (*revista humorista)*	unavailable	Palm Garden
Oct. 23, 1950	Concert of zarzuela arias	Victoria de Los Angeles	Town Hall

Date of Production	Title/Description of Production	Director/Company/ Sponsor	Location
Fall 1956	*Marina*	Teatro Lírico Experimental	Nuevo Círculo Dramático
1962	*Cecilia Valdés*	Performers included Cuban singer Martha Pérez and Venezuelan tenor Alfredo Sadel	Carnegie Hall
July 1969	*Fiesta in Madrid* (a version of *La Verbena de la Paloma*)	Tito Capobianco and members of the New York City Opera	City Center
Apr. 19, 1973	Recital of zarzuela arias	Monserrat Caballé	Carnegie Hall
Jan. 24, 1974	*Marina,* concert version with piano accompaniment	unavailable	Carnegie Recital Hall
June 1974	*La Viuda Alegre* (5)	Miguel De Grandy, dir., Victor del Corral, prod.	City Center
1974–75	*Luisa Fernanda, Los Gavilanes, La Verbena de la Paloma*	Miguel De Grandy, dir., José Bovantes, prod.	Town Hall
1981–82	*La Corte de Faraón*	Repertorio Español	Teatro Repertorio Español
Dec. 1983	*Viva la Zarzuela,* a concert of zarzuela selections	Asociación Pro Zarzuela en América	Alice Tully Hall
1983 (1986)	*Doña Francisquita,* staged with piano accompaniment	Repertorio Español	Teatro Repertorio Español
Dec. 1, 1984	Zarzuela arias in concert	Asociación Pro Zarzuela en América	Carnegie Hall
1985	*Spanish Zarzuela Favorites*	Ilya Martínez and Rafael LeBron with the Brooklyn Philharmonic	Prospect Park Bandshell
1985–86	*Luisa Fernanda*	Repertorio Español	Repertorio Español
Feb. 3, 1985	*Songs of Spain,* a solo concert including zarzuela arias	Alfredo Kraus	Alice Tully Hall
Mar.–Aug. 1985	*La Verbena de la Paloma*	Thalia Spanish Theatre	Thalia Theater
Aug. 1985	*Antología de la Zarzuela*	Plácido Domingo with José Tamayo and Co.	Madison Square Garden
Sept. 20, 1985	Zarzuela Recital (9)	Mario Valdivielso, baritone, and Josu Gallastegui, from Amigos de la Zarzuela	Museum of the City of New York
Nov. 2, 1985	*Zarzuela in Concert*	Evangelina Colón and friends (3 singers, 4 dancers); cosponsored by the Spanish Consulate	Alice Tully Hall

Date of Production	Title/Description of Production	Director/Company/ Sponsor	Location
Nov. 3, 6, 10 13, 17, 20, 1985	*El Barberillo de Lavapiés*	Concertante Musical Society	Rincón Taino
Nov. 11–12, 1985	*El Barberillo de Lavapiés*	"	William Redfield Theater
Dec. 12, 1985	*El Barberillo de Lavapiés*	"	El Museo del Barrio
Apr.–Aug. 1986	*Los Gavilanes*	Thalia Spanish Theatre	Thalia Theatre
Apr. 1986 (week)	*Antología de la Zarzuela*	José Tamayo and Co.	Madison Square Garden
Oct. 18, 1986	Zarzuela selections	José Carreras and the Metropolitan Opera Orchestra	Avery Fischer Hall
Nov. 8, 1986	Zarzuela Gala Concert	Singers and pianist sponsored by Amigos de la Zarzuela	Cami Hall
1987	*La Corte de Faraón*	Repertorio Español	Repertorio Español/ Equitable
1987	*La Revoltosa*	Thalia Spanish Theatre	Thalia Spanish Theatre
1988	*Molinos de Viento*	"	"
1988	*La Generala*	Repertorio Español	Repertorio Español/ Equitable
1989	*La del Manojo de Rosas*	Thalia Spanish Theatre	Thalia Spanish Theatre
1990	*El Barbero de Sevilla*	"	"
1991	*Los Claveles*	"	"
1992	*Las Leandras*	"	"
1992	*Los Jíbaros Progresistas* (Manuel González); *Luisa Fernanda*	Repertorio Español	Repertorio Español/ Equitable
1993	*Luisa Fernanda*	"	Repertorio Español
1994	*¡Y se Armó la Mojiganga!*	"	Repertorio Español/ Equitable
1994	*La Tempranica*	Thalia Spanish Theatre	Thalia Spanish Theatre
1995	*La Dolorosa*	"	"

Note: This is not a comprehensive catalog, but it is representative. The appendix is meant to show how programming of Spanish-language zarzuela and related lyric theater in New York changed over the course of a century. To obtain information on productions, I surveyed microfilm copies of the Spanish-language newspaper *La Prensa,* New York daily edition, 1932–50 (an incomplete run is available at the New York Public Library). Data were also obtained from a survey of current newspapers, including the *New York Times,* the *Village Voice,* and the *New York Daily News;* examination of clippings files obtained from the Billy Rose Theatre Collection of the New York Public Library; and consultation of two periodicals, *Reporter Teatral* and *Revista Hispanica Moderna,* the journal published by the Hispanic Institute of America. Most of the information on productions prior to 1930 was obtained from Richard Aldrich, *Concert Life in New York, 1902–1923* (New York: G.P. Putnam's Sons, 1941); Pablo Figueroa, *Teatro: Hispanic Theatre in New York City, 1920–1976,* El Museo del Barrio exhibition catalog, April 22–June 3, 1977; and Nicolás Kanellos, *A History of Hispanic Theatre in the United States: Origins to 1940* (Austin: University of Texas Press, 1990).

a. Luis Baralt was a celebrated scholar, playwright, director, and leader in the establishment of the modern theatrical movement in Cuba beginning in the 1920s. One of his aims was to make serious theater that connected to contemporary experience. He was the director of the influential Cuban theatrical company La Cueva (The Cave) in the 1930s. Information on Baralt and his contributions to contemporary theater can be obtained in Natividad González Freire, *Teatro cubano, 1927–61* (Cuban Theater, 1927–61), 2d ed. (Havana: Ministerio de Relaciones Exteriores, 1961).

Names of Theaters Mentioned and Their Locations

Alice Tully Hall: Lincoln Center, Broadway at West Sixty-seventh St.
Avery Fisher Hall: Lincoln Center
El Calpe Americano: 366 Third Ave., between Twenty-sixth and Twenty-seventh Sts.
Casa Galicia: West Sixty-fourth St. (during the 1920s)
CAMI Hall: 165 West Fifty-seventh St.
Carnegie Hall: 154 West Fifty-seventh St.
Center Theater: Forty-ninth St. and Sixth Ave.
Central Opera House: 205–15 East Sixty-seventh St.
Centro Español: N/A
City Center: 131 West Fifty-fifth St.
Cosmopolitan Opera House: 135 West Fifty-fifth St.
El Museo del Barrio: Fifth Ave. and 104 St.
Fifth Avenue Theatre: Broadway and Twenty-eighth St.
Hamilton House: N/A
McMillan Theater: 116 St. and Broadway (Columbia University)
Museum of the City of New York: 103 St. and Fifth Ave.
Nuevo Círculo Dramático: 1129 Sixth Ave. (between Forty-third and Forty-fourth Sts.)
Park Theater: 5 Columbus Circle, once known as "New York's Foreign Opera House," according to Richard Davis, *A History of Music in American Life*, 3 vols. (Malabar, Fla.: Robert E. Krieger, 1982).
Radio Teatro Hispano (Radio T.H.): 116 St. and Fifth Ave.
Repertorio Español: 138 East Twenty-seventh St.
Rincón Taíno: 113 East Twelfth St.
Teatro Campoamor: 116 St. and Fifth Ave.
Thalia Spanish Theatre: 41–17 Greenpoint Ave., Sunnyside (Queens)
Theatre Mansfield: 256 West Forty-seventh St.
Webster Hall: 119 East Eleventh St.
William Redfield Theatre: 354 West Forty-fifth St.

Appendix B

Program Summaries for Hispanic Theaters at Two New York Locations, 1932–41

The following summary lists the kinds of programs offered by various New York Hispanic theaters between 1932 and 1941. Because the theaters most renowned for Spanish-language productions frequently changed names, general directors, and programming format, I have organized the summary according to location. The data are drawn from my surveys of New York's largest Spanish-language newspaper, *La Prensa,* and have been supplemented by discussions included in Nicolás Kanellos, *A History of Hispanic Theatre in the United States: Origins to 1940* (Austin: University of Texas Press, 1990).

Theater at 125 Street

Apollo (intermittent and Sunday programs)

Year	Company/Artists	Type of Program
1926–27	Compañía de Bufos Cubanos, Christina R. Inclán	Weekly performances of *bufos cubanos*
1927	Trío Borinquen	
1928	Compañía Española de Zarzuelas, Comedias y Variedades, directed by Ramón Reynado	
1928	(Galician) La Compañía Narcisín	Melodrama, zarzuela, Galician drama, and Puerto Rican dramas, including Erasmo Vando's *De Puerto Rico al Metropolitano o El Caruso Criollo*

Teatro Español (came under new management and was renamed in 1929)

Programming by the Miranda brothers alternated Spanish, Cuban, and Puerto Rican shows mixed with lyric theater, vaudeville, and musical revues.

Year	Company/Artists	Type of Program
1930	Gran Compañía de Zarzuela Española, Gran Compañía de Zarzuelas Cubanas, Scandals and Follies	Spanish zarzuela, Cuban zarzuela, and American vaudeville, frequently on the same bill, including *bufos cubanos: Cuba en el Año 2000; El Espiritista, El Negro que Tenía el Alma Blanca, Los Africanistas, Ked Chocolate, La Mulata, El Tabaquero o Un Negro en Sevilla,* and *Menéalo que se Empelota*
1933–36		Periodic performances of Spanish zarzuela
1934–36	Grupo Artístico Cervantes (an amateur ensemble)	Two- and three-act comedies such as *Los Gatos*

Theater at 110 St. and Fifth Ave.

Teatro San José

This theater featured programming designed to appeal to diverse Hispanic nationalities, including shows related to Hispanic life in New York, Caribbean negritude, and Puerto Rican nationalism.

Year	Company/Artists	Type of Program
1931	Compañía Fernando Luis (Cuban)	Standard zarzuelas and Cuban zarzuelas
1932	Rodrigo Lila y su Compañía	*Revistas* such as *El Hombre que Asesino, Una Noche en España, Modernismo, Bata-Klan, El Bodeguero, Carnaval de Amor, La Alegría de Vivir*
	Compañía Revistas de Sergio Rojas	Musical revues and workers' dramas, including the Puerto Rican *revista: Cuando la Vida Suena,* featuring songs by Rafael Hernández

Variedades (after 1933)

The staged works at the Variedades remained under the direction of Fernando Luis. After 1933 films received top billing.

Year	Company/Artists	Type of Program
1933	Compañía de Revistas de Fernando Luis y Francisco Gómez	Films receive top billing, but *revistas* with a creole perspective also appear, such as *La Floración,* a Puerto Rican revue with an overt political theme, and *Cayó la Tirana,* a concert of mountain music
1933	Cuarteto Canario musical presentations	Cuban and Puerto Rican

Teatro Borinquen (from 1935)

Under this name the theater offered social dramas, as well as works staged in English.

Teatro Latino (after 1941)

Under this name, the theater was primarily a movie house, but *revistas,* musicals and *operetas* were offered in filmed versions.

Theater at 116 St. and Fifth Ave

Campoamor (1934–36)

Originally this theater operated as the Mt. Morris Theater, beginning in 1913. When it opened in 1932 under Hispanic management (led by the team of Marcial Flóres and Fernando Luis), it was renamed for the Spanish romantic poet Ramón del Campoamor.

Year	Company/Artists	Type of Program
1934–35	Miguel De Grandy joins the regular cast of singers, dancers, and *bufo* actors, including "El Negrito," Alberto O'Ferrill	*Revistas* such as *Fin de Año, Una Feria de Puerto Rico*
1935	Companies from Spain and Latin America, particularly Cuba, Argentina, Mexico, and Puerto Rico, appeared for special presentations	Shows included a week-long homage to Puerto Rican composer Rafael Hernández
1936	Compañía de Zarzuelas Españolas	A week of zarzuelas including *Los Claveles*
1936	Eliseo Grenet and his orchestra	Cuban *revistas*

El Teatro Cervantes (July 1936–Feb. 1937)

As with the Teatro Latino, the theater began to emphasize film but also offered variety acts and *revistas* such as *De Puerto Rico a Nueva York.*

El Teatro Hispano (1937–50)

Year	Company/Artists	Type of Program
1937–40	Data unavailable	A wide array of *revistas, bufos,* and *variedades*
1939–50s	Under the general direction of Señor del Pozo, Mexican orchestra	Movies and three daily stage shows, at 2:00, 5:30, and 9:00 P.M., except on

Year	Company/Artists	Type of Program
	leader whose vaudeville troupe became the theater's stock company	Sundays, when four shows were given, at 1:30, 4:30, 7:00, and 9:30
Oct. 1939	La Gran Compañía de Bufos Cubanos y Zarzuela Española arrived from Cuba on its tour of the United States, Spain, and Puerto Rico	The featured film was *Tres Argentinos en Paris,* and the traveling stage show included a revue called *Cuba, España, y Puerto Rico*
Feb. 1941	Cuban company of Leopoldo Fernández arrived	A special series of Cuban *bufo* dramas
Nov. 1941	Marita Reid and Co. performed regularly	The featured stage show was the zarzuela *La Condesa María*

Appendix C

A Comparison of Musical Productions at Three Hispanic Theaters in the New York Metropolitan Area

Repertorio Español, 138 East Twenty-seventh St., New York

Staged Zarzuelas

La Corte de Faraón	Opened in 1981, revived in 1987
Doña Francisquita	Opened in 1983, placed in repertory, performed again in 1986
Luisa Fernanda	Opened in 1985, placed in repertory, performed again in 1986 and in 1992
Los Jíbaros Progresistas	1991, showcase production of this contemporary zarzuela by Puerto Rican composer Manuel González
La Generala	Opened in 1988
La Viuda Alegre	Opened in 1990

Other Musical Productions

The Fantasticks	1980
El Cónsul (opera)	Opened in 1990, 1992
¡Y se Armó la Mojiganga!	Opened in 1994
Pilar Rioja (flamenco dance)	Ongoing yearly engagements

Productions That Include Zarzuela Excerpts

¡Habana!	A musical anthology, opened in 1982; still in repertory 1986–87, revised and performed in 1988
Puerto Rico: Encanto y Canción	Opened in 1984, still in repertory 1986–87
La Revista de la Zarzuela	Opened in 1988, placed in repertory
Cuentos Afro-Caribeños	Opened in 1996, still running in 1999

Thalia Spanish Theatre, Sunnyside, Queens

Staged Zarzuelas

La Verbena de la Paloma	Opened in April 1985, ran for five months
Los Gavilanes	Opened in April 1986, ran for five months
La Revoltosa	1986, 1987
La Tabernera del Puerto	1987
Molinos de Viento	1988
La del Manojo de Rosas	1989
El Barbero de Sevilla	1990
Los Claveles	1991
Las Leandras	1992
Potpourri de Zarzuela	1993
La Tempranica	Opened in 1994
Potpourri de Zarzuela	1994
Potpourri de Zarzuela	1995
La Dolorosa	1995
Agua, Azucarillos, y Aguardiente	1996
La del Soto del Parral	1997
La del Soto del Parral	1998
La Parranda	1999

Other Musical Theater

La Brujita	Children's musical play (1977)
El Globo Felíz	Children's musical play (1978)

La Asociación de Teatro Musical, Union City, New Jersey

Staged Zarzuelas

La Viuda Alegre	June 13, 1982
La Leyenda del Beso	Nov. 20–21, 1982
Las Leandras	Apr. 16–17, 23–24, 1983; revived Mar. 1986
Luisa Fernanda	Nov. 26–27, 1983
Los Gavilanes	June 1983
La Viuda Alegre	Revived Apr. 28–29, 1984

Other Musical Productions

Fiddler on the Roof	Apr./May 1982, the premiere performance of this company, in English
Ochún Mayéye	Sept. 11–12, 18–19, 1992, a folkloric Afro-Cuban

	musical based on a legend about the Yoruba deity Ochún
Man of La Mancha	Oct. 29–31, 1982, in English
Godspell	Dec. 10–12, 1982, in English
Roko!	Sept. 1983, another folkloric Afro-Cuban work
Italy and Its Music	June 8, 1986, a concert of opera arias, duets, and songs

Glossary

Apropósito: An introductory dramatic form in the style of an entr'act.

Auto: A Spanish dramatic work in one act preceded by a prologue, or *loa. Autos* were most often treatments of sacred or allegorical subjects and were performed on religious feast days, such as the feast of Corpus Christi.

Autos sacramentales: Short religious dramas.

Baile: Literally, a dance. In Mexico the freer, more rambunctious *bailes* contrasted with the well-mannered *danzas.* In the theater this term may refer to an entr'act where dance is the primary attraction. Also popular were *bailes cantados,* which were sung from start to finish.

Bufo: A term meaning "comic," or "comedy," frequently used to refer to a theatrical genre with a mocking, joking flavor.

Bufos cubanos: Cuban light theater in the comic, or *bufo,* tradition.

Bolero: A Spanish dance in triple meter originating in the late eighteenth century and frequently performed by a pair of dancers with castanets. The nineteenth-century Cuban *bolero* is a duple-meter dance and song form characterized by distinctive interlocking rhythmic patterns.

Cacucha: A popular dance in triple meter of Andalusian origin. It is related to the *fandango.*

Canción cubana: A song complex that embodies Afro-Cuban forms and styles of singing.

Carretero: A wagon cart driver.

Castizo: Traditional, very Spanish; pure Castilian.

Catalanes: People from the Spanish province of Catalonia.

Chispa: Literally, spark. In Latin America the term may refer to a dance as well.

Chispero/a: A drunk.

China: China or Chinese; also a peasant girl or girl of mixed ancestry; also a term of endearment.

Chulapa: A pretty girl of lower-class status.

Coloquio: A dialogue song.

Comedia: A full-length drama (lasting sometimes two to three hours) in several (usually three) acts, frequently featuring elaborate stage machinery, gaudy costumes, and expensive sets and pageantry.

Cómicos: A term for comic actors.

Contradanza: The Spanish version of the English country dance made popular in the eighteenth-century French courts as the *contredanse*. The dance included rapid figures in duple meter, in the square dance tradition. The *contradanza* became extremely popular in Cuba.

Coplas: Couplets, or two-line sets. Most typically this term refers to a four-line stanza or strophe with a rhyme scheme of *abcb. Coplas* are frequently part of longer song forms such as the *romance* or *villancico,* but they might also be performed as separate works.

Corrales: Courtyards, which were turned into theater sites by enterprising performers.

Costumbrista: Featuring local custom and color.

Criollismo: A perspective that takes pride in recognizing the non-European contributions to blended ancestry that were devalued during colonial rule; a perspective born of, or nurtured in, New World settings.

Criollo: A term referring to persons, traditions, or products born in the New World but bearing European ancestry (akin to the French *créole*).

Da capo aria: A song form, characteristic of Italian opera, in which the opening section returns to close the performance, resulting in an overall ABA structure. The repeated section is typically an opportunity for the performer to ornament or elaborate on the original material.

Danzas: Elegant, well-measured, and stately dances; another name for the *contradanza* in Cuba and Puerto Rico.

Danzón: A Cuban social dance derived from the *contradanza.* The figures of the *danzón* were more complex; developments of the *danzón* include the *mambo* and the *cha-cha-chá.*

Décima: Poetic song form featuring a series of ten lines; often improvised, sometimes in competition.

Dengue: Literally, a tantrum; also a frenzied type of dance.

Écloga: Eclogue, an ancient form of pastoral poem. By the fifteenth century the *écloga* was a well-established dramatic genre made popular by Juan del Encina (1468–1529).

Entremés: Literally, "Between acts." The term refers to a brief entr'act drama that took several forms and that frequently punctuated the set acts of comic and tragic plays such as the *comédias* of the seventeenth and eighteenth centuries.

Estribillo: A refrain.

Espectáculo: A show or spectacle.

Espectáculos de hora: Hour-long shows.

Fiesta de música: A multiact stage piece featuring song and dance alternating with spoken drama and verse. Such productions generally minimized stage machinery and elaborate pageantry.

Fiesta de zarzuela: Originally a one-act work featuring music and spoken verse as well as elaborate costumes and stage effects.

Fiestas de la Zarzuela: Literally, celebrations at the Zarzuela Palace. The term was used to describe the earliest zarzuelas in the sixteenth and seventeenth centuries. These were short plays without elaborate settings in which instrumental music and song were paramount.

Fin de fiesta: Literally, "end of the performance"; another popular entr'act form serving to punctuate and define a longer drama as well as entertain viewers during set changes and transitions. The term was often connected to the staged *mojiganga,* which also provided a jolly closing to an evening of entertainment and commonly closed performances of early zarzuelas.

Funciones completas: A complete evening of entertainment lasting several hours, which might include a substantial drama, such as a *comedia,* along with other, shorter presentations.

Funciones por horas: Hour-long events or programs.

Gallego/a: A Spaniard from Galicia.

Gavotas: A baroque court dance in duple meter.

Género chico: Literally, "minor genre"; used to refer to relatively informal one-act zarzuelas.

Género grande: A major dramatic genre. See *zarzuela grande.*

Género ínfimo: A nineteenth-century development of zarzuela. The genre was a decadent form of lyric theater based on the French variety shows and featuring crude humor and action.

Gitano/-na: A Gypsy.

Gorgoritos: Trills, associated with coloratura in contemporary practice.

Grilles: Literally, grills; a seating area in the theater.

Guajiro/-ra: A Cuban peasant; someone from the hinterlands; in Colombia or Venezuela, a person from the Guajira Peninsula; also a type of rural music of strong Hispanic influence featuring songs known as *puntos* and ensembles of string instruments such as the *guitarra, tres,* or *laúd.*

Guaguancó: A popular Cuban dance of the rhumba type.

Guaracha: Cuban song and dance music reflecting Afro-Cuban influence of multilayered rhythms and call-and-response sections using a soloist and chorus. The form became popular with dance bands and in theatrical works of the nineteenth and twentieth centuries.

Guineo: A Mexican dance with African influence.

Habanera: A nineteenth-century Cuban song and dance form featuring a slow to moderate duple meter and a characteristic dotted-eighth–sixteenth rhythm followed by two even eighths. Its name reflects its origins in Havana, from which city it spread to Spain, other European countries, and Latin America.

Humorada: A short comic skit originally serving as an entr'act in the course of a full evening's theatrical entertainment. The term used to indicate the humorous nature of a drama or zarzuela.

Indígena: Indigenous; of Native American or Amerindian ancestry.

Jacalones: The popular, outdoor tent stages featuring *tandas* in nineteenth-century Mexico.

Jácara: Originally a literary form; later a popular light theatrical form performed between acts of a longer, more serious work. *Jácaras* traditionally concerned the plight of the rascals or villains in a play and were sung by one to six persons. By the seventeenth century this form had expanded to the proportions of a small comic opera with more popular and less aristocratic appeal than the earlier between-act form enjoyed. Musically the *jácara* developed as a lively ballad song with reference to street folk and high-spirited character. In the seventeenth and eighteenth centuries sacred *jácaras* also existed.

Jarabe: A lively Mexican folk dance featuring choreography suggesting sensuous courtship; according to Stevenson, a favorite with revolutionary soldiers.

Jota: Spanish folk dance and song. The song developed from ancient poetic forms; the lively dance takes several forms, one of which was originally associated with the province of Aragon and another type, freer in style, comes from Navarre.

Jugete: Literally, a plaything, a little card game, or a jest or joke. The *jugete* was a brief, fast-paced between-act drama mixing verse, music, and drama.

Lírico/-a: Lyric, sung, or songlike, as in *drama lírico.*

Loa: Literally, "praise"; used to describe the prologue to a Spanish dramatic work. The *loa* was a common feature of sixteenth- and seventeenth-century lyric theater. *Loas* were frequently positioned before the first act of a longer drama in an evening's entertainment. The *loa* might include praise for specific patrons, as well as a laudatory introduction to the genre, the medium, or the artists involved.

Madrileños: Residents of Madrid.

Majo/-a: Fashionable men and women of Madrid's lower classes, including Gypsies, of the late eighteenth and early nineteenth centuries.

Melólogo: An Argentinean stage work combining features of the *tonadilla* and the *sainete.*

Mendigo/-a: A beggar.

Mestizo: A person of mixed ancestry, usually Spanish and indigenous.

Minuetes de corte: Minuets in the style of the eighteenth-century court traditions.

Mojiganga: Originally another type of between-act entertainment; later a short burlesque or satiric piece, popular well into the eighteenth century. Plots often featured carnival-like elements of role reversal, such as humans dressing as animals, the poor besting the rich, or mortals overcoming the grip of death.

Montuno: Rhythmic and harmonic vamp used in Afro-Cuban dance and salsa music.

Montero: A hunter.

Moro: Moor, Muslim.

Negrito/-a: Literally, "little and black." The adjective was used to refer to Negro characters in *bufo* dramas and on the vaudeville stage. Although appearing as an endearment, the term bore a deprecatory sense as well, for the stage character was often portrayed in blackface.

Ñáñigo: Person belonging to one of the Afro-Cuban confraternities associated with the maintenance of African linguistic and ritual tradition on the island. Originally the Ñañigo were Carabalí, persons descended from tribes living along the border region between Nigeria and Cameroon. Over time membership in the group expanded to include persons of different ancestries, sometimes including white Creoles. The overriding group aesthetic continued to emphasize Afro-Cuban perspectives.

Opereta: Spanish operetta in the style of the comic satires blending spoken dialogue, song, and other entertainment that emerged in Central Europe during the mid-nineteenth century with the works of Offenbach, Strauss, and Lehár. Although this genre is clearly akin to the zarzuela, Spanish composers and audiences generally viewed *opereta* as a different branch of popular music drama. In the United States these distinctions have blurred.

Palcos: Box seats in the theater; theater boxes.

Pan de xarabe: A traditional Mexican dance (see *jarabe*).

Parodia: A parody scene.

Pasatiempo: Literally, a pastime; used to indicate the nature of a dramatic work or zarzuela.

Payo/-a: A word Gypsies use to refer to a non-Gypsy; also a peasant.

Peninsulares: Persons born on the Iberian Peninsula; Spanish and Iberian colonists.

Peones: Laborers; farmworkers.

Pequeñas zarzuelas: Brief (literally, small) zarzuelas, another term for the *género chico.*

Polaca: Literally, "Polish"; used in Spain and Latin America to refer to the triple-meter dance the polonaise.

Revista: A revue. The format developed in France in the late 1800s and spread to the rest of the world in the following century. The theatrical genre began as an opportunity to "review" the successes of an entire year in one large work. By the time the genre arrived in Spain, it was equally customary to create new collections of song, dance, and drama, without relying on the past year as an excuse to hold together the loosely combined numbers. When the genre spread to Hispanic America, it was less well known and was promoted by local theater and zarzuela companies. In the 1920s Spanish Americans would use the *revista* as an opportunity for satire and caricature of local politicians and politics. The irreverent nature of the *revista,* coupled with its growing tendency toward salacious innuendo and display, led some governments, like that of Avila Camacho in Mexico, to censor the form. For an engaging extended discussion of the *revista* in Mexico consult *Las Divas,* by Pablo Dueñas (1994).

Romance: In Spain, a balladlike song with a poetic text typically set as a series of sixteen-syllable strophes and dealing primarily with historical or legendary figures. The *villancico* bore characteristics of the *romance,* and in Spanish America the *décima* and the *corrido* (Mexico) developed from the *romance* tradition.

Romanza: Another term for *romance;* also, a song form influenced by romantic opera.

Romerías: Small traveling circuses.

Rumba: A type of Afro-Cuban, urban, collective celebration. The song and dance forms associated with these fiestas developed into separate genres featuring songs typically accompanied by an ensemble of Afro-Cuban drums known as *tumbadoras* or congas.

Sainete: A dramatic composition in one act, generally featuring comic, lower-class characters. The eighteenth-century Spanish author Juan de la Cruz made the *sainete* a vehicle for exploring local customs.

Salsa: Literally, sauce; used to refer to twentieth-century dance music based on Cuban and Puerto Rican traditions, popular throughout Latin America and the United States.

Sarao: An old-style, well-mannered Spanish dance. The term was later applied to a salon-style gathering of persons of high social status that included musical performance and dancing.

Seguidilla: A verse form featuring strophes of four or seven lines, each featuring between five to seven syllables. *Seguidillas* are frequently set to music in 6/8 meter and also represent one of the most popular Spanish dance forms.

Son: The tune used for dance songs; also, a Cuban song tradition forming a complex of genres. Originally accompanied by plucked string instruments and African-derived percussion instruments, these songs typically feature a call and response between a solo singer and chorus. Also found in Mexico.

Tanda: A segment of an entire evening of entertainment created by linking together several independent and unrelated works, including one-act plays, circus segments, dance numbers, and zarzuelas. Low-cost tickets were sold for each *tanda,* and patrons could choose how many to attend in an evening. In the case of longer works, such as a two- or three-act opera, each act would be considered a *tanda. Tandas* became extremely popular in Latin America after 1850.

Teatro por horas: A theater or company specializing in hour-long functions.

Telenovelas: Soap operas. Unlike their counterparts in the United States, Spanish and Latin American soap operas are usually designed to run for a finite period of time, more like a miniseries.

Tertulias: A salon-style gathering of intellectuals, artists, and musicians—a Spanish American version of a *soireé musicale.*

Tirana: A dance song frequently tied to folkloric practice in the northwestern region of the Iberian Peninsula, most notably the Spanish regions of Asturias and Galicia, as well as the countryside surrounding the Miño River extending into the Portuguese province of Minho.

Títeres: Puppeteer groups.

Tonada: A designation equivalent to "song." Distinctive characteristics are a melody sung in a monotone or recitation-like manner set to music of isometric rhythm. The *tonada* has a folkloric character and is considered to be a very expressive form. In Cuba it is the tune used to sing or recite *décimas.*

Tonadilla: A little song. In the theater such a song was often the last item in an *entremés.*

Tonadilla escénica: Literally, a scenic *tonadilla;* an eighteenth-century development from the *entremés* of classical zarzuelas and *comedias.* This new kind of drama featured songs, dancing, and even orchestral accompaniment. It was designed for a small number of singers (typically one to four) and lasted twenty minutes or less. *Tonadillas* featured music drawing on regional folk song and dance and local character types in funny or satiric plots. They were fashionable in the theaters of Madrid in the eighteenth century and were typically enjoyed and then discarded within a seven-day cycle.

Tono: Mode; liturgical chant song; a cappella folk song.

Vaudeville: A sequence of music, dance, and drama, often only thinly bound together by a theme or plot.

Villancico: A form of Spanish poetry that alternates a refrain, an *estribillo,* with one or more strophes called *coplas* or *pies.* Poetically each strophe features two kinds of lines, a *mudanza* (a change) or a *vuelta* (a return). The musical settings of this poetic form have varied from the thirteenth century to the present era, and thus the term's implications vary as well. *Villancicos* were popular additions to stage drama. Sixteenth-century *villancicos* include polyphonic, homophonic, and even single-voice settings. Seventeenth-century performance practice for both the *villancico* and the *romance* caused the distinction between the two genres to blur. It became a popular practice to add *estribillos* to *romances,* and in both the *villancico* and the *romance* it was common to perform the *estribillos* as instrumental settings. In the twentieth century the term *villancico* has become almost synonymous with "Christmas carol."

Zarabandas: A courtly dance popular well before the eighteenth century.

Zarzas: Bramble or blackberry bushes.

Zarzuela grande: Nineteenth-century form featuring one or two acts, akin to the French *opéra comique,* Italian opera buffa, or Viennese operetta. *Zarzuela grande* might treat serious subjects and even approach grand opera.

Zarzuelero: A person who composes or performs zarzuela.

Sources: In preparing this glossary, I consulted several standard reference sources, including *The New Grove Dictionary of Music and Musicians, The Harvard Dictionary of Music, The Oxford*

Spanish Dictionary, and *The Garland Encyclopedia of Music.* In addition, I am indebted to the following sources: Gerard Béhague, *Music in Latin America: An Introduction* (Englewood Cliffs, N.J.: Prentice-Hall, 1979); Patricia Bentivegna, "A Study of Three *Zarzuelas Madrileñas* Together with a Historical Outline of the Zarzuela" (Master's thesis, Columbia University, 1955); Pablo Dueñas, *Las divas en el teatro de revista mexicano* (The divas of Mexico's theatrical revues) (Mexico City, D.F.: Asociación Mexicana de Estudios Fonográficos, 1994); John Koegel, "Music: Nineteenth and Twentieth Centuries," in *Encyclopedia of Mexico,* ed. Michael Weiner (Chicago: Fitzroy and Dearborn, 1997), 2:984–97; Mary Montaño, "The Manuel Areu Collection of 19th-Century Zarzuelas" (Master's thesis, University of New Mexico, 1972); Craig Russell, ed., *Santiago de Murcia's "Códice Saldívar No. 4": A Treasury of Secular Guitar Music from Baroque Mexico,* vol. 1: *Commentary* (Urbana: University of Illinois Press, 1995); and Robert Stevenson, *Music in Mexico: A Historical Survey* (New York: Thomas Y. Crowell, 1952).

Notes

Introduction

1. It is not surprising to find the Virgin Mary symbolized by a dove in this fiesta and the dramas that celebrate it. The figure of the dove (*paloma*) is a popular symbol of both a messenger of love and the beloved in Spain and its colonies. John Koegel notes that doves often appear in both learned and folkloric Mexican poetry and song. The Festival of the Dove draws on a sacred, devotional reading of this symbol of love. See John Koegel, "Canciones del país: Mexican Musical Life in California after the Gold Rush," *California History* 78 (Fall 1999): 160–219.

2. After the Thalia Spanish Theatre began presenting zarzuela in 1985, the company continued to produce at least one zarzuela per year. As of 1999 it was the only New York company to be that consistent.

3. Perhaps the most overtly rebellious use of the zarzuela can found in the Philippines, where new *sarsuelas,* using Tagalog instead of Spanish, became popular during that country's movements for independence from Spain and the United States. For an examination of the "seditious" nature of the Philippine zarzuela, see Amelia Lapeña-Bonifacio, *The "Seditious" Tagalog Playwrights: Early American Occupation* (Manila: Zarzuela Foundation of the Philippines, 1972).

4. In 1980 Lionel Salter described the zarzuela as an expired genre and wrote that "the zarzuela appears to have run its meteoric course" (*The New Grove Dictionary of Music and Musicians* [1980], s.v. "zarzuela"). Critics of the zarzuela's dominance in popular musical life prior to 1950 include Chase and Sopeña Ibañez, and even dedicated revivalists such as Plácido Domingo are candid about the sloppy performance traditions that stigmatized many zarzuela productions in Spain and abroad. See Gilbert Chase, *The Music of Spain* (New York: Dover, 1959); Federico Sopeña Ibañez, *Historia de la música española contemporánea* (Madrid: Ediciones Rialp, 1958); and Plácido Domingo, *My First Forty Years* (New York: Knopf, 1983).

5. René Buch, interview with the author, New York City, July 11, 1985.

6. This argument recalls views expressed by Gilbert Chase in his *Handbook of Latin American Studies* (Cambridge, Mass.: Harvard University Press, 1943), 446. Robert Stevenson uses Chase's perspectives to bolster his argument for more studies of music that "touches the lives of many," noting that by applying ourselves to the so-called mediocre popular and commercially distributed music, we may "be able to reach nearer to the souls of the commonalty" (Robert Stevenson, *Music in Mexico* [New York: Thomas Crowell, 1952], 165–66). René Buch is in no way a champion of the mediocre (nor are most fans of zarzuela), but he *is* interested in reaching a wider public that would include those common souls about whom Stevenson speaks. The popular, yet frequently neglected zarzuela has also gained new attention from scholars who are coming to realize the impact this genre has had on the development of popular and classical music and theater in Spain and Latin America. Volumes 2 and 3 (1996–97) of *Cuadernos de música iberoamericana* contain thirty-three articles by scholars from Spain, Argentina, Chile, Colombia, Cuba, Mexico, and Venezuela concerning the history, characteristics, reception, and production of zarzuela.

7. René Buch, interview, July 11, 1985.

8. See Janet Sturman, "Zarzuela in New York: Contributions of Lyric Theatre to Hispanic Identity" (Ph.D. diss., Columbia University, 1987).

9. Much of the historical data used for the first three chapters of this book remains available only to readers of Spanish. There is a need for a detailed English-language compilation of this research in a widely available publication, and for this reason I cover the historical background of the genre in Spain and the New World in some detail. My historical overview is intended to be only representative, however, not comprehensive. My primary goal is to present a frame for my ethnographic research into contemporary productions.

10. These terms are not necessarily interchangeable, as I discuss in chapter 6.

11. Luis Valdez, *Early Works: Actos, Bernabe, and Pensamiento Serpentino* (Houston: Arte Publico, 1971), 12.

12. Valdez uses the pejorative term *gabacho* to denote the white European, a group he sees as too frequently setting the standards by which various aspects of Chicano experience are evaluated. A focus on the Spanish colonial heritage, claims Valdez, too often "obscures the indio fountains of Chicano culture" (see Valdez, *Early Works,* 7, 11).

13. The writings of Krister Malm and Roger Wallis remain the most important scholarly treatments of the recording industry's effects on traditional music production and the presentation of identity. See also "Patterns of Change," in Simon Frith and Andrew Goodwin, *On Record: Rock, Pop, and the Written Word* (New York: Pantheon Books, 1990).

Chapter 1: From the Spanish Court to Madison Square Garden

1. According to Bentivegna, although *El Laurel de Apolo* was originally intended for performance in one of the palaces of retreat, the one in the Pardo known as La Zarzuela, the birth of the prince Felipe Próspero caused the king to return to Madrid. The premiere

performance was delayed until March 4, 1658, when it took place in the Coliseo del Buen Retiro, a sumptuous theater built in 1639 and on which the theater in La Zarzuela was modeled (see Patricia Bentivegna, "A Study of Three *Zarzuelas Madrileñas* Together with a Historical Outline of the Zarzuela" [Master's thesis, Columbia University, 1955], 12–14).

2. See Louise Stein, *Songs of Mortals, Dialogues of the Gods: Music and Theatre in Seventeenth-Century Spain* (Oxford: Clarendon, 1993), 264.

3. Scholars view *El Laurel de Apolo* as the first work deserving of the name *zarzuela* because it unfolds in two acts, and its sung episodes form an integral part of the drama. Both features later emerged as essential characteristics of the seventeenth-century zarzuela. See D. Emilio Cotarelo y Mori, *Historia de la zarzuela o sea el drama lírico en España, desde su origen a fines del siglo xix* (Madrid: Tipografía de Archivos, 1934), 99.

4. This remarkable company, under the direction of Blanche Artis Lewis, stands out among American companies producing zarzuela because of its frequent collaborations with the Chicago Baroque Ensemble and its general support of early music, exemplified by the production of Torrejón y Velasco's operatic version of *La Púrpura de la Rosa.* This said, the majority of the zarzuelas the group has offered (all fully staged with orchestra) have been the late romantic favorites.

5. As noted in the introduction, this historical overview is not exhaustive. The endnotes and bibliography indicate the sources on which I based my work. The bibliography includes important works that I have examined but do not directly cite and that offer additional details regarding the history of zarzuela.

6. In *Songs of Mortals* Louise Stein examines in detail the genres of theater that gave rise to the zarzuela in the seventeenth century. This important work provides a critical appraisal of music's function in these dramatic forms and offers criteria for separating them into distinct genres.

7. Of all genres, the *romance*—its development, its transmission throughout the Luso-Hispanic world, and the resultant retentions and variants it inspired—has received the most scholarly attention. The bulk of the research has considered the romance from a literary perspective. The extensive publications of Margit Frenk Alatorre on these matters represent this tradition at its finest. Her numerous publications include Margit Frenk Alatorre, *Cancionero de romances viejos* (Mexico City: [Dirección General de Publicaciones], 1961) and *Cancionero folklorico de México,* 5 vols. (Mexico City: Colegio de México, 1975–85).

8. The *corrales* quickly became permanent theaters. According to Chase, the open square was fitted with a "rude stage and benches." An awning was provided for the actors, but there was no corresponding roof for the spectators. In Madrid, one of the first cities to boast such theaters, the *corrales* were named for the streets on which they were located. Two famous examples are the Corrales Príncipe, built in 1579, and the Cruz, built in 1538. See Gilbert Chase, *The Music of Spain* (New York: Dover, 1959), 94–95. José Subirá includes attractive pictures of the *corrales* in *Historia de la música española e hispanoamericana* (Barcelona: Salvat Editores, S.A., 1953), 331.

9. Stein directs our attention to the work of Margit Frenk Alatorre, who has written on the appropriation of these popular songs by the growing urban middle class.

10. Stein, *Songs of Mortals,* 48.

11. Ibid., 12.

12. Directors at institutions such as the Siglo de Oro festival in El Paso and Repertorio Español regularly program works by Lope de Vega and devote attention to historical performance traditions. They also highlight the ties between de Vega's *comedias* and the modern zarzuela tradition during their seasonal offerings of zarzuela. In 1983 Repertorio Español went further, stitching together Lope de Vega's drama *La Discreta Enamorada* with music from *Doña Francisquita,* by the nineteenth-century composer Amadeo Vives.

13. Cotarelo, *Historia de la zarzuela,* 42. The translation in the text is my own, as are all subsequent translations, unless indicated otherwise.

14. José Deleito y Piñuela, *Origen y apogeo del género chico,* (Madrid: Revista de Occidente, 1949), 243.

15. Cotarelo, *Historia de la zarzuela,* 43.

16. The preceding segment was a *loa* and the closing one a *mojiganga,* a short comic act frequently including music and characters who wear animal masks or who traverse the divisons between living and dead, human and not human.

17. Chase, *Music of Spain,* 98.

18. Stein, *Songs of Mortals,* 297. Stein also discusses the politics underlying the seventeenth-century Spanish approach to opera and approaches represented in native forms of lyric theater, including zarzuela, in Louise Stein, "Opera and the Spanish Political Agenda," *Acta Musicologica* 63 (1991): 125–67.

19. Stein, *Songs of Mortals,* 297.

20. See Subirá, *Historia de la música española,* 439–41.

21. Although some of these operas were originally presented in the Italian language, by 1840 the audience in the theaters grew to expect such works to be presented in Spanish translation.

22. Chase, *Music of Spain,* 123.

23. William M. Bussey, *French and Italian Influence on the Zarzuela: 1700–1770,* Studies in Musicology, no. 53 (Ann Arbor: UMI Research Press, 1982), 74–76.

24. Although Chase reports that this zarzuela captured the hearts of the public, it is not the first zarzuela created by the team of Ramón de la Cruz and Antonio Rodríguez de Hita. Both men had worked with *tonadillas,* and the formats overlapped. The manuscript to *La Maja Petardista* (a *tonadilla* for three people with music by José Castel) provides an example. Annotations indicate that the work was sung in Ramón de las Cruz and Antonio Rodríguez de Hita's zarzuela *Las Segadoras,* which premiered in 1768 (see José Subira, *Tonadillas teatrales inéditas: Libretos y partituras, con una descripción sinóptica de nuestra música lírica* [Madrid: Tipografía de Archivos, 1932], 88).

25. Chase, *Music of Spain,* 126.

26. H. V. Hamilton, "Zarzuela," in *Grove's Dictionary of Music and Musicians,* 2d ed., ed. J. A. Fuller-Maitland (Philadelphia: Theodore Presser, 1916), 104.

27. The *verbena,* or festival, at the heart of this drama honors Madrid's patron saint, Mary, Virgin of the Dove. Originally associated with Madrid's poorer neighborhoods,

it is one of the most colorful and is held on the eve of the Feast of the Assumption, August 15.

28. For a more detailed discussion of the *tonadilla,* including its early connection with religious music and drama, the development of its various forms, and an authoritative inventory of composers and librettists, consult José Subirá's monumental text *Tonadillas teatrales.*

29. Chase, *Music of Spain,* 129.

30. Subirá, *Tonadillas teatrales,* 29.

31. Chase, *Music of Spain,* 132.

32. Ibid.

33. Federico Sopeña Ibañez, *Historia de la música española contemporánea* (Madrid: Ediciones Rialp, 1958), 20–21.

34. Cotarelo, *Historia de la zarzuela,* 181.

35. Ibid., 179.

36. Ibid., 242.

37. Ibid., 335–36.

38. Lionel Salter and Jack Sage, "Zarzuela," *The New Grove Dictionary of Music and Musicians,* ed. Stanley Sadie (London: Macmillan, 1980), 651.

39. For a discussion of recent Madrid productions of Barbieri's *El Barberillo de Lavapiés,* see Richard Traubner, "¿Qué Pasa? ¡Zarzuela!" *Opera News* 62 (July 1997): 27.

40. See Bentivegna, "Three *Zarzuela Madrileñas,*" for more details on Madrid's main theaters.

41. Stormy political conditions had long characterized Spanish government, but the split of the monarchy in 1833 caused by King Ferdinand's decision to name his daughter Isabella as heir rather than his brother Carlos opened the way for ambitious statesmen such as Espartero, Narváez, and O'Donnell to seize power. As the historian Raymond Carr explains, this period was defined by a string of military coups, known as *pronunciamentos.* These officer's rebellions led to a succession of governments that reached a climax in 1898 when Spain battled Cuba, the United States, and the Philippines in wars for independence and lost the last of its New World colonies. See Raymond Carr, *Modern Spain, 1875–1980* (Oxford: Oxford University Press, 1980), 1–2.

42. Bentivegna, "Three *Zarzuelas Madrileñas,*" 50.

43. Salter and Sage, "Zarzuela," 651.

44. Bentivegna, "Three *Zarzuelas Madrileñas,*" 59.

45. As noted earlier in this chapter, *La Verbena de la Paloma* was labeled a *sainete* by its creators, although it is frequently cited as an example of the *género chico* and is designated as such on many programs and printed scores. Another, both affectionate and descriptive, term for this drama is *zarzuelito* (little zarzuela). The interchangeable application of these terms is discussed later in the chapter.

46. See Victor Sánchez, "La crisis de la zarzuela grande en la obra de Tomás Bretón" (The crisis of zarzuela grande in the works of Tomás Bretón), *Cuadernos de música iberoamericana* vols. 2–3 (1996–97): 205–12.

47. See Bentivegna, "Three *Zarzuelas Madrileñas,*" 40, 57.

48. Chase, *Music in Spain,* 146.

49. Ibid.

50. See Armando de María y Campos, *Archive de teatro cronicas: De enero a diciembre de 1946* (Mexico City: Compañia de Ediciones Populares, 1947).

51. Author's interviews with Josefina Trelles Solomon, New York City, 1983–87, and Nelly Vuksic, New York City, February 14, 1985. Musical director Pablo Zinger also noted his distaste for the work as "a placid imitation of Italian opera—heavy, formulaic . . . painful" (Zinger, "The Spanish Songbook," *Opera News* 62 [July 1997]: 13).

52. Cotarelo, *Historia de la zarzuela,* 13, 17.

53. Salter and Sage, "Zarzuela," 651.

54. See ibid. for a summary.

55. Plácido Domingo, *My First Forty Years* (New York: Knopf, 1983), 7.

56. Richard Traubner, *Operetta: A Theatrical History* (London: Victor Gollancz, 1984), 430.

57. Antonio Iglesias, "Spain Experiences a Revival," *Musical America,* November 15, 1951; R. P., "Zarzuelas from Spain on Disks," *New York Times,* May 22, 1955, p. 16X.

58. Herbert Weinstock, "Music from Spain," *Saturday Review,* January 31, 1953, p. 38.

59. Richard Traubner, "Zarzuela Goes on Display," *New York Times,* August 4, 1985, pp. 9, 24.

60. Ibid.

61. Anonymous, "Zarzuela Emerges Victorious," *Variety,* September 5, 1979, p. 63.

62. Traubner, "Zarzuela Goes on Display," 24. In the 1990s even fewer productions of zarzuela took place at this namesake theater. Traubner attributes this decline to fact that the Teatro de la Zarzuela had been serving as Madrid's principal opera house; perhaps more attention will be devoted to zarzuela now that the Teatro Real has reopened. See Traubner, "¿Qué Pasa? ¡Zarzuela!" 26.

63. The recording label is French, but the funding is from a Spanish bank, the Caja de Madrid, and the project is helped enormously by the new scores being released by ICCHU and SGAE. See Traubner, "¿Qué Pasa? ¡Zarzuela!" 27.

64. Richard Traubner, telephone interview with the author, July 23, 1999.

65. Ibid.

Chapter 2: Zarzuela in the New World

1. See Domingo's official Web site at <http://www.placidodomingo.com>, where he also includes stage pictures of both his parents as they appeared in zarzuelas and Spanish operas.

2. Alejo Carpentier skillfully describes a Cuban concept of *criollismo* in his essay "How the Negro Became Creole." His celebration of Creole culture makes it clear that he rejects any assumption of Cuban culture's inferiority to European culture. It also indicates the political nature of the designation, especially in connection with the growing nationalist sentiment that developed in literary and cultural movements as each of Spain's col-

onies won its independence. See Alejo Carpentier, "Cómo el negro se volvió criollo," *Conferencias,* ed. Virgilio López Lemus (Havana: Editorial Letras Cubanas, 1987), 215–22. For a related discussion, see also Carpentier, "América latina en la confluencia de coordenadas históricas y su repercusión en la música" in *Ese músico que llevo dentro,* ed. Zoila Gómez (Havana: Editorial Letras Cubanas, 1980), 3:336.

3. In addition to such classic texts as Aimé Césaire, *Discours sur le colonialisme* (Paris: Présence Africaine, 1956), and Frantz Fanon, *Black Skin, White Masks* (New York: Grove, 1962 [1952]), the more recent work by Verena Stolcke, *Marriage, Class, and Colour in Nineteenth-Century Cuba: A Study of Racial Attitudes and Sexual Values in a Slave Society* (Ann Arbor: University of Michigan Press, 1989), is a valuable resource.

4. See Rebecca Scott, *Slave Emancipation in Cuba: The Transition to Free Labor, 1860–1899* (Princeton, N.J.: Princeton University Press, 1985), for additional discussion of racial categories and population statistics. Katherine Hagedorn, *Divine Utterances: The Translation of Memory in Afro-Cuban Performance* (Washington, D.C.: Smithsonian Institution Press, forthcoming), includes a consideration of racial categories and corresponding status; see especially chapter 6.

5. The foremost source regarding the slave trade is Philip Curtin, *The Atlantic Slave Trade: A Census* (Madison: University of Wisconsin Press, 1969). Another perspective is offered by José Luciano Franco, *La presencia negra en el Nuevo Mundo* (Havana: Casa [de las Américas], 1968).

6. Robert Stevenson, *Music in Mexico: A Historical Survey* (New York: Thomas Crowell, 1952), 173.

7. Ibid., 174.

8. Gerard Béhague, *Music in Latin America: An Introduction* (Englewood Cliffs, N.J.: Prentice-Hall, 1979), 60.

9. Gilbert Chase, *Music in Spain,* 2d ed. (New York: Dover, 1959), 261. Three songs by Hidalgo, the most important Spanish theater composer of this period and a regular collaborator with Calderón, are preserved in a manuscript located at the Sutro Library, in San Francisco, California. They document the journey of this music to the New World, particularly Mexico. See John Koegel, "New Sources of Music from Spain and Colonial Mexico at the Sutro Library," *Notes: Quarterly Journal of the Music Library Association* 55, no. 3 (Mar. 1999): 583–613.

10. Carlos Vega, *Panorama de la música popular Argentina, con un ensayo sobre la ciencia del folklore* (Buenos Aires: Editorial Losada, S.A., 1944), 293. See also Ann Livermore, *A Short History of Spanish Music* (New York: Vienna House, 1972), 224.

11. Robert Stevenson analyzes *La Púrpura de la Rosa* and places it in its historical context in his introduction to his edition of Torrejón y Velasco's score. He also includes a detailed discussion of musical spectacles in seventeenth-century Spain and the origins of Peruvian theater. See Robert Stevenson, ed., *La Púrpura de la Rosa,* by Tomás Torrejón y Velasco (Lima: Instituto Nacional de Cultura, 1976).

12. The exact nature of the score is a matter of speculation, since it is lost. Other scores by Sumaya, however, indicate his interest in Italian opera, and the duke of Linares, Vice-

roy Don Fernande de Alencastre Noroña y Silva, for whom *La Parténope* was performed, was a devoteé of Italian opera. See Stevenson, *Music in Mexico,* 148–53. According to Aurelio Tello, Sumaya was the most important Mexican musician in the first half of the seventeenth century. He held a post as *maestro de capilla* (the master musician responsible for all musical performance and composition in the cathedral and its chapels) in Mexico City and later moved to the cathedral in Oaxaca, where he worked from 1732 to 1745. Until Tello's recent identification of predecessors, many important historians of Mexican music, including Beristaín y Souza, Olavarría y Ferrari, Robert Stevenson, Alba Herera y Miguel Galindo, Jesús Estrada, and Gabriel Saldívar, considered him to be the first Mexican-born chapel master.

13. John Koegel, "Music: Nineteenth and Twentieth Centuries," in *Encyclopedia of Mexico,* ed. Michael Weiner (Chicago: Fitzroy and Dearborn, 1997), 2:985.

14. Vega, *Panorama,* 293.

15. Otto Mayer-Serra, *Panorama de la música mexicana desde la Independencia hasta la actualidad* (Panúco, Mexico: El Colegio de México, 1941), 35.

16. Rine Leal, *Breve historia del teatro cubano* (Havana: Editorial Letras Cubanas, 1980), 50.

17. Ibid., 55–56.

18. Ibid., 56.

19. Robert Stevenson, *Music in Mexico,* 172–223.

20. Béhague, *Music in Latin America,* 60.

21. Anthony M. Pasquariello, "The Evolution of the *Sainete* in the River Platte Area," *Latin American Theatre Review* 17 (Fall 1983): 14–24.

22. For more detailed discussion of the Argentine *sainete,* consult the work by Pasquariello cited in the previous note.

23. Vicente Gesualdo, *Historia de la música en la Argentina* (Buenos Aires: Impresiones Diagonal, 1971), 149.

24. This claim is strongly argued with regard to Mexico and Cuba by Sally Bissell in "Manuel Areu and the Nineteenth-Century Zarzuela in Mexico and Cuba" (Ph.D. diss., University of Iowa, 1987), 231.

25. Mary Montaño, "The Manuel Areu Collection of 19th-Century Zarzuelas" (Master's thesis, University of New Mexico, 1972); Bissell, "Manuel Areu."

26. Vega, *Panorama,* 293. D. Emilio Cotarelo y Mori does not mention the 1853 date for Cuba and instead notes that theater records for 1855 indicate the arrival of several companies that would later settle in Havana, Matanzas, and Pinar del Río (*Historia de la zarzuela o sea el drama lírico en España, desde su origen a fines del siglo xix* [Madrid: Tipografía de Archivos, 1934], 511, 553–54). In short, by any account, Cuba was one of the first, if not the first, New World country to benefit from the nineteenth-century traveling zarzuela troupes.

27. Antonia Saenz, *El Teatro en Puerto Rico,* 2d ed. (San Juan: University of Puerto Rico, Colección UPREX, 1970).

28. Montaño, "The Manuel Areu Collection," 36.

29. Bissell, "Manuel Areu," 233.

30. Ibid., 75.

31. Ibid., 81.

32. Ibid., 83; appendixes A and B show how several of these works found their way to New York theaters.

33. Bissell, "Manuel Areu," 236; see also Patrick J. Smith, *The Tenth Muse: A Historical Study of the Opera Libretto* (New York: Schirmer Books, 1970), 294.

34. See Emilio Casares Rodicio, "Historia del teatro de los bufos, 1866–1881: Crónica y dramaturgia," *Cuadernos de música iberoamericana* 2–3 (1996–97): 73–118.

35. See Bissell, "Manuel Areu," 240–46; see also Gloria Carmona, "La música en México en la época de Juárez, Lerdo y Díaz (1868–1879)," in *Período de la independencia a la revolución (1810 a 1910),* vol. 3 of *La música de México,* pt. 1, *Historia,* ed. Julio Estrada, 5 vols. (Mexico City: Instituto de Investigaciones Estéticas, Universidad Nacional Autónoma de México, 1984), 122.

36. See Bissell, "Manuel Areu," 96–98, for details.

37. These remarks by Ramon Berdejo, journalist for *El Correo Español,* appear in Antonio Magaña Esquivel, *Los teatros en la Ciudad de Mexico, D.F.* (Mexico City: Colección Popular de México, 1974), 33.

38. Eugenio Pereira Salas, *Historia de la música en Chile (1850–1900)* (Santiago: Editorial del Pacífico, S.A. [Publicaciones de la Universidad de Chile], 1957), 301.

39. Esquivel, *Los Teatros,* 126.

40. Bissell, "Manuel Areu," 165, 174–75.

41. Pereira Salas, *Historia de la música en Chile,* 301.

42. Ibid., 302.

43. Chase, *Music in Spain,* 303.

44. Vega, *Panorama,* 294.

45. Bissell, "Manuel Areu," 251; see also Gerónimo Baqueiro Foster, *La música en el período independiente,* vol. 3 of *Historia de la música en México* (Mexico City: Secretaría de Educación Pública, Instituto Nacional de Bellas Artes, 1964), 336.

46. Bissell, "Manuel Areu," 252.

47. Miranda argues that for Mexicans, the century ended in 1910, 100 years after independence; see Ricardo Miranda, "La zarzuela en México: 'Jardin de senderos que se bifurcan . . . ,'" *Cuadernos de música iberoamericana* 2–3 (1996–97): 452.

48. Ibid., 468–74.

49. Plácido Domingo, *My First Forty Years* (New York: Knopf, 1983), 14.

50. Catherine Dower, *Puerto Rican Music Following the Spanish-American War* (Lanham, Md.: University Press of America, 1983). See also Emilio Pasarell, *Orígenes y desarrollo de la afición teatral en Puerto Rico—siglo XX*), vol. 2 (Rio Piedras: Editorial Universitaria, Universidad de Puerto Rico, 1967); Saenz, *El Teatro en Puerto Rico.* In 1985 Puerto Rico boasted three professional companies devoted to lyric theater and zarzuela: the Fundación Teatral, the Fundación Puertorriqueña, and the Pro-Arte Lírico de Puerto Rico (Evangelina Colon, Puerto Rican–born soprano, interview with the author, New York City, February 7, 1985).

51. Leopoldo Escalante, interview with the author, New York City, June 11, 1986.

52. Data obtained from the author's interviews with Evangelina Colón, Nelly Vuksic, Josefina Trelles, and Irene Markoff in New York City, 1985.

53. Domingo, *My First Forty Years,* 5–6.

54. Collectors of dance and traditional music, such as Vicente T. Mendoza, have determined that some of the musical examples they gathered in the early twentieth century originated in colonial theater. Such findings also indicate how widely the music dispersed from the urban centers to the countryside. For an introductory discussion of the impact of theatrical music and dance on the general, nonurban public in Hispanic America, see John Koegel, "Nuevas fuentes musicales para danza, teatro y salón de la Nueva España," *Heterofonía: Revista de investigación musical* 30, nos. 116–17 (1997): 20–21.

Chapter 3: A Side Trip to Cuba

1. Federico Chueca's *La Gran Vía* was an incredibly popular *género chico* work both in Spain and abroad. Bentivegna notes that the work marked the first definite success of the *género chico* in Madrid. It combined the popular *revista* form with a favorite theme: life in Madrid (Patricia Bentivegna, "A Study of Three *Zarzuelas Madrileñas* Together with a Historical Outline of the Zarzuela" [Master's thesis, Columbia University, 1955], 77). In Latin America *La Gran Vía* spawned many imitations and parodies. For example, Pereira lists the following Chilean versions: *Gran Vía Chilena* (1892) and *Gran Vía Mapocho* (1895), both arranged by José Serrano; *El Gran Calidoscopio* (The Big Kaleidoscope, 1894), a panorama of Santiago by Salvador Pereira; and *La Gran Avenida* (1897), by Guillermo Wetzer. See Eugenio Pereira Salas, *Historia de la música en Chile (1850–1900)* (Santiago: Editorial Del Pacífico, S.A. [Publicaciones de la Universidad de Chile], 1957), 303.

2. Ann Livermore, *A Short History of Spanish Music* (New York: Vienna House, 1972), 224.

3. Catherine Dower, *Puerto Rican Music Following the Spanish-American War* (Lanham, Md.: University Press of America, 1983), x.

4. In his *Breve historia del teatro cubano* (Havana: Editorial Letras Cubanas, 1980), Riné Leal reports that Covarrubias's company included such famous individuals as Andrés Prieto, Manuel García, Isidoro Maíquez, the singer María del Rosario Sabatini, Antonio Hermosa, Mariana Galino, the dancer Manuela Gamborino, and her sister, the *tonadilla* artist Isabel Gamborino. With due respect to Leal, this group could not have worked together over the next twenty-one years, as he claims, without some shifts in personnel. Slonimsky and Béhague both place García in Paris from 1807 to 1809 and in Italy from 1811 to 1816. In 1819 García returned to Paris, where he stayed until 1824. After a year in London he traveled to New York in 1825 with a dramatic troupe including his son Manuel, his daughter María (Maliban). García's influence, then, was hardly limited to Cuba. He shaped public taste for lyric drama in Spain, Italy, France, Mexico, and the United States. His work is testimony to the international influence of a stellar performer and

teacher, as well as to the international appeal of lyric forms such as the *tonadilla.* His experience also indicates the importance of the traveling dramatic repertory ensemble in introducing lyric theater, especially Spanish lyric forms, to new audiences.

5. Alejo Carpentier, *La música en Cuba* (Mexico: Fondo de Cultura Económica, 1946), 178.

6. See Leal, *Breve historia,* 30.

7. Carpentier, *La música en Cuba,* 134–42.

8. Ibid., 140.

9. Ibid., 144.

10. Ibid., 143.

11. Leal, *Breve historia,* 78.

12. Edwin T. Tolón, *Teatro lírico popular de Cuba* (Miami: Ediciones Universal, 1973), 27.

13. Carpentier, *La música en Cuba,* 143.

14. Tolón, *Teatro lírico,* 30.

15. Livermore, *A Short History,* 234.

16. Tolón, *Teatro lírico,* 48. Tolón relates how he, as impresario, came to arrange this premiere at the request of Lecuona himself and how he needed to send the scores to Colón, Panama, to secure the services of these two outstanding performers, who were there for the celebration of the opening of the Panama Canal.

17. Ibid., 51.

Chapter 4: Creating *The Land of Joy*

1. Nicolás Kanellos, *A History of Hispanic Theatre in the United States: Origins to 1940* (Austin: University of Texas Press, 1990), xv.

2. Pablo Figueroa, *Teatro: Hispanic Theatre in New York City, 1920–76,* El Museo del Barrio exhibit catalog, April 22–June 3, 1977, p. 8.

3. As will be discussed in future chapters, El Paso emerged in the 1990s as the site of both the Siglo de Oro Festival of Spanish-language drama and an international zarzuela festival.

4. John Koegel, "Canciones del país: Mexican Musical Life in California after the Gold Rush," *California History* 78 (Fall 1999): 161.

5. Rosemary Gipson, "The Beginning of Theatre in Sonora," *Arizona and the West* (1967): 351.

6. Koegel, "Canciones del país," 27.

7. Ibid., 30. Koegel offers wonderful detail in this article for anyone wishing to know more about the history of Hispanic music and theatrical life in California, particularly in Los Angeles. His text includes detailed discussions of artists, companies, and programs at individual theaters.

8. Ibid., 28.

9. Gipson, "Theatre in Sonora," 351; see also Rosemary Gipson, "The History of Tucson Theater before 1906" (Master's thesis, University of Arizona, 1967), 14.

10. Kanellos, *History of Hispanic Theatre,* 4.

11. Gipson, "History of Tucson Theater," 10.

12. Kanellos, *History of Hispanic Theatre,* 5.

13. Koegel, "Canciones del país," 178.

14. Ibid.

15. Ibid.

16. Kanellos point out that the resident Hispanic theater companies in Florida were largely noncommercial, distinguishing them from groups in the Southwest and New York. For a discussion of theatrical development in Tampa and elsewhere in Florida, see Kanellos, *History of Hispanic Theatre,* 146–75.

17. Richard Davis, *A History of Music in American Life,* 3 vols. (Malabar, Fla.: Krieger, 1982).

18. Kanellos, *History of Hispanic Theatre,* 105.

19. Ibid., 107.

20. Ibid., 107–11.

21. The work was most often described as a "musical revue" in the English-language press, although the *New York Tribune* billed it as a zarzuela and the *New York World* called it an operetta. The variance in nomenclature can be partially explained by the flexible nature of these terms, as I have discussed in previous chapters. Also, the Spanish libretto of *The Land of Joy* was adapted to cater to an English-speaking audience. By adding English-speaking comedians who performed short sketches as preludes or interludes to the original scenes, the American producers made the show more of a revue than it was originally.

22. "Quinito" was the nickname of Joaquín Valverde y San Juan (1875–1918), son of Joaquín Valverde (1846–1910), the composer who collaborated with Federico Chueca on the music for the *género chico* work *La Gran Vía,* among other zarzuelas and *revistas* (Patricia Bentivegna, "A Study of Three *Zarzuelas Madrileñas* Together with a Historical Outline of the Zarzuela" [Master's thesis, Columbia University, 1955], 72, 81–82, 206). Bentivegna claims that one of the authors of this libretto was Mexican but offers little information about either. Olavarría lists José Elizondo as the Mexican author and Velasco as "a gentleman" (Enrique de Olavarría y Ferrari, *Indices a la reseña histórica del teatro en México, 1538–1911* [Mexico City: Editorial Porrua, 1968], 45, 3054).

23. The Billy Rose Theatre Collection of the New York Public Library at Lincoln Center has clippings from the *New York Globe, New York Times, New York Tribune, New York American, New York World, New York Mail, New York Telegraph, New York Sun,* and *Brooklyn Times,* as well as from current magazines of the period, such as *Life* and *Current Opinion,* all collected in unnumbered pages and folders in Mrs. Frank B. McGay, "Scrapbook of Concert, Opera, Theatre, Civic, and Cultural Programs Given in New York City between 1881–1954" (presented to the New York Historical Society by Thomas Larremore, 1881–1954).

24. Carl Van Vechten, *The Music of Spain* (New York: Knopf, 1918), 9.

25. See McGay, "Scrapbook."

26. *New York Globe,* November 2, 1917 (in McGay, "Scrapbook").

27. *New York Times,* November 12, 1917 (in McGay, "Scrapbook").

28. Kanellos, *History of Hispanic Theatre,* 111.

29. Ibid., 117.

30. Figueroa, *Teatro,* 8–9. Casa Galicia housed many theatrical performances in 1920–30. The schedule was heavily dominated by performances of Spanish zarzuelas, with works including *Los Gavilanes, La Princesa de Dólar* (The Dollar Princess), *El Conde de Luxemburgo* (The Count of Luxembourg), *Carceleras* (The Jailers), and *La Viuda Alegre* (see appendix A).

31. Ibid., 10.

32. See Kanellos, *History of Hispanic Theatre,* 144–45, as well as Figueroa, *Teatro,* 17.

33. Figueroa, *Teatro,* 16.

34. See John C. Miller, "Contemporary Hispanic Theatre in New York," in *Hispanic Theatre in the United States,* ed. Nicolás Kanellos (Houston: Arte Publico, 1984), 24–34.

35. Daniel Bendahan, *Hispanoamérica en la música del siglo XX* (Venezuela: Monté Avila Editores Latinoamericana, 1997).

36. Figueroa, *Teatro,* 16.

37. Ibid., 17.

38. Ibid., 17–18.

39. Miller, "Contemporary Hispanic Theatre," 25.

40. Beginning in the 1930s Columbia University and Barnard College supported the presentation of classic and serious modern Spanish drama. In a sense their goal to maintain tradition fit into the underground theater movement I referred to earlier. Occasionally a zarzuela was mounted at Columbia's McMillan Theater (see appendix A), but productions of works by Lope de Vega, Calderón, and García Lorca were more frequent. This emphasis on classics as fundamental repertoire has formed the programming policies of many contemporary Hispanic theaters and is perhaps most evident in the policies of Teatro Repertorio Español today.

Chapter 5: Profiles of Contemporary Producers of Zarzuela in the New York Metropolitan Area

1. A repertory company tries to sustain an ensemble of salaried actors, designers, directors, and sometimes playwrights. For each production the company draws on this ensemble. Such a format allows a company to run more than one production simultaneously. As a consequence, a production can run for a much longer period of time with less chance of a company becoming stale. The repertory format offers actors and their productions a great opportunity for artistic development.

2. René Buch, interview with the author, New York City, July 11, 1985.

3. Ibid.

4. Paul D. Colford, "And You Don't Have to Speak Spanish (The Story of Dramatic Growth)," *Newsday,* July 7, 1983, sect. 2, pp. 4–5.

5. John C. Miller, "Contemporary Hispanic Theatre in New York," in *Hispanic Theatre in the United States,* ed. Nicolás Kanellos (Houston: Arte Publico, 1984), 26.

6. These are not the only dance shows the company has offered. The 1998 season featured the flamenco dancer Andrea del Conte with Danza España. A new tango production called "Tango y Tango" appeared in the 1994–95 season.It replaced the previous "Tango and Folklore Argentino" series. (See Thalia's Web site, <http://www.queensnewyork.com/cultural/thalia>, for latest program listings.)

7. Silvia Brito, interview with the author, Sunnyside, New York, April 8, 1986.

8. Julie De Grandy, telephone interview with the author, July 15, 1999.

9. The production of *La Verbena* was a family affair, and De Grandy's then six-year-old namesake and grandson, now a highly respected lawyer and state senator, participated in the show. La Asociación Pro-Arte Grateli was founded by the Cuban performing artists Píli de la Rosa and Martha Pérez and remains under their direction today. Their productions are housed at the newly opened Miami-Dade County Auditorium (2901 West Flagler Street, Miami, FL 33135; 305/547–5414).

10. Silvia Brito, interview, April 8, 1986.

11. Much of that awareness was boosted by Plácido Domingo's worldwide tour with Tamayo's *Antología de la Zarzuela.*

12. This group has officers living in Manhattan and New Hyde Park, New York (on Long Island). Founded by the Spanish-born zarzuela aficionados Antonio and Carmen Pérez, it has been in operation since 1985 and sponsors performances featuring Spanish and Hispanic American singers.

Chapter 6: Identity and Choice

1. Ilan Stavans, *The Hispanic Condition: Reflections on Culture and Identity in America* (New York: HarperCollins, 1995), 30.

2. Ibid., 129.

3. In the 1980s and 1990s productions of zarzuela by the Chicago Opera Factory, directed by Blanche Artis Lewis, have been in English translation, and the University of Texas at El Paso, under the direction of Hugh Cardon, has produced zarzuela with English dialogue and Spanish song. Translation (discussed more in chapter 7) became more popular in the 1990s, and presentations with translated spoken dialogue include the production of *Luisa Fernanda* offered by the Jarvis Conservatory in Napa, California (1997). Plácido Domingo preferred to use projected supertitles for his production of *Doña Francisquita* during the 1997–98 season of the Washington Opera. More daring is Richard Traubner's complete translation (both songs and dialogue were delivered in English) of *La Verbena de la Paloma* and *La Gran Vía* for the Ohio Light Opera. Although becoming more popular, complete translations remain exceptions to the general rule.

4. The source for data on the Chicago Opera Factory is Blanche Artis Lewis, telephone interview with the author, August, 2, 1999. Although my emphasis in this chapter is on responses to full-scale productions of zarzuela in New York, it is important to note that elsewhere some notable exceptions exist to the norm in New York, where Hispanics form the majority of the audience. One such example is the 1999 summer production of *La*

Verbena de la Paloma and *La Gran Vía* by the Ohio Light Opera. This English-language production attracted a predominantly non-Hispanic audience. The city of Wooster does not have a sizable Hispanic population, and the production was not promoted with any special effort to attract patrons from the larger Hispanic communities in nearby Cleveland and Columbus.

5. After two years of regular attendance and observation, I distributed questionnaires to audiences at one zarzuela performance at each of the principal Spanish theaters, Repertorio Español, Thalia, and the ATM. After analyzing the results, I noted characteristic patterns among those who attend zarzuela in New York–area theaters. For more details on the questionnaires and methodology employed in distributing and analyzing the data, see Janet Sturman, "Zarzuela in New York: Contributions of Lyric Theatre to Hispanic Identity" (Ph.D. diss., Columbia University, 1987).

6. Although on a large scale the proportional relationships remain similar, the composition of the Hispanic population in New York has changed significantly in the past decade. In 1980 Mexicans made up 2 percent of the New York Hispanic population; in 1990 the ratio increased to 4 percent. The Mexican presence is thus slightly stronger in New York today than it was when I first began this study.

7. The Puerto Rican dominance in New York has diminished significantly since 1980, when Puerto Ricans constituted 60 percent of the Hispanic population of that city. Census figures for 1990 indicate that Puerto Ricans now make up 46–48 percent of New York's Hispanic population. This change is particularly noteworthy since the percentage of Puerto Ricans among U.S. Hispanics increased from 6 percent to 10.5 percent during the same decade. New York's Hispanic population has clearly become more diverse, more pan-Latino.

8. The population figures for New York vary depending on what census table one consults. See Roger Daniels, *Coming to America: A History of Immigration and Ethnicity in American Life* (New York: HarperCollins, 1990). Discrepancies exist even within the same census tract depending on the questions used to tally responses. For this reason table 2 uses percentages. These percentages, while rough, are adequate to clarify general relationships and to make it clear that the size of the group does not determine the extent of its influence in cultural matters.

9. An excellent overview of diversity among Hispanics in the United States can be found in Joan Moore and Harry Pachon, *Hispanics in the United States* (Englewood Cliffs, N.J.: Prentice-Hall 1985), 38–65.

10. Adelaida Reyes Schramm, "Ethnic Music, the Urban Area, and Ethnomusicology," *Sociologus* 29 (1979): 6.

11. Stavans, *The Hispanic Condition*, 27.

12. Respondents represented anywhere from 60 percent to 80 percent of the total audience on the days polled.

13. John Rockwell, "Cecilia Valdés: Alliance of Latin Arts," *New York Times*, April 4, 1974.

14. Anonymous, "Spanish Theater Is Projected Here—Producers of *La Leyenda del Beso* Plan the 'Get Acquainted Series' for This Season," *New York Times*, November 22, 1942.

15. See Janet Sturman, "Advertising and Latin Music at a New York City Jazz Club," *Current Musicology* (1984): 159–66, in which I explore various attempts to reinforce salsa's appeal to the larger society and particularly to segments of the society with socioeconomic leverage.

16. For many Americans, race is a question of black or white. This idea has been reinforced by the persistent use of the word *minority* as a synonym for *African Americans.* Although this practice was less common in the 1990s, the treatment of race and ethnicity in the United States has a legacy of simplistic categorization. Writing in 1985, Moore and Pachon point out that an obvious example of such a narrow vision of race is enshrined in the U.S. Census, which has never dealt adequately with the concept of mixed race. See Moore and Pachon, *Hispanics in the United States,* 3.

17. In 1985 Moore reported that for persons over twenty-five years of age, Anglo-Americans have completed a median of 12.1 years of school; blacks, 10.9; and Hispanics, 9.1. In general Cuban Americans tend to have a higher educational profile than other Hispanic groups, and most equal or exceed the Anglo-American averages. Puerto Ricans, on the other hand, have the lowest educational profile of Hispanics in the New York area, whereas in the Southwest, Mexicans have the lowest educational profile. See Moore and Pachon, *Hispanics in the United States,* 66–70; Lydia Chavez, "Striving but Still Lagging: Puerto Ricans Wonder Why," *New York Times,* June 5, 1986, pp. B1, B15.

18. Whereas 44 percent of all people polled said that they never attend opera in New York, 45 percent said that they do attend. At the extremes of the latter group, 15 percent reported that they attend less frequently than once a year, and 7 percent reported attending at least once a week.

19. Their age implies that they are less likely to be Puerto Rican. Puerto Ricans and North Americans of Hispanic descent constitute larger percentages of the casts that perform zarzuela in New York area than they do of the audiences for those performances. Still, as in the audiences, the percentage of Cubans who perform zarzuela far outweighs those of the others involved.

20. See Moore and Pachon, *Hispanics in the United States,* 93–95; John C. Miller, "Contemporary Hispanic Theatre in New York," in *Hispanic Theatre in the United States,* ed. Nicolás Kanellos (Houston: Arte Publico, 1984), 24–33.

21. Moore and Pachon, *Hispanics in the United States,* 102.

22. Of all respondents, 12 percent identified themselves as Puerto Rican.

23. Significantly, 79 percent of the respondents were attending Repertorio Español for the first time (the figure was 38 percent for the Thalia Spanish Theatre and 35 percent for the ATM), and only 19 percent (42 percent for Thalia and 48 percent for the ATM) attended other Spanish theaters in the metropolitan area. Repertorio Español also attracted the largest percentage of patrons born in the United States (26 percent, versus 8 percent at Thalia and 2 percent at the ATM). Furthermore, 22 percent of the patrons at Repertorio Español identified themselves in ways that did not suggest Hispanic ethnicity. Thalia attracted virtually the same number (21 percent) of non-Hispanic patrons, whereas the ATM attracted only 2 percent. A greater percentage of patrons at Repertorio

Español expressed a preference for seeing drama performed in English than in Spanish (19 percent, versus 4 percent at Thalia and 2 percent at the ATM).

Some of the differences among the three audiences may stem from sampling bias: the evening I polled the audience at Repertorio Español, two groups of students were attending, a group of students enrolled in a Spanish course from a high school in Pennsylvania and a group of Mexican college graduates whose New York tour package included an evening at Repertorio Español.

24. René Buch, interview with the author, New York City, July 11, 1985.

25. Ibid.

26. See Manuel Peña, *The Texas-Mexican Conjunto: History of a Working-Class Music* (Austin: University of Texas Press, 1985).

27. Domingo continues by praising traditional music of Mexico and Latin America. See Plácido Domingo, *My First Forty Years* (New York: Knopf, 1983), 201.

28. See Richard Traubner, "Zarzuela Goes on Display," *New York Times,* August 4, 1985, pp. 9, 24; Peter G. Davis, "Music," *New York Magazine,* August 26, 1985.

29. The full quotation runs as follows: "Masters in the art of remembrance, we suffer from a traumatic past and refuse to inhabit the future. Could we then assimilate in the Promised Land? My impression is that neither here nor there, Latinos shall always inhabit the hyphen. My generation will prove infuriating. Others will finally realize that Spanish is here to stay, never to vanish. What's more, our stubbornness will force many non-Latinos to come to us, to adapt to our ways" (Stavans, *The Hispanic Condition,* 199).

Chapter 7: An Analysis of Performance Practices

1. Scholars who have devoted considerable energy to the concept of distance in performance situations include Henry Kingsbury, who explores the rituals of classical concert behavior and the distance between performer and audience in his book *Music, Talent, and Performance* (Philadelphia: Temple University Press, 1988). Richard Schechner has explored the rituals of theatrical performance from many angles, but he also explores the distance between viewer (audience) and performer, noting that all theatrical events embrace both distance and familiarity and emphasize one vantage point over the other at different points throughout the event. The overall balance (favoring one position over the other) also differs from one context to another. See his *Essays on Performance Theory, 1970–1976,* rev. ed. (New York: Routledge, 1988), and *The Future of Ritual: Writings on Culture and Performance* (London: Routledge, 1993).

2. De Grandy used a similar approach with the closing *habanera* of *La Verbena de la Paloma,* discussed later in this chapter.

3. Silvia Brito, interview with the author, Sunnyside, New York, April 8, 1986.

4. Guadalupe Silva, "Final Zarzuela a Masterpiece in Terms of Historical Accuracy," *El Paso Times,* August 8, 1987, p. 6D.

5. See Enrique Fernández, "One Sings the Other Doesn't," *The Village Voice,* December 20, 1983.

6. My free translation of material from the review first published in *El Nacional,* Caracas, September 5, 1955. See Alejo Carpentier, *Ese músico que llevo dentro,* ed. Zoila Gómez (Havana: Editorial Letras Cubanas, 1980), 3:65.

7. Nico Castel, interview with the author, New York City, February 25, 1985. Castel has written a useful book on Spanish diction: *A Singer's Manual of Spanish Lyric Diction* (New York: Excalibur, 1994).

8. Thalia Spanish Theatre, *Annual Report '98,* 9.

9. See Kathleen Wilson Spillane's practical discussion of the steps involved in preparing supertitles for the 1995 production of *Doña Francisquita* at the University of New Hampshire: Spillane, "The Zarzuela as Source Material for College Opera Programs," *The NATS Journal* (Mar.-Apr. 1994): 22–23.

10. Hugh Cardon, interview with the author, El Paso, Texas, July 29, 1995.

11. Program notes for the Ohio Light Opera production of *La Verbena de la Paloma* and *La Gran Vía,* June 20, 1999.

12. Ibid.; this is Traubner's description of *La Gran Vía.*

13. Richard Traubner, telephone interview with the author, July 23, 1999.

14. Hugh Cardon, interview with the author, El Paso Texas, July 29, 1995.

15. Chapter 4 discusses some of the earlier productions that experimented with an English-Spanish mix.

16. Mary Montaño, cofounder of ¡Viva Zarzuela! and publicity director of Opera Southwest, both companies from Albuquerque, New Mexico, telephone interview with the author, June 7, 1994.

17. René Buch, interview with the author, New York City, July 11, 1985. The reaction of Spaniards to Repertorio Español's delivery was not uniform. In Madrid the company was received warmly, and Buero Vallejo, whom Buch describes as "the Arthur Miller of Spain," remarked after one production: "¡Qué bien dicen el verso sus actores! (How well your actors speak the poetry!) (René Buch, interview with the author, New York City, June 8, 1999).

18. Among these critics are most scholars who chronicle Hispanic theater. Both Miller and Kanellos record treatments of zarzuela but tend to dismiss these productions as less serious; they certainly do not treat them as works that address the political concerns of Hispanic American populations.

19. Dell Hymes, "Ways of Speaking," in *Explorations in the Ethnography of Speaking,* ed. Richard Bauman and Joel Scherzer (New York: Cambridge University Press, 1974), 449.

20. Ibid., 441.

21. Miguel De Grandy, correspondence with the author, May 23, 1986.

22. Without question the most popular *zarzuela grande* for American performances since 1980 has been *Luisa Fernanda.* Prior to that time, a New Yorker was more likely to hear selections in concert anthologies than to attend a fully staged presentation. In addition to being offered in live performances, *Luisa Fernanda* has also been a favorite of recording artists since the 1950s, and new releases of the complete zarzuela continue to appear. Favorite excerpts, especially the magnificent tenor aria "Romanza de Javier," which

begins "En este apacible rincón de Madrid" (In this peaceful corner of Madrid), appears on the 1996 CD *¡Viva la zarzuela!* (Auvidis Valois, V 4765), as well as on *Les voix d'or de la zarzuela* (The Golden Voices of Zarzuela), featuring Monserrat Caballé, Alfredo Kraus, Teresa Berganza, Plácido Domingo, Pilar Lorengar, and Jaime Aragall (Forlane [Alhambra—Columbia Records] UM 3926), and *Fiestas de la zarzuela, vol. 1,* a recital featuring Plácido Domingo (Anacruse [Alhambra—Columbia Records] UM 3906). In 1984 the Moss Music Group reissued the Columbia recording of *Luisa Fernanda* featuring Teresa Berganza in the title role with Rafael Frühbeck de Burgos conducting the Philharmonic Orchestra of Spain (Columbia MMG1151).

23. In his Ph.D. dissertation, "Sociología del teatro musical español" (Georgetown University, 1986), 106–9, Sixto Plaza proposes that the nature of the characters in zarzuela plots accounts for the genre's incredible popularity in Spain. Regarding *Luisa Fernanda,* Plaza argues that the title character's decision to follow her heart rather than tradition makes the work a modern drama. I am not convinced that this alone makes Luisa a modern woman, but I will agree that the emotional concerns of her character allow the work to transcend its historical and national context and appeal to diverse audiences.

24. Pablo Zinger, interview with the author, New York, June 3, 1995.

25. Indeed David Galán's 1997 cyber introduction to Madrid is organized entirely around characters, scenes, and songs from the zarzuela *La Verbena de la Paloma.* "The Madrid represented there," he writes, "is the Madrid I carry in my heart." See <http://www.ciudadfutura.com/madrid/>.

26. "Zarzuelas," an article originally written for *El Nacional,* Caracas, May 5, 1954, in Alejo Carpentier, *Ese músico que llevo dentro,* ed. Zoila Gómez (Havana: Editorial Letras Cubanas, 1980), 3:62.

27. Patrick J. Smith, "Fiesta in Madrid," *Musical America,* August 1969.

28. This is how Traubner handled his re-creation of *La Gran Vía* for the Ohio Light Opera in the summer of 1999.

29. In 1994 Madurga moved from New York City to Miami, where he now devotes himself to organizing annual concert programs of zarzuela. His series, known as "¡Viva la Zarzuela!" incorporates the talents of several Hispanic singers with whom he worked during his illustrious stage career on and off Broadway. Many of these artists have performed with the Thalia Spanish Theater and Repertorio Español.

30. Theodore W. Libby Jr., "Zarzuela: Joseph in the Pharaoh's Court," *New York Times,* January 26, 1982.

31. Pablo Zinger, interview with the author, New York, March 27, 1985.

32. The film was one of nine shown at New York's Second Festival of Films from Spain, sponsored by the Spanish Ministry of Culture in 1986. The festival was so successful with New York audiences that it was extended for an additional two weeks.

33. Jim Braden, "*Luisa Fernanda* Zarzuela More of a Musical Treat Than a Theatrical One," *El Paso Times,* July 31, 1992.

34. In 1997, for example, the Sonidos series was presented in cooperation with the American Composer's Orchestra, the fourth year for such collaboration. The Potpourri

de Zarzuela benefited from the artistic direction of Pablo Zinger, formerly musical director for Repertorio Español. Zinger also participated with the Thalia Outdoors series, presented in Thompson Hill Park, a city park serving residents of the borough of Queens. He turned his piano-playing skills to introducing music by Latin American composers as a member of a chamber trio also featuring clarinetist and saxophonist Paquito D'Rivera and cellist Gustavo Tavares.

35. René Buch remarked that Repertorio Español no longer presents full-scale zarzuelas because they have become too expensive to produce (interview, June 8, 1999). Issues arising in connection with financing zarzuela production will be discussed in chapter 8.

36. Author's observation of a rehearsal at Repertorio Español, New York, New York, July 15, 1985.

37. Carpentier, *La Música en Cuba* (Mexico: Fondo de Cultura Económica, 1946), 94.

38. Buch, interview, July 11, 1985.

39. Although Zinger worked as the full-time musical director for Repertorio Español throughout the 1980s and into the next decade, his involvement with the company's Hispanic Chamber Music series (first in 1996) was as a visiting artist.

40. The Cuban musician D'Rivera is better known as a Latin jazz saxophonist. His work in classical music reminds us of the connections between the classical and popular music worlds.

41. Pablo Zinger, interview with the author, New York, June 3, 1995.

42. Conchita Rodríguez, quoted by Silva, "Final Zarzuela," 6D.

43. On July 1, 1996, following the retirement of Martin Feinstein, Plácido Domingo took over as artistic director of the Washington Opera, in which capacity he selects the repertoire and casting and oversees all stages of the creative process. Domingo's decision to produce *El Gato Montés* (The Wild Cat), by Manuel Penella, for the 1996–97 season (the same year he produced it for the Los Angeles Opera) disappointed many who hoped that the famous tenor would promote zarzuela rather than Spanish opera but pleased fans who long for more Spanish-language productions on opera stages (including the Hispanic Friends of L.A. Opera; see <http://www.laopera.org/hispanics.htm>). The following year Domingo produced *Doña Francisquita* for the 1997–98 season.

44. Victor Chacón, interview with the author, El Paso, Texas, July 29, 1995.

45. Zinger, interview, June 3, 1995, and e-mail exchanges in September 1999.

46. I am grateful to my colleague Prof. Jay Rosenblatt for discussions that stimulated this observation.

Chapter 8: Support Networks for Artistic Production

1. The effect that the Internet will have on music production, distribution, and consumption has yet to be determined, but the impact promises to be considerable. Producers and fans of zarzuela have new access to a wealth of material concerning zarzuela in Christopher Webber's *Zarzuela!* Web site: <http://www.nashwan.demon.co.uk/zarzuela.htm>. In addi-

tion to providing a general introduction to the genre, Webber offers information on scores, recordings, and performers from around the world (he links to Pablo Zinger, for example). Links to CDs, sound files, plot synopses, current productions, composer biographies, and a gallery of artwork and photos featuring zarzuela are also available. If virtual production of zarzuela were ever to take place, this would be the site to consult.

2. Richard Traubner prepared a succinct and useful review of zarzuela recordings for the *Opera News* issue devoted to zarzuela. He notes the remarkable range of releases, which include a flood of 78-rpm records (some of which have been rereleased in compact disc format); LP and stereo formats pre-dating the 1980s (released by London International, Montilla, Angel, and Columbia); and new compact discs, including EMI's La Zarzuela series featuring new and old releases and the Auvidis Valois series of new performances of zarzuelas ranging from José de Nebra's *Viento Es la Dicha de Amor* to Sorozábal's *La Tabernera del Puerto.* I agree heartily with Traubner's applause for the Auvidis Valois collection; it is dificult to imagine any other series that can compete with the vitality and polish of these modern renditions. See Traubner, "¡Oid! Los compactos de zarzuela," *Opera News* 62 (July 1997): 24.

3. *Luisa Fernanda,* performed by the Jarvis Conservatory, compact disc, (JC 9702). The CD can be obtained by contacting the Jarvis Conservatory, 1711 Main Street, Napa, CA 94559; telephone, 707/255–5445.

4. Performers of non-Hispanic ancestry are regularly cast by the Chicago Opera Factory and formed the majority in the zarzuela productions offered by the Ohio Light Opera. College productions frequently involve performers of various background, and although it may seem surprising in a city such as El Paso, which comprises a sizable Hispanic population, Zarzuela at UTEP includes many non-Hispanic singers and actors.

5. I am grateful to Joe McClain for his contributions to this observation.

6. See Nicolás Kanellos, *A History of Hispanic Theatre in the United States: Origins to 1940* (Austin: University of Texas Press, 1990) and "An Overview of Hispanic Theatre," *Nuestro* (October 1985): 39–43.

7. Hugh Cardon, interview with the author, El Paso, Texas, July 29, 1995.

8. Mary Montaño, telephone interview with the author, June 7, 1994. See also Mary Montaño, "The Manuel Areu Collection of 19th-Century Zarzuelas" (Master's thesis, University of New Mexico, 1972).

9. Mary Montaño, telephone interview, June 7, 1994.

10. Ibid.

11. Richard Traubner, telephone interview with the author, July 23, 1999.

12. The contact address for the U.S. delegation of the SGAE is Delgado de la Sociedad General de Autores Españoles, 240 East Forty-seventh St., Suite 10B, New York, NY 10017.

13. For the 1987 festival Montaño's company produced *La Verbena de la Paloma,* with piano accompaniment, and in 1988 it produced *El Barberillo de Lavapiés* with full orchestra.

14. Mary Montaño, telephone interview, June 7, 1994.

15. Ibid.

16. Victor Chacón, telephone interview with the author, July 2, 1999.

17. This collection features 441 zarzuelas. According to Susanna Redondo, director of the Hispanic Institute of the Americas, the zarzuela collection at Columbia University began with the appointment of Federico de Onís in 1916 to the University's Spanish department (Redondo, interview with the author, October 29, 1986). He, along with Ramon Giménez, his wife, Zenobia Camprubí, and the composer Emilio de Torre, traveled regularly to Spain to collect scores and transcribe folk songs, which they used to teach students at the university's Spanish Institute. In the late 1950s this collection was divided: the scores were sent to the music library in Dodge Hall (on the main campus at Broadway and 116 St.), and the books were kept at Casa Hispánica (116 St., between Riverside Drive and Broadway). Today the Spanish Institute is known by the name it adopted in 1940: the Hispanic Institute of the Americas. An article in *Revista Hispánica Moderna* (1940) reports that the change was made to make people "aware of the prestigious history shared by Spanish speaking people, and so that people would know that the Institute was an American one and not a Spanish organization located in the United States" (86).

18. A documentary video of this production is available from KCOS-TV, El Paso.

19. See Pablo Zinger, "The Spanish Songbook" and "Son of Zarzuela," *Opera News* 62 (July 1997): 12–15, 16–19.

20. See <http://members.aol.com/PabloZinge/PabloZinger.html>.

21. Illness prevented Feliciano from honoring this engagement, and the role was filled by a local soprano, Yvonne Marmolejo, who managed to learn the part in only four days.

22. *Las Puertas de la mañana: Canciones argentinas de Carlos Guastavino* (Doors of the Morning: Argentine Songs by Carlos Guastavino), Ulises Espaillat, tenor; Pablo Zinger, piano (New Albion Records NA 058 CD). This compact disc features twenty songs by Carlos Guastavino, including the cycle *Siete Canciones* (Seven Songs), with text by Rafael Alberti.

23. Michael Schudson, *Advertising, the Uneasy Persuasion: Its Dubious Impact on American Society* (New York: Basic Books, 1986).

24. Ibid., xxi.

25. Ibid., xxii.

26. Ibid., ix.

27. Data reported here were obtained from responses to questionnaires that I distributed to audiences at a zarzuela performance at Repertorio Español, Thalia Spanish Theatre, and the ATM. These questionnaires were developed after two years of regular attendance, observation, and interviews at each of these theaters, and this prior experience helped me interpret the responses. For more details on the questionnaires and methodology employed in distributing them and analyzing the data, see Janet Sturman, "Zarzuela in New York: Contributions of Lyric Theatre to Hispanic Identity" (Ph.D. diss., Columbia University, 1987).

28. Newspaper Advertising Bureau, *Movie Advertisements and Reviews in Newspapers,* Research note 6 (New York: Newspaper Advertising Bureau, 1981).

29. See Richard Traubner, "Zarzuela Goes on Display," *New York Times,* August 4, 1985.

30. Peter G. Davis, "Music," *New York Magazine,* August 26, 1985.

31. Ibid., 109.

32. Paul D. Colford, "And You Don't Have to Speak Spanish (The Story of Dramatic Growth)" *Newsday,* July 7, 1983.

33. Silvia Brito, interview with the author, Thalia Spanish Theatre, Sunnyside, New York, April 8, 1986.

34. Guadalupe Silva, "Final Zarzuela a Masterpiece in Terms of Historical Accuracy," *El Paso Times,* August 8, 1987.

35. Velma Nieto, "*La Revoltosa* Superb Final Act to Second Zarzuela Festival," *El Paso Herald-Post,* August 6, 1987.

36. Jim Braden, "*Luisa Fernanda* Zarzuela More of a Musical Treat Than a Theatrical One," *El Paso Times,* July 31, 1992.

37. Dick Netzer, *The Subsidized Muse: Public Support for the Arts in the United States* (Cambridge: Cambridge University Press, 1978), 62.

38. Raul Cuervo, interview with the author, Union City, New Jersey, June 21, 1986.

39. Silvia Brito, interview with the author, Thalia Spanish Theatre, Sunnyside, New York, May 28, 1996.

40. Center for Arts Information, *New York City Arts Funding Guide,* ed. Ellen Thurston and R. Lewis (New York: Clearinghouse for Arts Information, 1985).

41. Victor Chacón, interview with the author, El Paso, Texas, July 29, 1995.

Chapter 9: Ends and Means

1. René Buch, interview with the author, Teatro Repertorio Español, New York City, June 8, 1999.

2. Silvia Brito, interview with the author, Thalia Spanish Theatre, Sunnyside, New York, June 10, 1999.

3. Pablo Zinger, "The Spanish Songbook," *Opera News* 62 (July 1997): 12–15.

4. Abner Cohen devotes all of *Two-Dimensional Man* (Berkeley: University of California Press, 1976) to explicating this conceptualization of politics and its symbolic expression in complex societies.

5. For example, it is hard to imagine Steven Blier confessing that he at first considered Rossini operas or German *Singspiel* to be "creepy," yet he admits to having initially felt this way about zarzuela. He writes: "The fact that no one but Spaniards sang these operas only confirmed their seeming inaccessibility. A recording of zarzuela by a non-Iberian seemed about as unlikely as an album of Yiddish folk music by Elisabeth Schwarzkopf" (Steven Blier, "Seduced by Zarzuela," *Opera News* 62 [July 1997]: 10).

6. These claims represent remarks voiced by directors, conductors, and performers. They mirror the views of individuals quoted directly and examined in previous chapters.

7. Repertorio Español's *¡Y se Armó la Mojiganga!* is a striking recent example. This contemporary comedy created by the Colombian director Jorge Alí Triana features rhythmic popular music by Germán Arrieta (known for his work with Colombian jazz and salsa) that directly contrasts with the operatic conceptions of zarzuela. Yet in 1994 Reper-

torio Español brought this production to the El Paso zarzuela festival, where it was presented alongside the production of the Spanish classic *La Tempranica* by the Thalia Spanish Theatre and the racy Mexican *revista Chin-chun-chán,* presented by the Compañía de Jorge Pais, from Mexico City.

8. The concept of pan-Hispanic identity that I present here contrasts with the one that Laurie Kay Sommers examines in "Inventing Latinismo: The Creation of 'Hispanic' Panethnicity in the United States," *Journal of American Folklore* (1991): 32–53.

9. For years the prevailing approach to studying ethnic communities, especially in urban areas, was to define the unit of investigation in terms of a geographical enclave. As Reyes-Schramm argued as early as 1979, this approaches denies the importance of interactions that cut across the boundaries of the enclave. Urban ethnic communities are shaped by wide-ranging connections. See Adelaide Reyes Schramm, "Ethnic Music, the Urban Area, and Ethnomusicology," *Sociologus* 29 (1979). Reprinted in Kay Kaufman Shelemay, ed., *Ethnomusicology: History, Definitions, and Scope* (New York: Garland, 1992), 297–318. Many such connections would be today described as "transnational." For a clear introduction to transnational theories, see Khachig Tölölyan, "The Nation State and Its Others: In Lieu of a Preface," *Diaspora: A Journal of Transnational Studies* 1 (Spring 1991): 3–7. Tölölyan defines transnational identity as individual identity shaped by the demands and loyalties to at least two "homes" in different nation-states. Such a perspective is useful for understanding the experiences and views of some Hispanic Americans, such as Mexican migrant workers, or, to a different degree, Puerto Ricans living on the mainland United States, but there are important exceptions, such as Cuban refugees. Again, such widely varying perspectives frustrate any simplistic conception of a single Hispanic identity existing outside the frame of limited, shared activity.

10. I attended a Cuban production of Severino Soutullo y Juan Vert's *La Leyenda del Beso* as part of the 1988 season by the Comedia Lírica Gonzalo Roig at the Gran Teatro de la Habana, Sala García Lorca (Prado y San Rafael), June 12, 1988.

11. For a rich discussion of how folkloric stage productions can be construed as de-Africanizing the African-derived practices they seek to present, see Katherine Hagedorn, *Divine Utterances: The Translation of Memory in Afro-Cuban Performance* (Washington, D.C.: Smithsonian Institution Press, forthcoming).

12. For a more detailed report of this emotional return visit, see Mireya Navarro, "An Exile Returns, Lured by the Memory of Cuba," (New York Times News Service, September 23, 1995), available at <http://www.latino.com/cuba923.html>.

Bibliography

Acuña, René. *El teatro popular en Hispanoamérica: Una bibliografía anotada* (Popular theater in Hispanic America: An annotated bibliography). Mexico City: Universidad Nacional Autónoma de México, 1979.

Aguirre, Yolanda. *Apuntes en torno al teatro colonial en Cuba (1670–1833)* (Notes concerning colonial theater in Cuba, 1670–1833). Havana: Universidad de la Habana, Dirección de Publicaciones, 1969.

Aldrich, Richard. *Concert Life in New York, 1902–1923.* New York: Putnam's, 1941.

Anonymous. "Zarzuela Emerges Victorious." *Variety,* September 5, 1979.

Arce Bueno, Julio C. "Approximación a las relaciones entre el teatro lírico y el cine mudo" (Approximation of the relationship between lyric theater and the silent cinema). *Cuadernos de música iberoamericana* 2–3 (1996–97): 273–80.

Arderíus, Francisco. *La ópera española y la zarzuela* (Spanish opera and zarzuela). Madrid: M. P. Montoya, 1882.

Arnau, Juan, and Carlos M. Gómez. *Historia de la zarzuela* (History of the zarzuela). Madrid: Tipografía de Archivos, 1934.

Arrom, José Juan. *Bosquejo histórico del teatro en Cuba desde sus orígenes hasta 1868* (A historical outline of theater in Cuba from its origins to 1868). New Haven, Conn.: Yale University Press, 1941.

Baqueiro Foster, Gerónimo. *Historia de la música en México,* vol. 3: *La música en el período independiente.* Mexico City: Secretaría de Educación Pública, Instituto Nacional de Bellas Artes, 1964.

Barth, Fredrik. Introduction. In *Ethnic Groups and Boundaries: The Social Organization of Culture Difference,* ed. F. Barth, 9–38. Boston: Little, Brown, 1969.

Béhague, Gerard. *Music in Latin America: An Introduction.* Englewood Cliffs, N.J.: Prentice-Hall, 1979.

———. *Performance Practice.* Westport, Conn.: Greenwood, 1984.

Bendahan, Daniel. *Hispanoamérica en la música del siglo XX* (Spanish America in the music of the twentieth century). Caracas: Monté Avila Editores Latinoamericana, 1997.

Bentivegna, Patricia. "A Study of Three *Zarzuelas Madrileñas* Together with a Historical Outline of the Zarzuela." Master's thesis, Columbia University, 1955.

Bissell, Sally Jane. "Manuel Areu and the Nineteenth-Century Zarzuela in Mexico and Cuba." Ph.D. diss., University of Iowa, 1987.

Blier, Steven. "Seduced by Zarzuela." *Opera News* 62 (July 1997): 10–11.

Braden, Jim. "*Luisa Fernanda* Zarzuela More of a Musical Treat Than a Theatrical One." *El Paso Times*, July 31, 1992.

Brenan, Gerald. *The Literature of the Spanish People: From Roman Times to the Present Day.* 2d ed. London: Cambridge University Press, 1953.

Brown, Thomas Allston. *A History of the New York Stage from the First Performance in 1732 to 1901.* New York: Dodd, Mead, 1903.

Bussey, William M. *French and Italian Influence on the Zarzuela: 1700–1770.* Studies in Musicology, no. 53. Ann Arbor: UMI Research Press, 1982.

Canepa Guzmán, Mario. *El teatro en Chile desde los indios hasta los teatros universitarios* (Theater in Chile from the Indians to the university theaters). Santiago, Chile: Arancibias Hermanos, 1967.

Carmona, Gloria. *Período de la independencia a la revolución (1810 a 1910)* (From the period of independence to the revolution, 1810–1910). Pt. 3 of *Historia* (History), vol. 1 of *La música de México* (The music of Mexico), ed. Julio Estrada, 2 vols. Mexico City: Instituto de Investigaciones Estéticas, Universidad Nacional Autónoma de México, 1984.

Carpentier, Alejo. "Cómo el negro se volvió criollo" (How the Negro became Creole). In *Conferencias*, ed. Virgilio López Lemus, 215–22. Havana: Editorial Letras Cubanas, 1987.

———. *Ese músico que llevo dentro* (The musician I carry within). Ed. Zoila Gómez. Vol. 3. Havana: Editorial Letras Cubanas, 1980.

———. *La música en Cuba* (Music in Cuba). Mexico: Fondo de Cultura Económica, 1946.

Carr, Raymond, *Modern Spain, 1875–1980.* Oxford: Oxford University Press, 1980.

Casares Rodicio, Emilio. "Historia del teatro de los Bufos, 1866–1881: Crónica y dramaturgia" (History of the Bufo theater, 1966–1881: Chronicle and dramaturgy). *Cuadernos de música iberoamericana* 2–3 (1996–97): 73–118.

Castel, Nico. *A Singer's Manual of Spanish Lyric Diction.* New York: Excalibur, 1994.

Castellanos, Jorge. *Cultura afrocubana* (Afro-Cuban culture). Miami: Ediciones Universal, 1988.

Center for Arts Information. *New York City Arts Funding Guide.* Ed. Ellen Thurston and R. Lewis. New York: Clearinghouse for Arts Information, 1985.

Césaire, Aimé. *Discours sur le colonialisme* (Discourse on colonialism). Paris: Présence Africaine, 1956.

Chase, Gilbert. *Handbook of Latin American Studies.* Cambridge, Mass.: Harvard University Press, 1943.

———. *The Music of Spain.* 2d ed. New York: Dover, 1959.

Chavez, Lydia. "Striving but Still Lagging: Puerto Ricans Wonder Why." *New York Times*, June 5, 1986.

Chenault, Lawrence R. *The Puerto Rican Migrant in New York City.* New York: Columbia University Press, 1938; repr., New York: Russell and Russell, 1970.

Cohen, Abner. Introduction. In *Urban Ethnicity,* ed. Abner Cohen, ix–xxiv. London: Tavistock, 1974.

———. *Two-Dimensional Man: An Essay on the Anthropology of Power and Symbolism in Complex Society.* Berkeley: University of California Press, 1976.

Colford, Paul D. "And You Don't Have to Speak Spanish (The Story of Dramatic Growth)." *Newsday,* July 7, 1983.

Corredor Alvarez, María José. "Aportaciones musicales de la Guerra de la Independencia a un nuevo género nacional: La zarzuela" (Musical contributions of the War of Indepenence to a new, national genre: The zarzuela). *Cuadernos de música iberoamericana* 2–3 (1996–97): 51–56.

Cotarelo y Mori, D. Emilio. *Historia de la zarzuela o sea el drama lírico en España, desde su origen a fines del siglo xix* (History of the zarzuela, or lyric drama, in Spain, from its origin to the end of the nineteenth century). Madrid: Tipografía de Archivos, 1934.

Curtin, Philip. *The Atlantic Slave Trade: A Census.* Madison: University of Wisconsin Press, 1969.

Daniels, Roger. *Coming to America: A History of Immigration and Ethnicity in American Life.* New York: HarperCollins, 1990.

Davis, Peter G. "Music." *New York Magazine,* August 26, 1985.

Davis, Richard. *A History of Music in American Life.* 3 vols. Malabar, Fla.: Robert E. Krieger, 1982.

DeCarlo, Tessa. "Company Box: Jarvis Conservatory." *Opera News* 63 (June 1999): 76.

Deleito y Piñuela, José. *Origen y apogeo del género chico* (Origin and apex of the minor genre). Madrid: Revista de Occidente, 1949.

Domingo, Plácido. *My First Forty Years.* New York: Knopf, 1983.

Dower, Catherine. *Puerto Rican Music Following the Spanish-American War.* Lanham, Md.: University Press of America, 1983.

Dueñas, Pablo. *Las divas en el teatro de revista mexicano* (The divas of Mexico's theatrical revues). Mexico City: Asociación Mexicana de Estudios Fonográficos, 1994.

Ericson, Raymond. "Pepita Embil, 'Queen of the Zarzuela,' Is Heard." *New York Times,* January 8, 1971.

Fanon, Frantz. *Black Skin, White Masks.* New York: Grove, 1962 [1952].

Fernández, Enrique. "One Sings the Other Doesn't." *Village Voice,* December 20, 1983.

Fernández-Cid, Antonio. *Cien años de teatro musical en España, 1875–1975* (One hundred years of musical theater in Spain, 1875–1975). Madrid: Real Musical, 1975.

Figueroa, Pablo. *Teatro: Hispanic Theatre in New York City, 1920–76.* El Museo del Barrio exhibition catalog, April 22–June 3, 1977.

Franco, José Luciano. *La presencia negra en el Nuevo Mundo* (The black presence in the New World). Havana: Casa de las Américas, 1968.

Freedman, Samuel G. "8 Theaters Get $1.3 Million in Grants." *New York Times,* September 6, 1984.

Frenk Alatorre, Margit. *Cancionero de romances viejos* (Songbook of old *romances*). Mexico City: Dirección General de Publicaciones, 1961.

———. *Cancionero folklorico de México* (Songbook of Mexican folk songs). 5 vols. Mexico City: Colegio de México, 1975–85.

Frith, Simon, and Andrew Goodwin. *On Record: Rock, Pop, and the Written Word.* New York: Pantheon, 1990.

Gesualdo, Vicente. *Historia de la música en la Argentina* (History of music in Argentina). Buenos Aires: Impresiones Diagonal, 1971.

Gibson, Charles. *Spain in America.* New York: Harper and Row, 1966.

Giménez, Alberto Emilio. "Presencia y arraigo de la zarzuela en Argentina" (The presence and popularity of zarzuela in Argentina). *Cuadernos de música iberoamericana* 2–3 (1996–97): 475–86.

Gipson, Rosemary. "The Beginning of Theatre in Sonora." *Arizona and the West* 9, no. 4 (1967): 349–64.

———. "The History of Tucson Theater before 1906." Master's thesis, University of Arizona, 1967.

Glazer, Nathan, and Daniel P. Moynihan, eds. *Beyond the Melting Pot: The Negroes, Puerto Ricans, Jews, Italians, and Irish of New York City.* Cambridge, Mass.: MIT Press, 1963.

———. *Ethnicity: Theory and Experience.* Cambridge, Mass.: Harvard University Press, 1975.

González Freire, Natividad. *Teatro cubano, 1927–61* (Cuban theater, 1927–61). 2d ed. Havana: Ministerio de Relaciones Exteriores, 1961.

Goodwin, Noel. "Zarzuela of the Spanish Heritage." *Opera,* April 1974.

Gordon, Milton. *Assimilation in American Life: The Role of Race, Religion, and National Origins.* New York: Oxford University Press, 1964.

———. *Human Nature, Class, and Ethnicity.* New York: Oxford University Press, 1978.

Greenfield, Charles. "Spain's King of Tenors." *Nuestro,* March 1985, pp. 21–25.

Hagedorn, Katherine. *Divine Utterances: The Translation of Memory in Afro-Cuban Performance.* Washington, D.C.: Smithsonian Institution Press, forthcoming.

Hall, Raymond. "Spanish as an Operatic Language." *New York Times,* March 22, 1931.

Hamilton, H. V. "Zarzuela." In *Grove's Dictionary of Music and Musicians,* 2d ed., ed. J. A. Fuller-Maitland, 590–92. Philadelphia: Theodore Presser, 1916.

Hamilton, Mary Neal. *Music in Eighteenth-Century Spain.* Urbana: University of Illinois, 1937.

Holden, Stephen. "A Month of Summerfare from Bach to Zarzuela." *New York Times,* July 13, 1984.

Holland, Bernard. "Domingo to Sing Zarzuela at Garden." *New York Times,* April 18, 1985.

Horowitz, Donald. "Ethnic Identity." In *Ethnicity: Theory and Experience,* ed. Nathan Glazer and Daniel P. Moynihan, 111–40. Cambridge, Mass.: Harvard University Press, 1975.

Hymes, Dell. "Ways of Speaking." In *Explorations in the Ethnography of Speaking,* ed. Richard Bauman and Joel Scherzer, 433–51. New York: Cambridge University Press, 1989 [1974].

Iglesias, Antonio. "Spain Experiences a Revival of Zarzuela." *Musical America,* November 15, 1951.

Kanellos, Nicolás. *A History of Hispanic Theatre in the United States: Origins to 1940.* Austin: University of Texas Press, 1990.

———. "An Overview of Hispanic Theatre." *Nuestro,* October 1985, pp. 39–43.

———. "An Overview of Hispanic Theatre in the United States." In *Hispanic Theatre in the United States,* ed. Nicolás Kanellos, 7–15. Houston: Arte Publico, 1986.

Koegel, John. "Canciones del país: Mexican Musical Life in California after the Gold Rush." *California History* 78 (Fall 1999): 160–87, 215–19.

———. "Mexican-American Music in Nineteenth-Century Southern California: The Lummis Wax Cylinder Collection at the Southwest Museum, Los Angeles." Ph.D. diss., Claremont Graduate University, 1994.

———. "Music: Nineteenth and Twentieth Centuries." In *Encyclopedia of Mexico,* ed. Michael Weiner, 2:984–97. Chicago: Fitzroy and Dearborn, 1997.

———. "New Sources of Music from Spain and Colonial Mexico at the Sutro Library." *Notes: Quarterly Journal of the Music Library Association* 55, no. 3 (Mar. 1999): 583–613.

———. "Nuevas fuentes musicales para danza, teatro y salón de la Nueva España" (New musical sources for dance, theater and salon in New Spain). *Heterofonía: Revista de investigación musical* 30, nos. 116–17 (1997): 9–37.

———. "Spanish and Mexican Dance Music in Early California." *Ars Musica Denver* 7, no. 1 (Fall 1994): 31–56.

Kingsbury, Henry. *Music, Talent, and Performance.* Philadelphia: Temple University Press, 1988.

Lapeña-Bonifacio, Amelia. *The "Seditious" Tagalog Playwrights: Early American Occupation.* Manila: Zarzuela Foundation of the Philippines, 1972.

Lapique Becali, Zoila. *Música colonial cubana* (Colonial Cuban music), vol. 1: *1812–1902.* Havana: Editorial Letras Cubana (Colección Cubana), 1979.

Leal, Riné. *Breve historia del teatro cubano* (Short history of the Cuban theater). Havana: Editorial Letras Cubanas, 1980.

Libby, Theodore W., Jr. "Zarzuela: Joseph in the Pharaoh's Court." *New York Times,* January 26, 1982.

Ligon, Betty. "Last Zarzuela Is Truly the Best." *El Paso Herald Post,* August 6, 1988.

Littlejohn, Stephen W. *Theories of Human Communication.* 2d ed. Belmont, Calif.: Wadsworth, 1983.

Livermore, Ann. *A Short History of Spanish Music.* New York: Vienna House, 1972.

López Chavarri, Eduardo. *Música popular española* (Spanish popular music). Barcelona: Editorial Labor, 1927.

Loza, Steven. *Barrio Rhythm: Mexican American Music in Los Angeles.* Urbana: University of Illinois Press, 1993.

Lyman, Stanford M., and William A. Douglas. "Ethnicity: Strategies of Collective Impression Management." *Social Research* 40 (1973): 344–56.

Lynes, Russell. *The Lively Audience: A Social History of the Visual and Performing Arts in America 1890–1950*. New American Series. New York: Harper and Row, 1985.

MacKinlay, Sterling. *Origin and Developement of Light Opera*. London: Hutchinson, 1927.

Magaña Esquivel, Antonio. *Los teatros en la Ciudad de Mexico, D.F.* (Theaters in Mexico City). Mexico City: Colección Popular de México, 1974.

Maldonado-Dennis, Manuel. *The Emigration Dialectic*. New York: International, 1980. English-language edition of *Puerto Rico y Estados Unidos: Emigración y colonialismo* (Puerto Rico and the United States: Emigration and colonialism). Mexico City: Siglo XXI, 1976.

Malm, Krister, and Roger Wallis. *Big Sounds from Small Peoples: The Music Industry in Small Countries*. London: Pendragron, 1984.

———. *Media Policy and Music Activity*. London: Routledge, 1992.

María y Campos, Armando de. *Archivo de teatro cronicas: De enero a diciembre de 1946* (Theatrical archive and chronicle from January to December 1946). Mexico City: Compañia de Ediciones Populares, 1947.

Martel, José, and Hymen Alpern, eds. *Diez comedias del siglo de oro* (Ten comedies of the Golden Era). 2d ed., rev. Leonard Mades. New York: Harper and Row, 1968.

Martin, Deborah. "Famed Cellist Persuaded Trumpet Player to Try Singing." *El Paso Herald-Post,* July 29, 1995.

Martínez Olmedilla, Augusto. *El maestro Barbieri y su tiempo* (Master Barbieri and his times). Madrid: Saez, 1950.

Mayer-Serra, Otto. *Panorama de la música mexicana desde la Independencia hasta la actualidad* (Panorama of Mexican music from independence to the present). Mexico: El Colegio de México, 1941.

McGay, Mrs. Frank B. "Scrapbook of Concert, Opera, Theatre, Civic, and Cultural Programs Given in New York City between 1881–1954." Presented to the New York Historical Society by Thomas Larremore.

Miller, John C. "Contemporary Hispanic Theatre in New York." In *Hispanic Theatre in the United States,* ed. Nicolás Kanellos, 24–34. Houston: Arte Publico, 1984.

———. "Hispanic Theatre in New York, 1965–1977." *Revista Chicano-Riqueña* 6, no. 1 (1978): 40–59.

Mindlin, Roger. *Die Zarzuela* (The Zarzuela). Zurich: Atlantis Verlag, 1965.

Miranda, Ricardo. "La zarzuela en México: 'Jardin de senderos que se bifurcan'" (The zarzuela in Mexico: A garden of forking paths). *Cuadernos de música iberoamericana* 2–3 (1996–97): 451–74.

Mitchell, J. C. "Perceptions of Ethnicity and Ethnic Behavior: An Empirical Exploration." In *Urban Ethnicity,* ed. Abner Cohen, 1–35. London: Tavistock, 1974.

Montaño, Mary Army. "The Manuel Areu Collection of 19th-Century Zarzuelas." Master's thesis, University of New Mexico, 1972.

Moore, Joan, and Harry Pachon. *Hispanics in the United States*. Englewood Cliffs, N.J.: Prentice-Hall, 1985.

Moore, Robin. *Nationalizing Blackness: Afrocubanismo and Artistic Revolution in Havana, 1920–1940*. Pittsburgh: University of Pittsburgh Press, 1997.

Muñoz, Matilde. *Historia de la zarzuela y el género chico* (History of the zarzuela and the minor genre). Madrid: Editorial Tesoro, 1946.

Nagore Ferrer, María. "La vida zarzuelística en Bilbao 1850–1936" (The zarzuela-influenced life in Bilbao). *Cuadernos de música iberoamericana* 2–3 (1996–97): 399–408.

Netzer, Dick. *The Subsidized Muse: Public Support for the Arts in the United States.* Cambridge: Cambridge University Press, 1978; New York: Twentieth Century, 1978.

Newspaper Advertising Bureau. "Movie Advertisements and Reviews in Newspapers." *Research Note 6.* New York: Newspaper Advertising Bureau, 1981.

New York Public Library. *Bulletin,* April 1922, p. 269.

Nieto, Velma. "*La Revoltosa* Superb Final Act to Second Zarzuela Festival." *El Paso Herald-Post,* August 6, 1987.

Olavarría y Ferarri, Enrique de. *Índices a la reseña histórica del teatro en México, 1538–1911* (Indexes to the collected history of theater in Mexico, 1538–1911). Mexico City: Editorial Porrua, 1968.

———. *Reseña histórica del teatro en méxico.* 3d ed., 5 vols. Mexico City: Editorial Porrua, 1961.

"Opera Nela at Tully Hall." *New York Times,* December 31, 1974.

Pasarell, Emilio J. *Orígenes y desarrollo de la afición teatral en Puerto Rico—siglo XX* (The origins and development of theatrical taste in Puerto Rico—twentieth century). Vol. 3. Rio Piedras, P.R.: Editorial Universitaria, Universidad de Puerto Rico, 1967.

———. *Panorama teatral de Puerto Rico en el siglo XIX* (Panorama of the theater in Puerto Rico in the nineteenth century). Printed under the auspices of the Ciclo de Conferencias sobre la Literatura de Puerto Rico. San Juan: Instituto de Cultura Puertorriqueña, 1972.

Pasquariello, Anthony M. "The Evolution of the *Sainete* in the River Platte Area." *Latin American Theatre Review* 17 (Fall 1983): 14–24.

Peña, Manuel. *The Texas-Mexican Conjunto: History of a Working-Class Music.* Mexican American Monographs, no. 9, Center for Mexican American Studies. Austin: University of Texas Press, 1985.

Peña y Goñi, Antonio. *España, desde la ópera a la zarzuela* (Spain, from opera to zarzuela). Ed. Eduardo Rincón. El libro de bolsillo, no. 49. Madrid: Editorial Alianza, 1967.

Peñin, José. "La vida de la zarzuela en la prensa venezolana" (The life of the zarzuela in the Venezuelan press). *Cuadernos de música iberoamericana* 2–3 (1996–97): 487–514.

Perdomo Escobar, José. *Historia de la música en Colombia* (History of music in Colombia). 3d ed. Bogotá: Editorial A B C, 1963.

Pereira Salas, Eugenio. *Historia de la música en Chile (1850–1900)* (History of music in Chile, 1850–1900). Publicaciones de la Universidad de Chile. Santiago: Editorial Del Pacífico, 1957.

———. *Historia del teatro en Chile desde sus orígenes hasta la muerte de Juan Casacuberta en 1849* (History of the theater in Chile since its origins to the death of Juan Casacuberta in 1849). Santiago: Ediciones de la Universidad de Chile, 1974.

Plaza, Sixto. "Sociología del teatro musical español" (Sociology of the Spanish musical theater). Ph.D. diss., Georgetown University, 1986.

R.P. "Zarzuelas from Spain on Disks." *New York Times,* May 22, 1955.

Reimers, David. *Still the Golden Door: The Third World Comes to America.* New York: Columbia University Press, 1985.

Repertorio Español. Internet Web page. <http://infolatino.com/News/970911nycb.html>.

Reyes de la Maza, Luis. *El teatro en México durante la Independencia (1810–1839)* (Theater in México during Independence). Cuidad Universitaria: Universidad Nacional Autónoma de México, 1969.

———. *El teatro en México en la época de Santa Anna* (The theatre in Mexico in the time of Santa Anna). Vol. 2 (1851–57). Ciudad Universitaria: Universidad Nacional Autónoma de México, 1979.

Reyes Schramm, Adelaida. "Ethnic Music, the Urban Area, and Ethnomusicology." *Sociologus* 29 (1979); repr. in *Ethnomusicology: History, Definitions, and Scope,* ed. Kay Kaufman Shelemay, 297–318. New York: Garland, 1992.

———. "Explorations in Urban Ethnomusicology: Hard Lessons from the Spectacularly Ordinary." *Yearbook for Traditional Music* 14 (1982): 1–15.

———. "The Role of Music in the Interaction of Black Americans and Hispanos in New York City's East Harlem." Ph.D. diss., Columbia University, 1975.

Rockwell, John. "Cecilia Valdés: Alliance of Latin Arts." *New York Times,* April 4, 1974.

———. "'Marina,' Zarzuela Is Tuneful Example of Rich Repertory." *New York Times,* January 23, 1974.

Rothstein, Edward. "Expert Tries to Sell Spanish Opera." *New York Times,* December 8, 1983.

Royce, Anya Peterson. *Ethnic Identity: Strategies of Diversity.* Bloomington: Indiana University Press, 1982.

Ruiz Elcoro, José. "Surgimiento y desarrollo de la zarzuela cubana: Estructura morfológica y análisis" (The emergence and development of Cuban zarzuela: Morphological structure and analysis). *Cuadernos de música iberoamericana* vols. 2–3 (1996–97): 423–38.

Russell, Craig, ed. *Santiago de Murcia's "Códice Saldívar No. 4": A Treasury of Secular Guitar Music from Baroque Mexico,* vol. 1: *Commentary.* Urbana: University of Illinois Press, 1995.

Saenz, Antonio. *El Teatro en Puerto Rico* (Theater in Puerto Rico). 2d ed. San Juan: University of Puerto Rico, Colección UPREX, 1970 [1950].

Sagardía, Angel. *Ruperto Chapí.* Madrid: Espasa-Calpe, 1979.

Salter, Lionel, and Jack Sage. "Zarzuela." In *The New Grove Dictionary of Music and Musicians,* ed. Stanley Sadie, 20:649–52. London: Macmillan, 1980.

Sánchez, Victor. "La crisis de la zarzuela grande en la obra de Tomás Bretón" (The crisis of zarzuela grande in the works of Tomás Bretón). *Cuadernos de música iberoamericana* 2–3 (1996–97): 205–12.

Schechner, Richard. *Essays on Performance Theory, 1970–1976.* Rev. ed. New York: Routledge, 1988.

———. *The Future of Ritual: Writings on Culture and Performance.* London: Routledge, 1993.

Schoenberg, Harold. "A Garden of Spain." *New York Times,* July 23, 1961.
———. "Musical Paella." *Newsweek,* June 9, 1969.
Schudson, Michael. *Advertising, the Uneasy Persuasion: Its Dubious Impact on American Society.* New York: Basic Books, 1986.
Scott, Rebecca. *Slave Emancipation in Cuba: The Transition to Free Labor, 1860–1899.* Princeton, N.J.: Princeton University Press, 1985.
Seeger, Charles. *Studies in Musicology 1935–1975.* Berkeley: University of California Press, 1977.
Sennett, Richard. *Classic Essays on the Culture of Cities.* Englewood Cliffs, N.J.: Prentice-Hall, 1978.
Shepherd, John. *Music as Social Text.* Cambridge: Blackwell/Polity, 1991.
Silva, Guadalupe. "Final Zarzuela a Masterpiece in Terms of Historical Accuracy." *El Paso Times,* August 8, 1987.
Singer, Roberta Louise. "My Music Is Who I Am and What I Do: Latin Popular Music and Identity in New York City." Ph.D. diss., Indiana University, 1982.
Smith, Patrick J. "Fiesta in Madrid." *Musical America,* August 1969.
———. *The Tenth Muse: A Historical Study of the Opera Libretto.* New York: Schirmer Books, 1970.
Sommers, Laurie Kay. "Inventing Latinismo: The Creation of 'Hispanic' Panethnicity in the United States." *Journal of American Folklore* 104 (1991): 32–53.
Sopeña Ibañez, Federico. *Historia de la música española contemporánea* (History of contemporary Spanish music). Madrid: Ediciones Rialp, 1958.
"Spanish Theater Is Projected Here—Producers of *La Leyenda del Beso* Plan the 'Get Acquainted Series' for This Season." *New York Times,* November 22, 1942.
Spillane, Kathleen Wilson. "The Zarzuela as Source Material for College Opera Programs." *NATS Journal* (Mar.–Apr. 1994): 19–24.
Stavans, Ilan. *The Hispanic Condition: Reflections on Culture and Identity in America.* New York: HarperCollins, 1995.
Stein, Louise K. "Opera and the Spanish Political Agenda." *Acta Musicologica* 63 (1991): 125–67.
———. *Songs of Mortals, Dialogues of the Gods: Music and Theatre in Seventeenth-Century Spain.* Oxford: Clarendon, 1993.
Stevenson, Robert. *Music in Mexico: A Historical Survey.* New York: Thomas Crowell, 1952.
———. "La primera compañía del ópera en el nuevo mundo" (The first opera company in the New World). *Américas,* January 1964.
———, ed. *La Púrpura de la Rosa,* by Tomás Torrejón y Velasco. Lima: Instituto Nacional de Cultura, 1976.
Stevenson, Robert, and José Antonio Guzmán Bravo. *Período virreinal* (The viceregal period). Pt. 2 of *Historia* (History), vol. 1 of *La música de México* (The music of Mexico), ed. Julio Estrada. Mexico City: Instituto de Investigaciones Estéticas, Universidad Nacional Autónoma de México, 1986.
Stolcke, Verena. *Marriage, Class, and Colour in Nineteenth-Century Cuba: A Study of Ra-*

cial Attitudes and Sexual Values in a Slave Society. Ann Arbor: University of Michigan Press, 1989.

Sturman, Janet. "Advertising and Latin Music at a New York City Jazz Club: Interrelationships That Shape the Musical Event." *Current Musicology* 37–38 (1984): 159–66.

———. "Zarzuela in New York: Contributions of Lyric Theatre to Hispanic Identity." Ph.D. diss., Columbia University, 1987.

———. "Zarzuela Productions in New York." *Yearbook for Traditional Music* 18 (1986): 103–13.

Suárez Radillo, Carlos Miguel. "The Spanish Influence: Theater in America." *Horizon* 29, no. 10 (Dec. 1986): 33–49.

Subirá, José. *Historia de la música española e hispanoamericana* (History of Spanish and Spanish American Music). Barcelona: Salvat Editores, 1953.

———. *Historia de la música teatral en España* (History of theatrical music in Spain). Barcelona: Editorial Labor, 1943.

———. *Historia y anecdotario del teatro real* (History and anecdotes of the royal theater). Madrid: Editorial Plus-Ultra, 1949.

———. *Tonadillas teatrales inéditas: Libretos y partitura, con una descripción sinóptica de nuestra música lírica* (Unpublished theatrical *tonadillas:* Librettos and scores, with a synoptic description of our lyric music). Madrid: Tipografía de Archivos, 1932.

Tamayo, Manuel. *El libro de la zarzuela* (The zarzuela book). Mexico City: Ediciones Daimon, 1982.

Tello, Aurelio. *Archivo musical de la Catedral de Oaxaca: Cantadas y villancicos de Manuel de Sumaya* (The musical archive of the Oaxaca Cathedral: Cantatas and festival songs of Manuel de Sumaya). Tesoro de la Música Polifónica en México, 7. Mexico City: CENIDIM, 1994.

Thalia Spanish Theatre. Internet Web page. <http://www.queensnewyork.com/cultural/thalia>.

Tölölyan, Khachig. "The Nation State and Its Others: In Lieu of a Preface." *Diaspora: A Journal of Transnational Studies* 1 (Spring 1991): 3–7.

Tolón, Edwin Teurbe. *Teatro lírico popular de Cuba* (Cuban popular lyric theater). Miami: Ediciones Universal, 1973.

Traubner, Richard. *Operetta: A Theatrical History.* London: Victor Gollancz, 1984.

———. "¡Oid! Los compactos de zarzuela." *Opera News* 62 (July 1997): 24.

———. "¿Qué pasa? ¡Zarzuela!" *Opera News* 62 (July 1997): 27.

———. "Zarzuela Goes on Display." *New York Times,* August 4, 1985.

Trottier, Richard W. "Charters of Pan-Ethnic Identity: Indigenous American Indians and Immigrant Americans." In *Ethnic Change,* ed. Charles Keyes, 271–305. Seattle: University of Washington Press, 1981.

Trudgill, Peter. *Sociolinguistics: an Introduction to Language and Society.* Rev. ed. New York: Penguin Books, 1983.

United States Department of Commerce, Bureau of the Census. *Bulletins of the Twelfth Census of the United States,* Oct. 6, 1900, to Oct. 20. Washington, D.C.: GPO, 1902.

———. "Composition and Characteristics of the Population by States, New York." In *Reports by States, with Statistics for Counties, Cities, and Other Civil Divisions—Nebraska to Wyoming.* Vol. 3 of *1910 Census of the United States.* 11 vols. Washington, D.C.: GPO, 1913.

———. "Country of Birth of Foreign-Born White [Population]." In *Composition and Characteristics of the Population by States.* Vol. 3 of *1920 Census of the United States.* 11 vols. Washington, D.C.: GPO, 1922.

———. "Table 17: Indians, Chinese and Japanese, 1910–1930, and Mexicans 1930 for Counties and Cities of 25,000 or More"; "Table 18: Foreign-born White by Country of Birth for Counties and Cities and Villages of 10,000 or More." In *Reports by States Showing the Composition and Characteristics of the Population for Counties, Cities, and Townships or Other Civil Divisions,* pt. 2, *Montana–Wyoming.* Vol. 3 of *1930 Census of the United States.* 8 vols. Washington, D.C.: GPO, 1933.

———. "Table 24: Country of Birth for the Foreign-Born White Population." In *Characteristics of the Population,* pt. 5, *New York.* Vol. 2 of *1940 Census of the United States: Population.* Washington, D.C.: GPO, 1943.

———. "Table 34a: Country of Birth for the Foreign-Born White Population for SMSAs, Urban Areas, and Urban Places of 10,000 or More." In *Characteristics of the Population,* pt. 32, *New York.* Vol. 2 of *1950 Census of the United States: Population.* Washington, D.C.: GPO, 1952.

———. "Table 99: Country of Origin of the Foreign Stock by Nativity, Color, and Sex for the State, SMSAs of 250,000 or More." In *Characteristics of the Population,* pt. 34, *New York.* Vol. 2 of *1960 Census of the United States: Population.* Washington, D.C.: GPO, 1960.

———. *Persons of Spanish Origin in the United States: November 1969.* Current Population Reports, ser. P-20, no. 213. Washington, D.C.: GPO, 1971.

———. "Table 141: Country of Origin for the Foreign Stock." *Characteristics of the Population,* pt. 34, *New York.* Vol. 1 of *1970 Census of the United States: Population.* 2 vols. Washington, D.C.: GPO, 1973.

———. "Population, by Spanish-Origin, Age, Sex and Marital Status" *State and Metropolitan Area Data Book—A Statistical Abstract Supplement.* Washington, D.C.: GPO, 1982.

———. "Table 16: Total Persons and Spanish Origin Persons by Type of Spanish Origin and Race." In *Characteristics of the Population,* ch. B, pt. 34, "New York." Vol. 1 of *1980 Census of the United States.* 2 vols. Washington, D.C.: GPO, 1982.

———. "Table 56: Summary of Social Characteristics"; "Table 59: Persons by Spanish Origin, Race and Sex." In *Characteristics of the Population,* ch. C, pt. 32, "New Jersey." Vol. 1 of *1980 Census of the United States.* 2 vols. Washington, D.C.: GPO, 1983.

Valdez, Luis. *Early Works: Actos, Bernabe, and Pensamiento Serpentino.* Houston: Arte Publico, 1971.

Valverde, Salvador. *El mundo de la zarzuela* (The world of zarzuela). Madrid: Editorial Palabras, 1979.

Van Vechten, Carl. *The Music of Spain.* New York: Knopf, 1918.

Van Winkle Keller, Kate, with John Koegel. "Secular Music to 1800." In *The Cambridge History of American Music,* ed. David Nicholls, 49–77. Cambridge: Cambridge University Press, 1998.

Vázquez Millares, Angel. "De la zarzuela española a la zarzuela cubana: Vida del género en Cuba" (From the Spanish zarzuela to Cuban zarzuela: The life of the genre in Cuba). *Cuadernos de Música Iberoamericana* 2–3 (1996–97): 439–50.

Vega, Carlos. *Panorama de la música popular Argentina, con un ensayo sobre la ciencia del folklore* (A panoramic overview of Argentine popular music, with an essay on the science of folklore). Buenos Aires: Editorial Losada, 1944.

Wallerstein, Immanuel. "Ethnicity and National Immigration in West Africa." In *Africa: Social Problems of Change and Conflict,* ed. Paul Van de Berghe, 478–82. San Francisco: Chandler, 1965.

Walsh, Stephen. "Time to Look and Listen." *Observer,* May 5, 1975.

Watson Espeñar, Maida, and Carlos José Reyes. *Materiales para una historia del teatro en Colombia* (Materials for a history of the theater in Colombia). Bogotá: Instituto Colombiano de Cultura, 1978.

Weinstock, Herbert. "Music from Spain." *Saturday Review,* January 31, 1953.

White, Theodore H. "America's Two Cultures." In *Our Troubled Press: Ten Years of the Columbia Journalism Review,* ed. Alfred Balk and James Boylan, 11–20. Boston: Little, Brown, 1971.

Wilson, John. "Opera: The Zarzuela, a Spanish Tradition." *New York Times,* December 11, 1983.

Yépez, Benjamin. "Noticias y zarzuelas en Colombia 1850–1880" (News and zarzuelas in Colombia, 1850–80). *Cuadernos de Música Iberoamericana* 2–3 (1996–97): 515–30.

Zarzuela! Internet Web page. <http://www.nashwan.demon.co.uk/zarzuela/htm>.

Zinger, Pablo. "Son of Zarzuela." *Opera News* 62 (July 1997): 16.

———. "The Spanish Songbook." *Opera News* 62 (July 1997): 12–19.

Zurita, Marciano. *Historia del género chico* (History of the minor genre). Madrid: Prensa Popular, 1920.

Interviews

Brito, Silvia, director, Thalia Spanish Theatre. Interview with the author, Sunnyside, N.Y., April 8, 1986.

———. Telephone interviews with the author, 1994.

———. Interview with the author, Sunnyside, N.Y., May 28, 1996.

———. Interview with the author, Sunnyside, N.Y., June 10, 1999.

Buch, René, artistic director, Repertorio Español. Interview with the author, New York City, July 11, 1985.

———. Informal interviews with the author, New York City, 1987.

———. Telephone interview with the author, November 2, 1992.
———. Telephone interview with the author, May 28, 1995.
———. Interview with the author, New York City, June 8, 1999.
Cardon, Hugh, director of Hispanic Music Association and professor of music, University of Texas at El Paso. Interview with the author, El Paso, Texas, July 29, 1995.
Castel, Nico, tenor, character actor, and diction coach, New York Metropolitan Opera. Interview with the author, New York City, February 25, 1985.
Chacón, Mauricio, and Frances Chacón, board members, Amigos de la Zarzuela. Interview with the author, New York City, April 29, 1986.
Chacón, Victor, artistic director of Zarzuela at UTEP, University of Texas at El Paso, 1996–98; president of Board of Directors and producer for the International Festival de la Zarzuela in El Paso, 1994–96. Interview with the author, El Paso, Texas, July 29, 1995.
———. Telephone interview with the author, July 2, 1999.
Colón, Evangelina, soprano. Interview with the author, New York City, February 7, 1985.
Cuervo, Raul, director, La Asociación de Teatro Musical. Interview with the author, Union City, N.J., June 21, 1986.
De Grandy, Julie. Telephone interview with the author, July 15, 1999.
De Grandy, Miguel, Cuban actor and baritone; guest director for Thalia Spanish Theatre (New York); artistic director, Teatro Pro-Arte Grateli (Miami). Informal discussion with the author, March 23, 1986.
———. Telephone interview with the author, April 4, 1986.
———. Correspondence with the author, May 23, 1986.
Escalante, Leopoldo, pianist; musical director for Thalia Spanish Theatre, 1985–87. Interview with the author, New York City, June 11, 1986.
González, Manuel, composer of modern zarzuela. Interview with the author, New York City, January 30, 1985.
Gottlieb, Aida, president, Latin American Productions. Interview with the author, Tarrytown, N.Y., March 3, 1985.
Lewis, Blanche Artis, director, Chicago Opera Factory and Ovation Artist Management. Telephone interview with the author, August 2, 1999.
Montaño, Mary, cofounder of "El Teatro de la Zarzuela," later called "¡Viva Zarzuela!" Telephone interview with the author, June 7, 1994.
———. Telephone conversations with the author, August 1999.
Redondo, Susana, director, Hispanic Institute, Columbia University. Interview with the author, New York City, October 29, 1986.
Traubner, Richard, scholar, author, and director. Telephone interview with the author, July 23, 1999.
Trelles Solomon, Josefina, Cuban-born translator and zarzuela fan. Regular conversations with the author, New York City, 1983–87.
Vuksic, Nelly, choral director and specialist in Argentinean music. Interview with the author, New York City, February 14, 1985.

Zinger, Pablo, conductor; pianist; author; musical director, Repertorio Español, 1983–95. Interview with the author, New York City, March 27, 1985.

———. Interview with the author, New York City, January 28, 1987.

———. Interview with the author, New York City, June 3, 1995.

———. Interview with the author, New York City, June 8, 1999.

Index

JANET L. STURMAN is an assistant professor of music at the University of Arizona, where she teaches courses in ethnomusicology, music literature, and general studies. She continues to be interested in the impact of Iberian practice on music in the Americas and has an article on that topic forthcoming in the *Garland Encyclopedia of Music in the United States and Canada.* Her current research centers on issues connected with southwestern border musics and on music and technology. Her writings in these areas appear in the journal *world of music* and in a forthcoming collection (from Wesleyan University Press) on music and technoculture edited by Leslie Gay and René Lysloff.

MUSIC IN AMERICAN LIFE

Only a Miner: Studies in Recorded Coal-Mining Songs *Archie Green*
Great Day Coming: Folk Music and the American Left *R. Serge Denisoff*
John Philip Sousa: A Descriptive Catalog of His Works *Paul E. Bierley*
The Hell-Bound Train: A Cowboy Songbook *Glenn Ohrlin*
Oh, Didn't He Ramble: The Life Story of Lee Collins, as Told to Mary Collins *Edited by Frank J. Gillis and John W. Miner*
American Labor Songs of the Nineteenth Century *Philip S. Foner*
Stars of Country Music: Uncle Dave Macon to Johnny Rodriguez *Edited by Bill C. Malone and Judith McCulloh*
Git Along, Little Dogies: Songs and Songmakers of the American West *John I. White*
A Texas-Mexican *Cancionero:* Folksongs of the Lower Border *Américo Paredes*
San Antonio Rose: The Life and Music of Bob Wills *Charles R. Townsend*
Early Downhome Blues: A Musical and Cultural Analysis *Jeff Todd Titon*
An Ives Celebration: Papers and Panels of the Charles Ives Centennial Festival-Conference *Edited by H. Wiley Hitchcock and Vivian Perlis*
Sinful Tunes and Spirituals: Black Folk Music to the Civil War *Dena J. Epstein*
Joe Scott, the Woodsman-Songmaker *Edward D. Ives*
Jimmie Rodgers: The Life and Times of America's Blue Yodeler *Nolan Porterfield*
Early American Music Engraving and Printing: A History of Music Publishing in America from 1787 to 1825, with Commentary on Earlier and Later Practices *Richard J. Wolfe*
Sing a Sad Song: The Life of Hank Williams *Roger M. Williams*
Long Steel Rail: The Railroad in American Folksong *Norm Cohen*
Resources of American Music History: A Directory of Source Materials from Colonial Times to World War II *D. W. Krummel, Jean Geil, Doris J. Dyen, and Deane L. Root*
Tenement Songs: The Popular Music of the Jewish Immigrants *Mark Slobin*
Ozark Folksongs *Vance Randolph; edited and abridged by Norm Cohen*
Oscar Sonneck and American Music *Edited by William Lichtenwanger*
Bluegrass Breakdown: The Making of the Old Southern Sound *Robert Cantwell*
Bluegrass: A History *Neil V. Rosenberg*
Music at the White House: A History of the American Spirit *Elise K. Kirk*

Red River Blues: The Blues Tradition in the Southeast *Bruce Bastin*
Good Friends and Bad Enemies: Robert Winslow Gordon and the Study of American Folksong *Debora Kodish*
Fiddlin' Georgia Crazy: Fiddlin' John Carson, His Real World, and the World of His Songs *Gene Wiggins*
America's Music: From the Pilgrims to the Present (rev. 3d ed.) *Gilbert Chase*
Secular Music in Colonial Annapolis: The Tuesday Club, 1745–56 *John Barry Talley*
Bibliographical Handbook of American Music *D. W. Krummel*
Goin' to Kansas City *Nathan W. Pearson, Jr.*
"Susanna," "Jeanie," and "The Old Folks at Home": The Songs of Stephen C. Foster from His Time to Ours (2d ed.) *William W. Austin*
Songprints: The Musical Experience of Five Shoshone Women *Judith Vander*
"Happy in the Service of the Lord": Afro-American Gospel Quartets in Memphis *Kip Lornell*
Paul Hindemith in the United States *Luther Noss*
"My Song Is My Weapon": People's Songs, American Communism, and the Politics of Culture, 1930–50 *Robbie Lieberman*
Chosen Voices: The Story of the American Cantorate *Mark Slobin*
Theodore Thomas: America's Conductor and Builder of Orchestras, 1835–1905 *Ezra Schabas*
"The Whorehouse Bells Were Ringing" and Other Songs Cowboys Sing *Guy Logsdon*
Crazeology: The Autobiography of a Chicago Jazzman *Bud Freeman, as Told to Robert Wolf*
Discoursing Sweet Music: Brass Bands and Community Life in Turn-of-the-Century Pennsylvania *Kenneth Kreitner*
Mormonism and Music: A History *Michael Hicks*
Voices of the Jazz Age: Profiles of Eight Vintage Jazzmen *Chip Deffaa*
Pickin' on Peachtree: A History of Country Music in Atlanta, Georgia *Wayne W. Daniel*
Bitter Music: Collected Journals, Essays, Introductions, and Librettos *Harry Partch; edited by Thomas McGeary*
Ethnic Music on Records: A Discography of Ethnic Recordings Produced in the United States, 1893 to 1942 *Richard K. Spottswood*
Downhome Blues Lyrics: An Anthology from the Post–World War II Era *Jeff Todd Titon*
Ellington: The Early Years *Mark Tucker*

Chicago Soul *Robert Pruter*
That Half-Barbaric Twang: The Banjo in American Popular Culture *Karen Linn*
Hot Man: The Life of Art Hodes *Art Hodes and Chadwick Hansen*
The Erotic Muse: American Bawdy Songs (2d ed.) *Ed Cray*
Barrio Rhythm: Mexican American Music in Los Angeles *Steven Loza*
The Creation of Jazz: Music, Race, and Culture in Urban America *Burton W. Peretti*
Charles Martin Loeffler: A Life Apart in Music *Ellen Knight*
Club Date Musicians: Playing the New York Party Circuit *Bruce A. MacLeod*
Opera on the Road: Traveling Opera Troupes in the United States, 1825–60 *Katherine K. Preston*
The Stonemans: An Appalachian Family and the Music That Shaped Their Lives *Ivan M. Tribe*
Transforming Tradition: Folk Music Revivals Examined *Edited by Neil V. Rosenberg*
The Crooked Stovepipe: Athapaskan Fiddle Music and Square Dancing in Northeast Alaska and Northwest Canada *Craig Mishler*
Traveling the High Way Home: Ralph Stanley and the World of Traditional Bluegrass Music *John Wright*
Carl Ruggles: Composer, Painter, and Storyteller *Marilyn Ziffrin*
Never without a Song: The Years and Songs of Jennie Devlin, 1865–1952 *Katharine D. Newman*
The Hank Snow Story *Hank Snow, with Jack Ownbey and Bob Burris*
Milton Brown and the Founding of Western Swing *Cary Ginell, with special assistance from Roy Lee Brown*
Santiago de Murcia's "Códice Saldívar No. 4": A Treasury of Secular Guitar Music from Baroque Mexico *Craig H. Russell*
The Sound of the Dove: Singing in Appalachian Primitive Baptist Churches *Beverly Bush Patterson*
Heartland Excursions: Ethnomusicological Reflections on Schools of Music *Bruno Nettl*
Doowop: The Chicago Scene *Robert Pruter*
Blue Rhythms: Six Lives in Rhythm and Blues *Chip Deffaa*
Shoshone Ghost Dance Religion: Poetry Songs and Great Basin Context *Judith Vander*
Go Cat Go! Rockabilly Music and Its Makers *Craig Morrison*
'Twas Only an Irishman's Dream: The Image of Ireland and the Irish in American Popular Song Lyrics, 1800–1920 *William H. A. Williams*

Democracy at the Opera: Music, Theater, and Culture in New York City, 1815–60 *Karen Ahlquist*
Fred Waring and the Pennsylvanians *Virginia Waring*
Woody, Cisco, and Me: Seamen Three in the Merchant Marine *Jim Longhi*
Behind the Burnt Cork Mask: Early Blackface Minstrelsy and Antebellum American Popular Culture *William J. Mahar*
Going to Cincinnati: A History of the Blues in the Queen City *Steven C. Tracy*
Pistol Packin' Mama: Aunt Molly Jackson and the Politics of Folksong *Shelly Romalis*
Sixties Rock: Garage, Psychedelic, and Other Satisfactions *Michael Hicks*
The Late Great Johnny Ace and the Transition from R&B to Rock 'n' Roll *James M. Salem*
Tito Puente and the Making of Latin Music *Steven Loza*
Juilliard: A History *Andrea Olmstead*
Understanding Charles Seeger, Pioneer in American Musicology *Edited by Bell Yung and Helen Rees*
Mountains of Music: West Virginia Traditional Music from *Goldenseal* *Edited by John Lilly*
Alice Tully: An Intimate Portrait *Albert Fuller*
Long Steel Rail: The Railroad in American Folksong (2d ed.) *Norm Cohen*
The Golden Age of Gospel *Text by Horace Clarence Boyer; photography by Lloyd Yearwood*
Aaron Copland: The Life and Work of an Uncommon Man *Howard Pollack*
Louis Moreau Gottschalk *S. Frederick Starr*
Race, Rock, and Elvis *Michael T. Bertrand*
Theremin: Ether Music and Espionage *Albert Glinsky*
Poetry and Violence: The Ballad Tradition of Mexico's Costa Chica *John H. McDowell*
The Bill Monroe Reader *Edited by Tom Ewing*
Music in Lubavitcher Life *Ellen Koskoff*
Zarzuela: Spanish Operetta, American Stage *Janet L. Sturman*

University of Illinois Press
1325 South Oak Street
Champaign, IL 61820-6903
www.press.uillinois.edu